This book constitutes the first detailed study of the later novels of Conrad. Gary Geddes here offers a strong challenge to the commonly accepted thesis that Conrad's writing suffered a decline after *Under Western Eyes* was completed. Professor Geddes demonstrates to the contrary that Conrad remained eloquently in control of his medium, working variations on the romance pattern (particularly the rescue of the individual in distress) and creating a form which might be called the *ironic romance*. Using the ironic romance as a basic structure for the analysis of social, psychological, and philosophical issues that particularly concerned him, Conrad moved into a new phase of artistic consolidation and experiment. His later novels are more highly stylized and more self-consciously shaped than the earlier work; they also explore many of the structural metaphors, such as sculpture and painting, that are anticipated in his early preface to *The Nigger of the 'Narcissus'*.

Critics have tended to misunderstand the later novels because they have neglected those techniques that deepen, modify, and render complexly ironic the surfaces of conventional romance which Conrad was working against. Professor Geddes' compelling interpretation not only promises a radical change in our understanding of the later novels, but also sheds new light on Conrad's entire canon.

Gary Geddes has published poetry, fiction, drama, and criticism. He teaches English at Concordia University in Montreal.

Also by the Author

Poetry
Poems (1971)
Rivers Inlet (1972)
Letter of the Master of Horse (1973)
Snakeroot (1973)
War & other measures (1976)

Anthologies
20th-Century Poetry & Poetics (1969, 1973)
15 Canadian Poets (1971, revised 1978)
Skookum Wawà: writings of the Canadian northwest (1975)
Divided We Stand (1977)

Editions
Heart of Darkness (1969)

Fiction
The Unsettling of the West (1980)

CONRAD'S
Later Novels

Gary Geddes

McGILL–QUEEN'S
UNIVERSITY PRESS

Montreal

© McGill-Queen's University Press 1980
ISBN 0-7735-0357-9
Legal deposit 2nd quarter 1980
Bibliothèque nationale du Québec

Design by Naoto Kondo
Printed in Canada by The Hunter Rose Company

This book has been published with the help of a grant from the Canadian Federation for the Humanities using funds provided by the Social Sciences and Humanities Research Council of Canada

*This book is for my parents
and for Howard O'Hagan and
Margaret Peterson*

Contents

Preface

Some years ago I attended a seminar at the meetings of the Modern Language Association in Denver, Colorado, on the subject of Joseph Conrad's later fiction. No place could have been further removed, in physical terms, from the wide expanse of sea upon which Conrad took his nautical apprenticeship or from the English countryside in which he served his long apprenticeship to the Muse of fiction. And yet there was something appropriate, something that the author of *Nostromo*, *The Secret Agent*, and *Under Western Eyes* would have appreciated about the location of this seminar, nestled among the Rocky Mountains, 5,280 feet above sea-level, on the site of a U.S. Mint and the headquarters for NORAD. While a feathering of fresh snow settled on the slopes, muffling all but the drone of the lifts, scholars and devotees of the work of Conrad gathered in the mammoth glass and concrete convention centre to hear three papers on the later novels, one on *Chance*, one on *The Rover*, and one on Conrad's fictional women.[1]

I mention this event because it was a significant occasion in Conrad studies. Although the conclusions reached in the papers and in the ensuing discussion were more tentative than might have been expected, it marked an important resurgence of interest in those neglected and misunderstood works of the later period, and a determination to challenge the prevailing opinion of Conrad's artistic growth so neatly and incorrectly summarized in the phrase, achievement and decline. Interestingly, the mountain setting of the seminar is an appropriate symbol for the arduousness of the task confronting the critic who would deal fairly with the whole of Conrad's canon. After the steep ascent of the great central novels, few readers have been able or willing to bring their full critical at-

tention to bear on all of the novels of the later period. Efforts
to scale these final peaks—*Chance*, *Victory*, *The Shadow Line*,
The Arrow of Gold, *The Rescue*, and *The Rover*—are too often
characterized, ironically, by the very exhaustion and failure
of critical nerve that has been attributed by his critics to the
later Conrad.

My aim in the following pages is to re-examine Conrad's
later novels in the context of his letters, essays, prefaces, and
A Personal Record with a view to casting some new light on
the nature of his aims and achievement after *Under Western
Eyes*. Unfortunately, these sources have been largely ignored
as a clue to Conrad's developing artistic concerns. Good intentions and evidence of craft are, of course, no guarantee of
success in fiction; the design may be there, but the novel may
still not work. That has not been my experience of the later
novels. I have found not only that they reward close attention, but also that they go a long way towards satisfying
those aims that Conrad expressed, through direct references
and veiled allusions, especially in his correspondence. My
hope is that these pages will challenge the notion that Conrad's writing suffered a decline and will assist in the belated
process of critical upgrading which the later novels deserve.
At least, I would like the reader to come away from this discussion convinced that there is much more in the novels of
this period than has commonly been thought.

I wish to thank those friends whose support and encourage-
ment made this book possible: Hugo McPherson, Rupert
Schieder, John Carroll, Robert Greene, Hugh MacCallum,
and Bill and Thelma Macht.

My thanks also go to *Mosaic* and *English Literature in Transition*, in which some of the material in chapters one and five
appeared, and to Marjorie Bonner Lowry and the Malcolm
Lowry Estate, for permission to include the poem 'Joseph
Conrad'.

To my wife Jan, whose love and commitment and naviga-
tional skills kept our domestic ship on course during the turbulent years of research and writing, I owe my own undying
regard.

Abbreviations

All references to Conrad's works are to the *Collected Works of Joseph Conrad*, published by J. M. Dent, and will be incorporated into the text and abbreviated—e.g. (*PR*, 98)—according to the following key:

AF	*Almayer's Folly*
AG	*The Arrow of Gold*
C	*Chance*
ET	*The End of the Tether*
HD	*Heart of Darkness*
LE	*Last Essays*
LJ	*Lord Jim*
MS	*Mirror of the Sea*
NN	*The Nigger of the 'Narcissus'*
N	*Nostromo*
NLL	*Notes on Life and Letters*
OI	*An Outcast of the Islands*
PR	*A Personal Record*
TR	*The Rescue*
R	*Romance*
RO	*The Rover*
SA	*The Secret Agent*
TSL	*The Shadow Line*
S	*Suspense*
TH	*Tales of Hearsay*
TU	*Tales of Unrest*
TW	*'Twixt Land and Sea*
UWE	*Under Western Eyes*
V	*Victory*
WT	*Within the Tides*

References to G. Jean Aubry's *Joseph Conrad: Life and Letters* (New York: Doubleday, 1927) will be similarly abbreviated to *LL*.

JOSEPH CONRAD

This wrestling, as of seamen with a storm
Which flies to leeward—while they, united
In that chaos, turn, each on his nighted
Bunk, to dream of chaos again, or home—
The poet himself, struggling with the form
Of his coiled work, knows; having requited
Sea-weariness with purpose, invited
What derricks of the soul plunge in his room.
Yet some mariner's ferment in his blood
—Though truant heart will hear the iron travail
And song of ships that ride their easting down—
Sustains him to subdue or be subdued.
In sleep all night he grapples with a sail!
But words beyond the life of ships dream on.

Malcolm Lowry

Introduction

Any re-examination of the later novels of Conrad must begin with a consideration of the achievement-and-decline thesis, since the intensity with which critics like Thomas Moser and Albert Guerard have dismissed some or all of the later works suggests, at least, a misunderstanding of Conrad's fictional aims and, possibly, a predilection for fictional modes and techniques that were no longer of paramount importance to Conrad.

The achievement-and-decline thesis, which takes its name from Thomas Moser's *Joseph Conrad: Achievement and Decline* (1957), is by no means a recent persuasion in Conrad criticism. During his lifetime, Conrad was faced with various reviews which suggested a falling-off in his work. Henry James had reservations about the narrative machinery of *Chance*; and three years after Conrad's death, John Galsworthy suggested the idea of a 'decline' in his 'Reminiscences of Conrad'.[1] A full-scale attack on the later novels did not take place, however, until 1952, with the publication of Douglas Hewitt's *Conrad: A Reassessment*. Hewitt argues that the later Conrad suppressed his awareness of evil, the dark vision of human affairs so powerfully expressed in *Heart of Darkness* and *Nostromo*. As a result of this suppression, Hewitt says, Conrad wrote nothing of real value after 'The Secret Sharer'; and, in every novel except *The Shadow Line*, his prose is faulty, his characters are one-dimensional, and his plots are melodramatic.

Thomas Moser concurs with Hewitt in the matter of Conrad's diminishing powers as a novelist. He argues vigorously, if less cautiously than Hewitt, that Conrad's failure stems from his determination to write about love, a subject which he could handle neither emotionally nor aesthetically. 'Why',

Moser asks, 'did Conrad cease those explorations into moral failure in the masculine world that had enabled him to achieve artistic success?'[2] In addition to his efforts to psychoanalyse Conrad on the basis of the later fiction, Moser also proposes to examine the so-called affirmations attributed to Conrad by such critics as Muriel Bradbrook, Paul Wiley, and Walter Wright; then, in a memorable chapter entitled 'Exhaustion of Creative Energy', he indicates his intention to

> show that the productions of Conrad's last years are virtually without a redeeming feature. They reveal that Conrad has exhausted his creative energy. He no longer has anything to write about and must rework old materials, cling to someone's memoirs, or, in the case of *The Rover*, spin nearly three hundred pages out of nothing. Even more seriously, the last novels show that Conrad has finally lost control of the basic tools of his craft. He can no longer focus on his subject: the novels contain beginnings but virtually no endings. The characters lack substance and Conrad can only assert their emotions and ideas—he cannot dramatize them. The prose of the last works is very faulty. When Conrad tries his hardest to make a scene important, the prose drifts into thin, vague pretentiousness. Although Conrad writes awkwardly at times in all of his novels (least so perhaps in *Lord Jim* and in the shorter sea-pieces), the prose of the last novels stumbles on every page. Sometimes he cannot execute a sentence. Besides the specific faults in technique, the last novels give a general feeling of weariness. All the characters, young and old, seem very tired, eager to sit or lie down. Moreover, the difficulty with which their creator manipulates them indicates clearly the source of their fatigue.[3]

Moser's demolition work seems, at first, so comprehensive as to leave no stone standing: he rejects the later novels, again with the exception of *The Shadow Line*, in terms of both content and form; and he adopts an irritatingly dismissive stance which makes his opinions difficult to take seriously. However, although Hewitt and Moser make surprisingly little effort to explain or substantiate their claims that the later Conrad can neither write convincingly nor manage any of the tricks of his craft, their thesis needs to be answered, if only because it has gained such widespread acceptance among critical works as diverse as Albert Guerard's *Conrad the Novelist* (1958), Frederick Karl's *A Reader's Guide to Joseph Conrad* (1960), and *Joseph Conrad: The Three Lives* (1979), and Bernard Meyer's *Joseph Conrad: A Psychoanalytic Biography* (1967). What began years ago as a dissatisfaction with certain aspects of the later novels has become, in the intervening years, an institution dedicated to lopping off, with some argument as to the proper place to begin and possible exceptions, the bulk of Conrad's writing after *Under Western Eyes*. So entrenched is this negative view of the later novels that Meyer can construct his psychoanalytic theories on it without question and a critic of Guerard's stature can be found arguing that 'the time has come to drop *Victory* from the Conrad canon'. [4]

Such surgical proceedings do little to encourage an open-minded response to the works of this difficult period. All four critics, Hewitt, Moser, Guerard, and Meyer, reveal a preference for psychological fiction, fiction that explores the individual's moral crisis from a position which might be described as internal, or subjective. They also seem predisposed towards the tragic mode. Hewitt makes clear his position when he singles out *Heart of Darkness* and 'The Secret Sharer' for special mention; Moser and Guerard share his interest in those works which dramatize a character's confrontation with his other self and, to use Guerard's words, they agree 'warmly that the best work of Conrad is the work of a tragic pessimist concerned with other kinds of masculine failure than sexual'. [5] Meyer also speculates that Conrad's apparent mental illness in 1910 caused him to avoid 'introspective journeys into the self' and to concern himself instead with the surfaces of life. [6] What these critics fail to recognize is that, in the later fiction, Conrad is not suppressing his awareness of evil, or of the complexity of human motivation; rather, he is allowing his psychological impulse to find a more generalized expression in work that is concerned with problems of conduct in society.

During the writing of *Nostromo*, Conrad wrote to H. G. Wells a letter which suggests that his own fiction might well take a broader, more obviously humanistic direction than it had in the earlier individual-oriented works:

But with my rooted idea of the whole value of the future (whatever we wish to make of it or find it) consisting in what we do endure and shape *today*. I can't help wishing you had emphasized that view—which surely is not foreign to your conviction. Is it? The future is of our own making—and (for me) the most striking characteristic of the century is just that development, that maturing of our consciousness which should open our eyes to that truth— or that illusion. Anything that would help open our intelligences towards a clearer view of the consequences of our social action is of the very greatest value—and, as such, a guide.

(*LL*, I, 323)

Certainly, the epic scale and the historical sensibility revealed in the work on which he was currently engaged indicate that this chronicler of the history of individuals in moments of extreme crisis was broadening his canvasses to include forces and events that are, properly speaking, not the primary concern of the psychological novel. Furthermore, after the completion of *The Secret Agent*, Conrad wrote to his agent Pinker to say that he would, in his subsequent fiction, be aiming at subjects such as labour and war that would be of greater public interest. At the same time, he was engaged in visiting the libraries for the initial research on the French Revolution and Napoleon in Elba, which would find its way eventually into the unfinished pages of *Suspense* and, in part, into *The Rover* and a short story called 'The Tale'.

John Palmer reaches a similar conclusion in *Joseph Conrad's Fiction* (1968), which contains an excellent short history of criticism relating to the problems of the later fiction, 'Achievement and Decline: A Bibliographical Note'. Palmer states his inclination to resist the idea of a 'decline' in Conrad and lends his support to the view of Conrad's moral and artistic growth and commitment to human solidarity as expressed by Morton Zabel in 'Chance and Recognition':

For Conrad, however existential he may have been by inclination, the commitment could never be arbitrary. It is a necessity which defines man as human, his moral consciousness as imperative, and his persistence in that consciousness as the fundamental law of life. From this germinal presentation of the case Conrad's drama of the self widens until, in his most ambitious books, it comes to include the larger workings of that law in society and politics, even in the destiny of nations and races. The growth in his thought from an idealistic conception of life to a critical one, from his temperamental romanticism to his later realism of values, is the drama of his genius in its difficult emergence, its strenuous self-discipline, and its eventual success.[7]

As Palmer and Zabel suggest, Conrad did not suddenly, out of exhaustion, ill health, or financial pressure, begin to write superficial stories of romantic love; nor did he lose his awareness of the destructive potential in human nature. As any reader of *The Nigger of the 'Narcissus'*, *Heart of Darkness*, *Nostromo*, and *The Secret Agent* can testify, Conrad saw this destructive potential as a threat not only to the individual, but also to the very fabric of society. James Wait and Donkin represent a threat to the safety and equilibrium of the *Narcissus* just as surely as Lord Jim's and Heyst's unbounded romanticism represents a threat to the little universe of their psyches. And the point which must be made in relation to *Victory* is that Heyst's commitment to certain abstractions, including the philosophy of non-involvement, leads not to an isolated tragedy, but rather to the disruption of many lives and the destruction of the Samburan community.

A preference for fiction that presents the drama of the self, at the expense of the wider, more social manifestations of Conrad's moral imperatives, has led critics to misinterpret Conrad's aims in the later novels. The subject of these works is not, as Moser suggests, romantic love; if there is a single subject or theme that underlies the later novels it is the theme of solidarity or human community, of which love is but a single aspect. Conrad is concerned to analyse various aspects of society, particularly those kinds of action which might destroy human solidarity and those which might lead to its restoration. That is why he chose to employ throughout the later novels the romance pattern of the rescue of the individual in distress (Flora, Heyst, Lena, the young captain in *The Shadow Line*, Rita, Hassim, Immada, Réal, and Arlette are all victims of some perfidy enacted upon them as a result of the warped values, ideals, or institutions of society). Conrad once advised his friend Norman Douglas to try writing a 'novel of analysis on the basis of some strong situation' (*LL*, II, 68), which describes his own fictional technique in the later novels perfectly. The romance pattern provides the 'strong situation' around which Conrad is able to conduct his analysis of certain values, ideas, and premises relative to the problem of community.

Conrad is not unaware of the dangers inherent in his use of the romance pattern of the rescue of the individual in distress. Although it represents a profoundly important and useful archetype for the fictional rendering and analysis of the breakdown and possible restoration of harmony within the community, the romance pattern is continually modified, or undercut, by ironic and mythic elements in the novels. Conrad frequently manipulates his character relations, for example, so that there are not only rescues within rescues, but also various false 'rescuers' against which the qualities of the genuine rescuer can be measured. Also, he undercuts the romance pattern, and its potential for sentimentality and melodrama, by filtering events through the consciousness of an ironic narrator. What results from this challenge to his talents as a novelist is a unique form which is best described as the ironic romance.

The ironic romance makes rather unusual demands upon the critic. Examined superficially, it may not be easily distinguishable from pure romance, in which everything must be subordinate to plot; that is no doubt the reason for the complaint, by critics such as Hewitt, Moser, and Guerard, that certain characters lack depth and complexity and that the novels' endings are hackneyed. The reader of the later novels must bring his critical attention to bear on fictional components other than these if he is to comprehend properly the function and significance of the romance pattern. He cannot expect the same kind of psychological depth as in the earlier works, in terms of naturalistic detail in the characterization, but he will find instead that the larger psychology of the novel, perhaps generalized and embodied in several characters and rendered by way of a certain patterning of events, a certain texturing of the prose, has a degree of effectiveness that is quite surprising; and whatever may be lost as a result of psychological reduction is more than compensated for by the increased philosophical and, for lack of a better term, sociological dimensions of the work of fiction.

My approach to the novels, as these comments suggest, is mainly by way of technique, a procedure which Conrad tried in vain to encourage on more than one occasion:

> My writing life extends but only over twenty-three years, and I need not point out to an intelligence as alert as yours that all that time has been a time of evolution, in which some critics have detected three marked periods—and that the process is still going on. Some critics have found fault with me for not being constantly myself. But they are wrong. I am always myself. I am a man of formed character. Certain conclusions remain immovably fixed in my mind, but I am no slave to prejudices and formulas, and I shall never be. My attitude to subjects and expressions, the angles of vision, my methods of composition will, within limits, be always changing—not because I am unstable or unprincipled but because I am free. Or perhaps it may be more exact to say, because I am always trying for freedom—within my limits.[8]

No critic, however, has taken Conrad at his word and attempted a detailed examination of those 'angles of vision', 'methods of composition', and 'attitudes to subjects and expressions' in the later novels, which Conrad insisted would, within limits, be always changing. The central premise of this study is that Conrad never lost interest in fictional experiment, in extending the possibilities of his craft with each new work. He often spoke of the novel upon which he was currently engaged as an experiment in technique: he described *Nostromo* as 'more of a Novel pure and simple than anything I've done since *Almayer's Folly*' (*LL*, I, 316); and he saw *The Secret Agent* as a 'new departure in *genre* and a sustained effort in ironical treatment of a melodramatic subject' (*LL*, II, 60), a description which anticipates his directions in the later novels. Similarly, each of the later novels represented for Conrad not, as Moser suggests, an exhausted return to old subjects or the spinning of pages out of nothing, but rather an artistic challenge to find the right form with which to analyse and give imaginative expression to the subject to which he had been temperamentally drawn.

There is ample evidence to support the belief that Conrad viewed his own development as a novelist primarily in terms of technique. Writing towards the end of his life to his friend and critic Richard Curle, Conrad tried to suggest the manner in which his own work might be approached most profitably; he begins by referring to a critic, real or imagined, who had used the word 'historical' in connection with Conrad's novels:

> My own impression is that what he really meant was that my manner of telling, perfectly devoid of familiarity as between author and reader, aimed essentially at the intimacy of a personal communication, without any thought for other effects. As a matter of fact, the thought for effects is there all the same (often at the expense of mere directness of narrative), and can be detected in my unconventional grouping and perspective, which are purely temperamental and wherein all my 'art' consists. This, I suspect, has been the difficulty the critics felt in classifying it as romantic or realistic. Whereas, as a matter of fact, it is fluid, depending on grouping (sequence) which shifts, and on the changing lights giving varied effects of perspective.
>
> It is in those matters gradually, but never completely mastered that the history of my books really consists.
>
> (*LL*, II, 317)

Written within thirteen months of his death, this letter offers an extremely useful and interesting bit of hindsight to Conrad's critics; in fact, it suggests an approach that would do much to dispel certain misconceptions that underlie so many discussions of the later novels. As this letter suggests, Conrad was primarily concerned with exploring various *ways of telling* whatever came to his hand, whether incidents dredged up from memory or events derived from the memoirs of other writers.

I do not mean to suggest that the later novels have not had their supporters. Numerous critics, including Ian Watt, Paul Wiley, F. R. Leavis, Muriel Bradbrook, Edward Said, Don-

ald Yelton, and Lawrence Graver, have written sympathetically and perceptively about one or more of them. However,
it must be admitted that their collective efforts have been insufficient to cast off the shroud of disapproval that is the
legacy of the achievement-and-decline thesis. Royal Roussel's
The Metaphysics of Darkness (1971) praises *Chance*, but dismisses Conrad's subsequent work as re-runs in which no new
spiritual discoveries are made; that new formal experiments
must have implied new discoveries in terms of content does
not seem to have occurred to Roussel. John E. Saveson's *Conrad, The Later Moralist* (1974), while extremely useful as a
guide to social and intellectual influences on Conrad's work
after *Lord Jim*, especially the Nietzschean elements, does not
take the novels after *Victory* seriously enough to include them
for discussion. *Conrad's Romanticism* (1974), by David Thorburn, contains a very fine account of Conrad's fictionalizing
process and narrative skills in *A Personal Record* and *The
Mirror of the Sea*, but adopts all of the old clichés about 'Conrad's failing energies' and 'the disappointing novels of his last
years'. [9]

The failure of the resolve to reassess the later novels is nowhere more apparent than in one of the most recent studies to
appear, the long-awaited biography by Frederick Karl, *Joseph
Conrad: The Three Lives* (1979). Karl writes of Conrad with
very few new insights, as if the unpublished letters, to which
he has had almost exclusive access, merely confirmed what he
had always thought about Conrad. His remarks about *The
Arrow of Gold* are fairly typical of his approach to the later
novels: 'The first hundred pages of *The Arrow* are more like
the notes for a novel than the novel itself. It is all beginnings;
forward movement of any kind is frustrated by long di-
alogues or scenes which remain static . . . the "setting up" of
George and his companions vis-à-vis Rita appears like a still
life without sufficient colour.' [10] The still-life image, which
originates with Leo Gurko, ought to have alerted Karl to a
fundamental feature of the art of *The Arrow of Gold*: images of
painting, as the letters suggest, turn out to be structurally important, determining not only the method of presenting
character, but also the kind of narrative frame that is used.
The colour is there all right; in fact, colour, design, composition, lighting—all the components of painting—are there, at
the expense of mere physical action. Remarkably, Conrad is

exploring that strange No Man's Land between the sequential literary arts and the spatial visual arts; as Hogarth's work took on a dynamic, sequential quality in 'The Rake's Progress' that is characteristic of narrative, so Conrad in *The Arrow of Gold* explores the more static, spatial qualities characteristic of painting.[11]

The importance of such technical considerations cannot be too strongly emphasized, as a way of both coming to terms with the art of the later novels and suggesting the serious limitations of the achievement-and-decline thesis. What Moser calls the 'feeling of weariness' in these works can be easily explained in the case of *The Arrow of Gold* by relating it to a deliberate downgrading of plot and an increase in the degree of interiorization, where event is replaced by the intersection of surfaces and psychology.[12] In *The Rover*, the so-called weariness relates not to Conrad's tiredness as author, but rather to images of sleep and paralysis and statuary imposed on the novel by the patterns of myth and romance.

I Chance

The Sympathetic Structure

In the early pages of *Under Western Eyes*, the Teacher of Languages who, out of a complex of different motives, pieces together the diary, disclaims any ability to fathom and to render in words the personality of Razumov. He insists that he has had his imagination 'smothered out of existence a long time ago under a wilderness of words. Words, as is well known, are the great foes of reality. I have been many years a teacher of languages. It is an occupation which at length becomes fatal to whatever store of imagination, observation, and insight an ordinary person may be heir to' (*UWE*, 3). When events of the novel have run their course, Razumov, too, has had his fill of words; once a prize-essayist, a deceiver, a spy, and a fake professor, he has achieved a brief measure of freedom and self-respect before his death by confessing to Natalie Haldin. Deaf at last, he moves in 'absolute silence' (496), no longer prey to the temptations and deceptions of the word.

Behind these sobering events and pronouncements, of course, stands the novel itself, as proof that words have power to communicate and that structures, however frail and transitory, may be built against the encroaching silence. Certainly not a new insight to Conrad, the failures and limits of language as a guide in human affairs became a central concern during the later period, particularly in *Chance*, *Victory*, and *The Rescue*. In many ways, *Chance* is an exploration of precisely those matters relating to imagination and language concerning which the Teacher of Languages professed to being inept.

At one point Marlow observes that he was once called a 'consummate hypocrite' (*C*, 264) and that this calumny affected him adversely for a disproportionate length of time; and he concludes with the observation: 'See the might of suggestion? We live at the mercy of a malevolent word. A sound, a mere disturbance of air, sinks into our very soul sometimes' (264). He alludes to the effect that words have had on Flora, who has been called unscrupulous, a fool, an adventuress; he compares her with her father, the financier de Barral, who 'had been carried away out of his depth by the unexpected power of successful advertising' (264). This reference deliberately recalls the initial account of de Barral's financial rise and fall on the strength of a single word:

> He was a mere sign, a portent. There was nothing in him. Just about that time the word Thrift was to the fore. You know the power of words. We pass through periods dominated by this or that word—it may be development, or it may be competition, or education, or purity or efficiency or even sanctity. It is the word of the time. Well just then it was the word Thrift that was out in the streets walking arm in arm with righteousness, the inseparable companion and backer up of all such national catch-words, looking everybody in the eye, as it were. The very drabs of the pavement, poor things, didn't escape the fascination.
>
> (74)

Like his forerunner Mr. Kurtz, de Barral is a hollow man, prime target for the corrupting effects of language, whether that vocabulary is economic, religious, political, or ethical.

Marlow thinks briefly of de Barral's career in terms of the words 'glory' and 'splendour', but comes quickly to the conclusion that 'No! Neither of these words will fit his success' (75). He comments, sarcastically, that de Barral is a 'true democrat', which he goes on to define as someone who 'would have done business (a sharp kind of business) with the devil himself' (75). When the outer narrator protests that Marlow exaggerates, Marlow replies: 'My way of putting things! My dear fellow, I have merely stripped the rags of business verbiage and financial jargon off my statements. And you are startled! I am giving you the naked truth. It's true that nothing lays itself open to the charge of exaggeration more than the language of naked truth. What comes with a shock is admitted with difficulty' (80).

Conrad is concerned in *Chance* to strip away the verbiage and jargon from the vocabulary of human conduct. At every level of composition—character relations, narrative point of view, and linguistic texture—language, particularly ethical terminology, is put to the test.

Conrad makes several explicit references in the novel to the limitations of conventional ethics. He speaks of the 'unreasonable complications the idealism of mankind puts into the simple but poignant problem of conduct on this earth' (325). Marlow calls Anthony's ship, the *Ferndale*, the 'most unrestful ship that ever sailed out of any port on earth' (376); then he goes on to explain that he is not speaking technically:

> I am not alluding to her sea-going qualities. Mr. Powell tells me she was steady as a church. I mean unrestful in the sense, for instance, which this planet of ours is unrestful—a matter of uneasy atmosphere disturbed by passions, jealousies, hates and the troubles of transcendental good intentions, which, though ethically valuable, I have no doubt cause often more unhappiness than the plots of the most evil tendency.
>
> (376)

At another point, in response to Flora's unwarranted feelings of guilt and remorse over her suicidal impulses, Marlow observes: 'I thought it was very likely some obscure influence of common forms of speech, some traditional or inherited feeling—a vague notion that suicide is a legal crime; words of old moralists and preachers which remain in the air and help to form all the authorized moral conventions' (214).

It is precisely these words and the moral conventions, or ideal conceptions, they embody that are Conrad's chief targets in *Chance*. My purpose in this chapter is to argue that Conrad was very serious when he insisted in the Author's Note to *Chance* that 'My intention was to interest people in my vision of things which is indissolubly allied to the style in which it is expressed' (x).

In *Chance*, as in all of his novels, Conrad is writing 'a novel of analysis on the basis of some strong situation' (*LL*, II, 68). The 'strong situation' around which *Chance* is constructed is Flora de Barral's experience with her governess. This austere, Medusa-like creature, Marlow informs us, is no normal woman but one with 'ungovernable passions; yet suppressed by the very same means which keep the rest of us in order: early training—necessity—circumstances—fear of consequences; till finally there comes an age, a time when the restraint of years becomes intolerable—and infatuation irresistible' (*C*, 103). Encroaching age and expectations crushed by the financial collapse of de Barral provoke the governess to lash out at Flora from the depths of her disappointment. Ironically, Flora had considered her the embodiment of wisdom and authority, so that when the governess appeared to her 'like an emanation of evil' (117), she 'set free in Flora that faculty of unreasoning terror lying locked up at the bottom of all human hearts . . .' (118). By calling Flora a fool, a 'vulgar, silly non-entity' (122) and her father a thief, the governess breaks Flora's hold on reality. Not only is Flora reduced to a state of shock, but also her very conception of herself is shattered: 'Her abominable experience with the governess had implanted in her unlucky breast a lasting doubt, an ineradicable suspicion of herself and others' (232). The experience is analogous, in terms of intensity and effect, to Jim's jump from the *Patna* and Razumov's betrayal of Haldin; in terms of moral responsibility, however, Flora's situation, like that of the young Rita de Lastaola in *The Arrow of Gold*, is beyond her control. Marlow informs us, in one of his least satisfactory descriptions, that her life is 'the saddest desecration, the withered brightness of youth, a spirit neither made cringing nor yet dulled but as if bewildered in quivering hopelessness by gratuitous cruelty; self-confidence destroyed . . . ill-luck' (312).

Chance operates on several important levels and it is on these levels that Conrad's methods of 'analysis' are employed. First, the novel is concerned with Flora's 'progress' through an unsympathetic and uncomprehending world; second, with the efforts of Marlow to piece together into a meaningful whole the fragments of Flora's story, an assortment of facts, impressions, and hearsay. Finally, there is the verbal texturing of the whole novel, through which Conrad draws attention to the nitty-gritty of human communication and the role of language therein. On the first level, Flora's story is conceived in terms of a series of encounters between herself and various characters in the novel. Just as our understanding of Lord Jim results from seeing him through the actions and comments of characters such as Stanton, Brierly, and Gentle-man Brown, so also our understanding of the psychology of Flora's situation depends on the subtlety with which Conrad renders each of these encounters. The important difference between the character relations in *Chance* and *Lord Jim* is that in *Chance* we are interested not so much in each character's opinion or corresponding problem as in his emotional response to Flora and her needs. In a very definite sense, the attitude of each character to Flora is a measure of that character's capacity for understanding.

Flora's first major emotional encounter, after her experience with her governess, is with de Barral's bourgeois cousin. This cardboard-box manufacturer, who possesses all the civic virtues and represents the Protestant work ethic, is one of Arnold's Barbarians. He is an 'odious personage' (166), entirely materialistic, who hopes to grab de Barral's supposed nest-egg by caring for the displaced Flora. Flora's relatives prove to be 'people without any fineness of either feeling or mind, unable to understand her misery' (163); a 'spirit of selfishness' (164) pervades their home and in the 'ugliness of their conduct' (164) they subject Flora to a sort of 'moral savagery' (163). Marlow cannot decide whether the cousin was 'more absurd than cruel or more cruel than absurd' (169). 'It was as though Flora had been fated always to be surrounded by treachery and lies stifling every better impulse, every instinctive aspiration of her soul to trust and to love' (174–75).

These relatives, who are motivated solely by self-interest thinly disguised as Christian charity, are totally lacking in understanding and sympathy. Their closest counterparts in Conrad's fiction are the ugly colonizers in 'An Outpost of Progress' and *Heart of Darkness*. Marlow's evident scorn for them reflects a general distaste that Conrad himself felt for the products of Christianity. Writing to Edward Garnett about Tolstoy, in terms almost identical to those quoted above, he said:

> Moreover, the base from which he starts—Christianity—is distasteful to me. I am not blind to its services but the absurd Oriental fable from which it starts irritates me. Great, improving, softening, compassionate it may be but it has lent itself with amazing facility to cruel distortions and is the only religion which, with its impossible stan-

dards, has brought an infinity of anguish to innumerable souls—on this earth.[1]

Beneath his Christian facade, de Barral's cousin's 'fangs' (168) can be seen; he moves with 'appalling versatility from sarcasm to veiled menace' (170). The kind of care which this scripture-quoting relative offers to Flora is sterile, like the promise of immortality to a starving child. 'What humanity needs', Conrad explains in 'The Life Beyond', 'is not the promise of scientific immortality, but compassionate pity in this life and infinite mercy on the Day of Judgment' (*NLL*, 69).

Two lesser encounters dislocate Flora from her familiar environment. Cast off by her only relatives, she is sent to care for a wealthy old maid. But the old woman lacks the capacity to understand; she can only make demands on people and, consequently, dismisses Flora for not being naturally cheerful. Flora's short experience as a tutor for a German family is equally disastrous. She mistakes the husband's advances for genuine sympathy: 'She thought him sympathetic—the first expressively sympathetic person she had ever met' (*C*,181). The ensuing events, reminiscent of *Pamela*, are nearly fatal for Flora; and she is saved from suicide en route back to England only by the 'quiet matter-of-fact attention of a ship's stewardess' (181). The point to be made here, as elsewhere in Conrad's fiction, is that in a hostile and uncomprehending universe, work, an unconscious devotion to the task at hand, offers at least the chance of sanity and survival.

When Flora returns to her friends the Fynes, she has become alienated not only by her inability to conceive of her own worth, but also by the lack of a significant role or social function. Ironically, the 'good intentions' (123) of the Fynes prove to be more disastrous than the obvious ill-will of her relatives. Mr. Fyne, who has an uncomplicated 'masculine imagination' (107), can see the fall of de Barral only as a great financial loss to Flora. Mrs. Fyne, on the other hand, 'felt under a sort of moral obligation not to be indifferent' (107) to Flora. Her 'patient immobility by the bedside of that brutally murdered childhood did infinite honour to her humanity' (139), the more so because she did not find Flora particularly sympathetic. Nevertheless, the anecdote about the Fyne dog reveals that, for all their apparent compassion, their 'undeniable humanity' (135), the Fynes lack imaginative sympathy. When Flora complicates matters in the cozy household by eloping with Mrs. Fyne's brother, Captain Anthony, the nature of the Fynes' interest and friendship alters radically. Although he too has eloped, Mr. Fyne sees Flora's affair as 'sheer lunacy' (242). Mrs. Fyne's response is more complicated, however; her maternal feelings for Flora quickly turn to competitive jealousy. In her lack of imagination, she is blind to the real motives for Flora's flight with Anthony and is prepared to believe the worst. As Marlow observes: 'in dealing with reality Mrs. Fyne ceases to be tolerant. In other words, she can't forgive Miss de Barral for being a woman and behaving like a woman' (189). Her adverse response to Flora's elopement reveals that Mrs. Fyne's feminism, like her compassion, is merely an 'intellectual exercise' (187). Furthermore, the alteration in her sentiments displays 'the inspiration of a possibly unconscious Machiavellism!' (194). Even Mr. Fyne, whose sympathy and sentiments 'had more stability' (190), is persuaded by his wife to conduct an interview with Captain Anthony which works 'infernal violence' (328) on Flora's marriage. As their name suggests, these two friends of Flora are fine people; but their lack of imaginative sympathy renders them two of her most deadly enemies.

Ironically, the more intimate a character's relationship with Flora, the more damage Flora receives. Her deliverer, Marlow informs us, is a 'hermit-like but not exactly misanthropic sailor' (223); he is *un galant homme* (233), and one who is unusually susceptible to the sufferings of mankind. Like Flora, Captain Anthony has had a debilitating childhood—as the son of Carleon Anthony, a poet who fed his family generously on ideals and clichés but starved them of love and understanding. Like Heyst in *Victory*, Anthony has 'an ideal conception of his position' (262), but is ill-equipped to tackle the realities of life. He sees in the frightened Flora the possibility of a total possession which will substantiate his conception of himself as a saviour of mankind; and he comes to regard himself as the 'rescuer of the most forlorn damsel of modern times' (238). Because he idealizes his relationship with Flora, Anthony is unable to overcome the sexual-emotional paralysis which settles upon him after his session with his brother-in-law Fyne, in which the seeds of doubt about Flora's motives are sown. The 'egoism of his vanity—or of his generosity' (331) drives him to honour his commitment to care for Flora, although he no longer believes that she cares for him. In his inexperience and ignorance, Anthony inflicts upon Flora a 'new perfidy of life taking upon itself the form of magnanimity' (336).

For both of them Anthony's idea proves but a 'flaming vision of reality' (262). Anthony undergoes such a radical transformation that his faithful chief-mate, Franklin (an appropriate name for a knight's assistant from the lower ranks) is forced to admit: 'I feel sometimes as if I must shake him by the arm: "Wake up! Wake up! You are wanted, sir . . ."' (303). Like Lord Jim, Anthony is a victim of his own egomania. His frustration at his failure to consummate his marriage expresses itself in the form of an unrealistic but seemingly more sophisticated love of mankind: his 'thoughts were inclined to pity every passing figure, every single person glimpsed under a street lamp' (346–47). Flora inspires in him something more, or other, than love: 'Something as incredible as the fulfillment of an amazing and startling dream in which he could take the world in his arms—all the suffering world—not to possess its pathetic fairness but to console and cherish its sorrow' (348). This misdirected emotion, not unlike that of the idiot Stevie in *The Secret Agent*, stems from 'a situation almost insane in its audacious generosity' (350). As Marlow muses, while Anthony became enslaved by his own generosity to Flora he 'probably was beginning at bottom to detest her—like the governess, like the maiden-lady, like the German woman, like Mrs. Fyne, like Mr. Fyne' (396).

If Flora's situation with the Fynes was suicidal, joining Captain Anthony on board the *Ferndale* is positively explosive. Not only does she have her husband and a hostile crew to contend with, but also her insensitive father. When de Barral is released from prison, he remains the prisoner of his own blindness and obsession. His presence on board the *Ferndale*, like that of James Wait on the *Narcissus*, serves as a disintegrating force. Flora, perhaps irrationally, expects peace and support from her father, but is disappointed because he is totally selfish and unimaginative in his dealings with people. And yet, although he is as morally obtuse as Sotillo in *Nostromo* and MacWhirr in *Typhoon*, de Barral does give Flora a sense of her own existence—not of her worth, but of her existence: 'There was in him no pity, no generosity, nothing whatever of these fine things—it was for her, for her very own self, such as it was, that this human being cared' (380). By making Flora his *raison d'être*, the substitute for his lost fortune, de Barral acts as an anchor, a staying force in her life. It is one of the supreme Conradian ironies—and a clear indication that the novel is not soft or 'sentimental' in its psychology—that this grotesque creature with his debased ideals and pure selfishness should be Flora's only source of comfort and, indirectly, the catalyst in her reunion with Anthony and with life.

Finally, Flora is thrown together with Powell, the young second mate 'whom the chance of his name had thrown upon the floating stage of that tragi-comedy' (272). Marlow observes that Powell is 'simple and his faculty of wonder not very great. He's one of those people who form no theories about facts' (261). Somewhat more inquisitive than Winnie Verloc in *The Secret Agent*, Powell nevertheless has a similar conviction that things do not bear much looking into; he is too engrossed in the duties and satisfactions of his new position to do more than wonder at the strange conditions on board the *Ferndale*: the unusual living quarters, the separate dining arrangements for the officers, the general discontent among the crew, and so on. What finally arouses Powell's curiosity, however, is the intensity of the chief mate's concern for the safety of Captain Anthony. Franklin, the 'thick chief mate' (274) with melancholy eyes and 'his head sunk beneath his shoulders' (277), as if the burden of his love for his captain were too much to bear, pronounces himself a good, faithful friend, but one who has been ill-used. Franklin sees Flora as a curse, a black-eyed *femme fatale*, who is engaged in 'devil's work' (305). Powell discovers that Franklin's jealous devotion and persistence have 'opened his understanding a measure' (300); so that, although he had no initial interest in Flora's affairs or in interfering with his captain's life, Powell inadvertently becomes the saviour of Flora and her unhappy marriage.

Of course the novel is nowhere as simple as this brief account of character relations suggests. Because of what he calls his 'unconventional grouping', Conrad never reveals all his information about characters or scenes at once. One of the incredible features of his technique in *Chance* is the way in which he withholds vital information, slips in tempting morsels, returns after many pages to complete a scene. The novel has, in fact, a remarkable rhythm and symmetry, if examined closely; what may appear, at first glance, to be digressions or wrong-turns (the long section on the collapse of de Barral, for example) are revealed, finally, to be very crucial to our understanding of the novel. What seems to be background material, which the painter calls negative space, turns out to be foreground. Thus the importance of Marlow as narrator, de Barral's world as an indicator of current social values, and the ethical terminology employed to give imaginative expression to the character relations.

The ethical vocabulary that Conrad employs here is substantial and includes the following words or phrases: tolerance, humanity, pity, magnanimity, generosity, fineness, honesty, good intentions, moral obligation, sympathy, love, matter-of-fact attention. Too often the real motivation or sentiment behind conduct turns out to have been closer to this second list of words: selfishness, treachery, rapaciousness, cruelty, egoism, Machiavellism, deceit, self-interest, anger, vanity, indifference, hatred. The three terms which predominate in the novel and which seem realistic, or workable, in moral terms are 'sympathy', 'imagination', and 'understanding', qualities associated almost exclusively with Marlow and, to a lesser degree, Powell. Inevitably, the question most often asked in the novel, by Flora, Powell, and Marlow is, Do you understand?

I have gone into considerable detail in discussing the character relations not only to establish the centrality of sympathy or understanding in *Chance*, but also to emphasize, by contrast with the roles of the other characters, the thematic and structural significance of Marlow. Because he is so much a part of the machinery of narration in the novel, there is a tendency to overlook Marlow's larger significance, a tendency to see him merely as a device. While admitting that Marlow is needed 'to watch a subtly complex situation and interpret it in its finest, most ambiguous shades', Edward Crankshaw nevertheless concludes that '*Chance* is not about Marlow at all'.[2] Similarly, Frederick Karl reads *Chance* as a 'novel of the maturation of a girl to a young lady'; therefore he complains, quite understandably, that the variety of narrators is nothing more than an awkward 'means of achieving the complicated apparatus'.[3] It must be admitted that Marlow is directly in-

volved in Flora's life only three times: first, in unintentionally
intruding upon her attempted suicide; second, in listening to
her confession on a street-corner in London's East End; and
finally, in bringing together Powell and the widowed Flora.
But *Chance* is not only the story of Flora's maturation; it is
also the story of Marlow's efforts to bring under imaginative
control the various facts concerning Flora, and his responses
to these facts.

Marlow's task is first one of historical reconstruction. In
order to make sense of Flora's situation, he has to engage in
some elementary research; he ferrets out the facts of her life
from the Fynes, from Powell, and from his own encounters
with her. As the narrator observes, Marlow is the 'expert in
the psychological wilderness. This is like one of those Red-
skin stories where the noble savages carry off a girl and the
honest backwoodsman with his incomparable knowledge
follows the track and reads the signs of her fate in a footprint
here, a broken twig there, a trinket dropped by the way'
(311). Marlow cannot adequately penetrate to the essential
'truth' of Flora's situation by means of abstract theorizing,
but must render it in terms of the elements of art: 'The purely
human reality is capable of lyrism but not of abstraction.
Nothing will serve for its understanding but the evidence of
rational linking up of characters and facts' (310). 'Fiction', as
Conrad explains in his essay on Henry James, 'is history,
human history, or it is nothing . . . and a novelist is a historian, the preserver, the keeper, the expounder, of human experience' (*NLL*, 17). The importance of this imaginative reconstruction, Marlow explains to the narrator, arises from
our general

> inability to interpret aright the signs which experience (a
> thing mysterious in itself) makes to our understanding
> and emotions. For it is never more than that. It always
> remains outside of us. That's why we look with wonder at
> the past. And this persists when from practice and
> through growing callousness of fibre we come to the
> point when nothing that we meet in that rapid blinking
> stumble across a flick of sunshine—which is our life—
> nothing, I say, which we run against surprises us any-
> more. Not at the time, I mean. If, later on, we recover the
> faculty with some such exclamation: 'Well! Well! I'll be

hanged if I ever, . . .' it is probably because this very
thing that there should be a past to look back upon, other
people's, is very astounding in itself when one has the
time, a fleeting and immense instant to think of it.
(282–83)

Through this by-play between Marlow and the narrator, a
kind of dialectic or ironic counterpoint is established, which
allows for the clarification of important issues in the novel.
When the narrator asks Marlow whether their 'inestimable
advantage of understanding what is happening to others'
(117) has any value other than that of amusement, Marlow
states emphatically: 'But from that same provision of understanding, there springs in us compassion, charity, indignation, the sense of solidarity; and in minds of any largeness an
inclination to that indulgence which is next to affection' (117–
18).

Marlow's function in *Chance* parallels that of the novelist,
which Conrad describes as 'rescue work, this snatching of
vanishing phases of turbulence, disguised in fair words, out
of the native obscurity into a light where the struggling
forms may be seen, seized upon, endowed with the only possible form of permanence in this world of relative values—
the permanence of memory' (*NLL*, 13). By holding up this
rescued fragment, the novelist is able to 'show its vibration,
its colour, its form; and through its movement, its form, its
colour, reveal the substance of its truth—disclose its inspiring
secret' (*NN*, x). The analogy is by no means far-fetched,
since the same phrase appears on the lips of Fyne in *Chance*, as
he thinks of Flora and Anthony taking on the responsibility
for her ex-convict father: 'They mean to drag him along with
them on board the ship straight away. Rescue work' (247).

In *Chance*, Marlow engages in imaginative rescue work; in
fact, one might argue that the subject of *Chance* is not so
much the story of Flora de Barral as the *rescue* of the story of
Flora de Barral from the dust and ashes of obscurity.[4] In
terms of the romance pattern Anthony is the knight who rescues Flora, but it is really Marlow who rescues the facts about
Flora, who analyses them and gives them imaginative shape.
He is, of course, undertaking the central Conradian task of
making us 'see'—that is, of making us understand.

Thus the significance of his speculations, his conjecture, his

sallies back and forth in time, the fragmentation of his narrative. Misunderstanding Conrad's aims in *Chance*, Frederick
Karl says of the narrative technique: 'One is tempted to suggest that Conrad was coming close to a satire on the Conradian method.'[5] One is tempted to suggest that Karl's observation comes unwittingly close to the truth; for Conrad is
aiming in *Chance* not at a satire but at an *elaboration* of his essential method. And this method of coming to terms with
the truth of experience is, as he suggests in the Author's
Notes to his novel, 'indissolubly allied' (*C*, x) to the vision of
imaginative sympathy that we have seen emerging from his
pages.

In comparison to the other characters in *Chance* who have
dealings with Flora, Marlow stands out as an inquisitive man.
He makes no claim to the 'pure compassion' of the Fynes, the
religiosity of de Barral's cousin, or the magnanimous idealism of Anthony; yet, he is the only one who fully understands Flora, the only one with sufficient imagination to
bring to fruition the prolonged 'courtship' between Powell
and the widowed Flora. Marlow's success in dealing with
Flora's story implies a peculiar attitude to experience. For
Marlow, things do bear looking into. Where Anthony's ideal
of generosity proves to be 'but a flaming vision of reality'
(262), Powell's curiosity is instinctive; it is more 'neutral'
(280). Marlow possesses this curiosity in abundance. His encounter in the East End with the pressman who had covered
de Barral's trial is important in this connection. The shallow
pressman, who was 'glad' that de Barral 'got seven years'
(86), disapproved of the convicted man's last gesture in court,
the raising of a hard-clenched fist above his head. Marlow
takes a significantly different view of de Barral's final gesture:

> The pressman disapproved of that manifestation. It was
> not his business to understand it. Is it ever the business of
> any pressman to understand anything? I guess not. It
> would lead him too far away from the actualities which
> are the daily bread of the public mind. He probably
> thought the display worth very little from a picturesque
> point of view; the weak voice, the colourless personality
> as incapable of an attitude as a bedpost, the very fatuity of
> the clenched hand so ineffectual at that time and place—
> no, it wasn't worth much. And then, for him, an accom-

plished craftsman in his trade, thinking was distinctly 'bad
business.' His business was to write a readable account.
But I, who had nothing to write, permitted myself to use
my mind as we sat before our still untouched glasses. And
the disclosure which so often rewards a moment of detachment from mere visual impressions gave me a thrill
very much approaching a shudder. I seemed to understand that, with the shock of the agonies and perplexities
of his trial, the imagination of that man, whose moods,
notions, and motives wore frequently an air of grotesque
mystery—that his imagination had been at last roused into
activity. And this was awful. Just try to enter into the
feelings of a man whose imagination wakes up at the very
moment he is about to enter the tomb.

(87)

Marlow describes himself as 'an investigator—a man of de-
ductions' (236), who is concerned with 'the facts of the case'
(425). The narrator contrasts Marlow's complicated hypoth-
eses and imaginative leaps with the 'artless talk' (284) of
Powell; and with the single-mindedness of Anthony whose
knowledge of Flora does not go beyond 'the bare outline of
her story' (333). Constantly we find Marlow 'piecing here
bits of disconnected statements' (222). Marlow makes mistakes as a result of faulty assumptions. He is scrupulously
faithful to facts, as far as they go; but, ultimately, the facts
must be supplemented by his own active imagination.

Unlike Powell and the pressman, Marlow theorizes about
facts; and in that 'moment of detachment from mere visual
impressions' (87) he perceives the essence of an object, a person, a gesture. His attitude to experience parallels that which
so often finds expression in Conrad's letters. The artist, Conrad wrote, 'is a much more subtle and complicated machine
than a camera, and with a much wider range, if in the visual
effects less precise' (*LL*, II, 302). In rejecting photographic realism, Conrad laboured to leave his work indefinite and suggestive, in order not to 'call attention away from things that
matter in the region of art'.[6] Conrad found his inspiration in
the forms and sensations of the real world, but he was a real-
ist only insofar as he was concerned with the truth underlying
every aspect of experience. 'All my concern', he explained,
'has been with the "ideal" value of things, events and people.

That and nothing else. The humorous, the pathetic, the passionate, the sentimental *aspects* came in of themselves—*mais en verité c'est les valeurs idéales des faits et des gestes humains qui se sont imposés à mon activité artistique'* (*LL*, II, 185).

In his art Conrad is striving for that deeper psychology that we have learned to associate with the works of Hawthorne. What matters in *Chance* is not Flora's story but rather the vision of things embodied in the novel's structure. Marlow is always speaking of his search for the psychology of events, the inwardness, the motivations. 'Don't you think that I have hit on the psychology of the situation?' (159) he asks the narrator about his assessment of Anthony. His existence is not merely passive, or aesthetic; he represents the ideal of imaginative sympathy which informs the whole novel. His relation to the world of *Chance* resembles Conrad's own relation to the world, as expressed in *A Personal Record*:

> The ethical view of the universe involves us at last in so many cruel and absurd contradictions, where the last vestiges of faith, hope, charity, and even of reason itself, seem ready to perish, that I have come to suspect that the aim of creation cannot be ethical at all. I would fondly believe that its object is purely spectacular: a spectacle for awe, love, adoration, or hate, if you like, but in this view—and in this view alone—never for despair! Those visions, delicious or poignant, are a moral end in themselves. The rest is our affair—the laughter, the tears, the tenderness, the indignation, the high tranquillity of a steeled heart, the detached curiosity of a subtle mind— that's our affair! And the unwearied self-forgetful attention to every phase of the living universe reflected in our consciousness may be our appointed task on this earth. A task in which fate has perhaps engaged nothing of us except our conscience, gifted with a voice in order to bear true testimony to the visible wonder, the haunting terror, the infinite passion and the illimitable serenity; to the supreme law and the abiding mystery of the sublime spectacle.
>
> (92)

It is Marlow's detached curiosity that enables him to listen to Flora's moving confession without becoming sentimentally involved. The steeled heart is not a cold heart or a heart of darkness; as the narrator observes, Marlow's eyes wear a 'slightly mocking expression, with which he habitually covers up his sympathetic impulses of mirth and pity before the unreasonable complications the idealism of mankind puts into the simple but poignant problem of conduct on this earth' (325).

The articulation of this vision of things was more important to Conrad than one might at first think. As a temperamental novel, one which is the product of one temperament appealing 'to all other innumerable temperaments', *Chance* reflects Conrad's major preoccupations at the time of composition. It was written during a crucial period in his life. Set aside in 1906 in order for Conrad to work on the corrections of *The Secret Agent*, *Chance* was not taken up again until June 1910 after the completion of *Under Western Eyes*; and before it was completed in March 1912, Conrad had weathered extreme domestic and professional stress. His wife Jessie had permanently injured her knee; his son John had been seriously ill; and Conrad's own health remained at best precarious. Although he had published *The Secret Agent*, *Under Western Eyes*, and several short stories, Conrad's financial situation continued to be a matter of grave concern. In addition to these trials, there was the disturbing fact of the unsympathetic reviews which greeted *The Secret Agent* and a number of his stories, including 'Gaspar Ruiz', 'The Brute', and 'Il Conde'.

Conrad's temperament, his Polish nationality, and his solitary lives as mariner and artist clearly marked him as an outsider. Furthermore, he had looked deeper than most men and seen strange things. There is little wonder, therefore, that the critics, faced with his sallies into the dark regions of the human heart, should have been blind to more specific artistic concerns and begun to generalize about the man behind the books. In a review of 'Gaspar Ruiz' and 'The Duel', W. L. Courtney described Conrad as a 'heartless wretch with a pose of brutality' (*LL*, II, 75). Conrad was understandably sensitive to these attacks on his public image; in a letter to Edward Garnett, he exclaimed: 'But the D[ai]ly News article is beyond everything the gloomiest pessimism as to the good feeling and common decency of daily criticism one could imagine' (*LL*, II, 76). Apparently the critic Arthur Symons also made a similar comment about Conrad. Writing to Garnett about Symons' article, Conrad expresses his disappointment: 'I read in a study (still unpublished) of Conrad that I gloat over scenes of cruelty and am obsessed by visions of spilt blood' (*LL*, II, 82). His reply to Symons is even more impassioned and to the point:

> One thing I am certain of is that I have approached the object of my task, things human, in a spirit of piety. The earth is a temple where there is going on a mystery play, childish and poignant, ridiculous and awful enough, in all conscience. Once in I've tried to behave decently. I have not degraded any quasi-religious sentiment by tears and groans; and if I have been amused or indignant, I've neither grinned nor gnashed my teeth. In other words, I've tried to write with dignity, not out of regard for myself, but for the sake of the spectacle, the play with an obscure beginning and an unfathomable dénouement.
>
> I don't think that this has been noticed. It is your penitent beating the floor with his forehead and the ecstatic worshipper at the rails that are obvious to the public eye. The man standing quietly in the shadow of the pillar, if noticed at all, runs the risk of being suspected of sinister designs. Thus I've been called a heartless wretch, a man without ideals and a poseur of brutality. But I will confess to you under seal of secrecy that I *don't believe* I am such as I appear to mediocre minds.
>
> (*LL*, II, 83–84)

Conrad's extreme sensitivity to public opinion had led him to compose *A Personal Record*. He considered the writing of this subtle and suggestive autobiography 'the chance of a lifetime' (*LL*, II, 88) because it gave him an opportunity to present himself as a man of sympathy and understanding, to underscore his aims as an artist. In this work the sea-life and writing career are rendered on parallel lines, since both had come under severe criticism. The life at sea, Conrad points out, 'does not prepare one for the reception of criticism'. 'Yes, you find criticism at sea, and even appreciation' (*PR*, 109). The importance to Conrad of his early letters of recommendation cannot be over-emphasized; they helped him through the difficult years in which he was criticized for leaving home and country to take up the rather indelicate and precarious life of a sailor. The sea had proved an exacting mistress, but not so ugly and insensitive as the priests of the mass media:

> There is a gentleman, for instance, who, metaphorically speaking, jumps upon me with both feet. This image has no grace, but it is exceedingly apt to the occasion. . . . It is not, indeed, pleasant to be stamped upon, but the very thoroughness of the operation, implying not only a careful reading, but some real insight into work whose qualities and defects, whatever they may be, are not so much on the surface, is something to be thankful for in view of the fact that it may happen to one's work to be condemned without being read at all.
>
> (*PR*, 106–7)

Inevitably, Conrad's resentment has been transformed into exquisite irony; like Titus Oates in the hands of Dryden, Courtney has been rendered immortal in his ignorance. Throughout *A Personal Record* Conrad attempts to justify himself on the grounds of artistic sobriety and conscience; and his efforts successfully call into question, as if the fiction itself were not enough, those naive accusations of 'want of patriotism, the want of sense, and the want of heart too' (110).

Chance, like *A Personal Record*, is a product of Conrad's desire to analyse the bases of human conduct and to elucidate some of the fundamentals of artistic integrity. In this novel he depicts a world where love has turned in upon itself, where men cannot communicate because they are trapped in the prisons of language, religion, philosophy, social convention, and self-love. Flora's desire to be believed in parallels Conrad's own hope of ultimately making himself understood. As he explained to his friend and critic R. B. Cunninghame Graham: 'I need not tell you this moral support of belief is the greatest help a writer can receive in those difficult moments' (*LL*, II, 14). 'What I am most grateful for', he wrote to Harriet Copes, 'is the artistic sympathy and the delicate intelligence of your praise' (*LL*, II, 304). Flora's intense need for understanding corresponds to the needs of Leggatt in 'The Secret Sharer' and Jim in *Lord Jim*, the epigraph of which is from Novalis: 'It is certain that any conviction gains infinitely the moment another soul will believe in it.'

In a letter to John Galsworthy (March 28, 1910), Conrad advised: 'And it is on the enunciation of the idea that you'll have to put stress if you want to guide the judgment of your contemporaries' (*LL*, II, 128). Written at the time when Conrad was getting up wind again to finish *Chance*, this statement is peculiarly descriptive of his intentions in that novel. In *Chance* he had been striving to give fictional shape to a concept of emotion or an attitude to reality—namely, that of imaginative sympathy. That his readers understood his intentions seems quite obvious in light of the Author's Note, written years later for the Collected Edition of his works. Dispensing with the criticism which had been directed at the novel's length and technique, Conrad recalled with pleasure the favourable response which *Chance* had received. 'The undoubted sympathy informing the varied appreciations of that book was', he explained, 'a recognition of my good faith in the pursuit of my art. . . . In that sort of foredoomed task which is in its nature very lonely also, sympathy is a precious thing' (ix). This sympathy assured Conrad that he was not 'drifting into the position of a writer for a limited coterie; a position which would have been odious to me as throwing a doubt on the soundness of my belief in the solidarity of all mankind in simple ideas and in sincere emotions' (ix). As a final answer to his critics, he adds: 'I have never sinned against the basic feelings and elementary convictions which make life possible to the mass of mankind and, by establishing a standard of judgment, set their idealism free to look for plainer ways, for higher feelings, for deeper purposes' (x).

It is not surprising, therefore, to find that the language and tone of the Author's Note closely resemble that of *A Personal Record* and the Preface to *The Nigger of the 'Narcissus'*. In the latter, written in 1897, Conrad had expressed his desire to 'arrest . . . the hands busy about the work of the earth . . . to make them pause for a look, for a sigh, for a smile . . .' (xii); ultimately, his aim was to 'awaken in the hearts of the beholders that feeling of unavoidable solidarity . . . which binds men to each other and all mankind to the visible world' (x). *Chance* is not only a dramatization of the creative ethic emerging from *A Personal Record* and Conrad's other writings, but also a reassertion of his faith in the role of the artist in society. Thus the importance of Marlow's almost religious practice of 'that old-maiden-lady-like occupation of putting two and two together' (326). If, as William York Tindall suggests, *Chance* is Conrad's portrait of the artist, it is not the ironic portrait of the artist as an aloof and dissociated young man.[7] (That description applies more readily to M. George in *The Arrow of Gold*.) Rather, it is the portrait of the artist as mature observer, as a sympathetic if somewhat idiosyncratic and sardonic worshipper of the spectacle. As Conrad explains in 'Books', the artist should 'look with a large forgiveness at men's ideas and prejudices' and 'be capable of giving tender recognition to their obscure virtues' (*NLL*, 9).

Chance is not, as Douglas Hewitt suggests, 'oversimplified and falsely romantic'; in fact, its ironic portrayal of the contemporary jungle of human relations and the shallowness and hypocrisy of religious and commercial motivations could hardly be more devastating.[8] No later novel, except perhaps *The Arrow of Gold* with its grotesque portraiture of European art circles, seems quite so bleak and uninhabitable. Obviously, a good deal of the resistance to *Chance* stems from its use of the romance pattern, in particular the ending in which Flora contracts a liaison with the faithful and persistent Powell. David Lodge's view is fairly typical. In his review of *The Turn of the Novel*, he agrees with Alan Friedman that the ending of *Chance*, like the ending of *Tess of the D'Urbervilles*, betrays the 'basic rhythm and impulse of the novel'; he claims that Friedman is correct 'to see a similar falsification in the marriage of Powell and Flora at the end of Conrad's *Chance*— a final twist in that ingeniously constructed novel designed, not to throw a new and interesting light on events, but to leave the reader with a comfortable, sentimental glow'.[9] Against a desperate panorama of meanness and the fact of her own painful and blighted youth, Flora's convenient marriage to Powell can hardly be regarded as a happy ending. Marlow's account of his last meeting with Flora is tinged with irony. Her version of her life with Roderick Anthony at this point in the novel must be read in the light of those events related to us by Marlow and Powell and the Fynes and, for that matter, by Flora herself at earlier stages in her life; otherwise, the reader is likely to be taken in by the rhetoric of romantic love: 'Roderick was perfect. . . . I loved and was loved. . . . All the world, all life, were transformed for me. . . . It was too good to last' (443–45). These moments, days, were the oases in a desperately unhappy saga of self-doubt and rage and depression, which she describes in terms of being 'on the rack' (444). This conversation, with a woman who, at enormous cost, has won a measure of freedom and self-respect, a certain poise and worldly wisdom, is brought properly into focus in the final moments of the meeting, when Marlow asks her, discreetly, about her relationship with Powell:

> I rose to go, for it was getting late. She got up in some agitation and went out with me into the fragrant darkness of the garden. She detained my hand for a moment and then in the very voice of the Flora of old days, with the exact intonation, showing the old mistrust, the old doubt of herself, the old scar of the blow received in childhood, pathetic and funny, she murmured, 'Do you think it possible that he should care for me?'
>
> (445–46)

Under the façade of control and well-being, behind the rhetoric of romantic love, Flora stands, with all the pathos of a character out of Chekhov, naked and exposed, doomed to have the spectre of self-doubt perpetually near at hand.

As the reader looks back upon the novel with the understanding of this final scene and its import clearly in mind, it is not difficult to see why Conrad chose to begin *Chance* with references to the sea and to the business of 'trying to get a ship' (6). Jocelyn Baines argues, mistakenly I believe, that the first section of *Chance* 'has only the most superficial relevance to the rest of the book'.[10] It seems to me, on the contrary, that the first chapter sets the scene beautifully for the progressive annihilation of Flora de Barral. In the early pages of the novel, a certain innocence, a wholesome busyness and integrity, attaches itself to Powell and his pursuit of a berth as an officer, after taking his exams. He rejoices in his success, exults in his future and 'the glamour of its romantic associations' (4). His mood resembles most that of the young captain in *The Shadow Line* after hearing the news of his first command. Then, just as quickly, Powell's success pales in the

knowledge that there is no immediate position available for
the exercise of his new status. He begins to envy even the
cabbies and boot-blacks and loafers for 'their places in the
scheme of the world's labour' (9).

When he finds himself the unexpected possesser of a berth
on the *Ferndale*, skippered by Captain Anthony, Powell once
again indulges his fantasies of success and good fortune during the mad preparations for his departure, with no qualify-
ing thoughts and hesitations to complicate or diminish his enjoyment of the moment. As he enters the gate at dockside,
however, in the presence of the dock policeman and accompanied by two rather questionable characters carrying his
luggage, Powell's conception of things is ruffled somewhat
by the spectacle of a mob from the shadows flying at the gate
closed behind him, like a scene from *Marat/Sade*: 'I was startled to discover how many night prowlers had collected in
the darkness of the street in such a short time and without my
being aware of it. Directly we were through they came surg-
ing against the bars, silent, like a mob of ugly spectres' (27).
This incident, the policeman's sombre assessment of the
scene, and the row which breaks out at a nearby public-house
inject an element of reality into Powell's initiation. Within
minutes he finds himself on board a ship with a cargo of dynamite and, perhaps more ominous for a normally super-
stitious sailor, with the potentially more explosive presence
of the captain's young wife. Suddenly, we are immersed in a
world of contradictions. Behind the warehouses and brick
walls, but hidden from the sight of passersby, is the broad expanse of the river dotted with shipping, the same river that
led into the heart of darkness. So, also, the promise of uncomplicated romance in his new position is qualified for
Powell, but more so for the reader who has the advantage
of Marlow's and the narrator's asides, by the existence of
a world that is either indifferent or antithetical to Powell's
vision.

This is precisely the lesson which Flora learns with such a
shock: that appearances lie, that initial impressions cannot always be relied upon. Conrad very carefully establishes a
moral framework in the early pages of the novel, so that
Flora's loss of faith in her senses and in her own capacities for
judgment are prepared for and are seen as part of a larger social problem. Marlow throws doubt upon the motives of

Powell's namesake, the shipping master. At first this seems a rather perverse and unacceptable slur, attributable to Marlow's determination to be difficult and mysterious; however, as events unfold, there is good reason to wonder at every motivation, to suspect that behind all appearances of order, well-being, and decency may be seen glimpses of chaos, discontent, and meanness. Carleon Anthony, introduced a few pages later in the second chapter, serves to underline the basic contradictions which we have seen emerging in the first chapter of *Chance*. This poet, Marlow informs us, who sings of social and domestic bliss and who aims 'to glorify the result of six thousand years' evolution towards the refinement of thought, manners, and feelings' (38), is, in reality, a bully: 'in his domestic life that same Carleon Anthony showed traces of the primitive cave-dweller's temperament' (38).

The first section of *Chance* establishes a moral framework within which to view the betrayal and subsequent brutalization of Flora at the hands of so-called friends, relatives, and employers; but it also, besides making clear the connections between Powell and the Anthonys, Marlow and the Fynes, and, of course, Marlow and Powell, makes possible a more satisfactory characterization of Marlow. In the early pages, Marlow is described by the narrator in terms of his dissimilarity to Powell. Marlow's orientation is vertical, intellectual; Powell's is horizontal, physical. 'Marlow, who was lanky, loose, quietly composed in varied shades of brown, robbed of every vestige of gloss, had a narrow veiled glance, the neutral bearing and secret irritability which go together with a predisposition to congestion of the liver' (32). Powell observes that Marlow looks as if he is 'up to a thing or two' (33), that 'he's the sort that's always chasing some notion or other round and round his head just for the fun of it' (33). The narrator offers numerous descriptions of both Marlow and Powell, one in particular which bears upon their mutual relation to the sea and which contains the same temple image quoted above from Conrad's letters in reference to his integrity as a writer:

Between two such organisms one would not have expected to find the slightest temperamental accord. But I have observed that profane men living in ships, like the holy men gathered together in monasteries, develop traits

of profound resemblance. This must be because the service of the sea and the service of a temple are both detached from the vanities and errors of a world which
follows no severe rule. The men of the sea understand
each other very well in their view of earthly things, for
simplicity is a good counsellor and isolation not a bad ed-
ucator. A turn of mind composed of innocence and scepticism is common to them all, with the addition of an
unexpected insight into motives, as of disinterested look-
ers–on at a game.

(33)

From this description it is apparent that the sailor's qualities
have been largely split down the middle, with the scepticism
and disinterested insight into motives going to Marlow and
the innocence and simplicity going to Powell.

John Palmer has argued that the limitations of *Chance* are
related not only to the tentativeness of the romance structure,
but also to the unpleasantness of Marlow's character as internal narrator; I have tried to suggest, however, that Marlow's
highly mannered and at times pompous, sarcastic, and sceptical observations are part of his characterization.[11] What could
be more fitting, and ironic, than the fact that out of this irritating, philosophizing sceptic, who hides behind a cloak of
misogyny and scorn for the world of commerce, religion,
government, and even justice, should come the most genuinely sympathetic voice in the novel? Marlow understands
Flora's dilemma, just as he senses the motivational complexity of the shipping master and Flora's many 'helpers'; he is, as
Conrad so aptly characterized himself, the 'man standing in
the shadow of the pillar' in the earth's temple, sinister only to
those mediocre minds that fail to perceive the sympathy and
compassion that move him.

The romance structure in *Chance* is tentative only in the
sense that it has been treated ironically. From the first page to
the last, Conrad has sought to undercut the romance pattern
at every level, delimiting the potential for sentimentality and
increasing the novel's complexity and suggestiveness. Conrad does a great deal to ensure that the romance pattern is seen
only as a convenient tool for the purposes of his analysis.
Marlow describes Anthony as an 'ass' (341); and, in case the
reader swallows the heroic caste of the subtitled parts (Part I,

The Damsel; Part II, the Knight) uncritically, Marlow mocks Anthony's ideal conception of his role: 'There are several types of heroism and one of them at least is idiotic. It is the one which wears the aspect of sublime delicacy. It is apparently the one of which the son of the delicate poet was capable' (328). To put the lid on firmly, Conrad even inserts a deliberate reference to the kind of literature which, ironically, some critics have accused him of reverting to in the later novels. Speaking of Powell's initially naive view of the relationship between Flora and Anthony, Marlow says: 'I suppose that to him life, perhaps not so much his own as that of others, was still in the nature of a fairy-tale with a "they lived happy ever after" termination. We are the creatures of our light literature more than is generally suspected in a world which prides itself on being scientific and practical and in possession of incontrovertible theories' (288). Conrad was quite accurate when he told his agent Pinker as early as 1907 that *Chance* was 'altogether different in tone and treatment' and that it would 'not be on popular lines. Nothing of mine can be, I fear' (*LL*, II, 54). Although the canvas and issues analysed in *Chance* were contemporary—even 'in the news'—Conrad's manner of analysis was anything but easy or popular.

Chance sets the pattern for all of the later novels in its ironic treatment of the romance pattern of the rescue of the distressed individual. Similarly, if the point that I have made about Marlow's curiosity and his manner of tracking down information that interests him being central to the novel's structure is accepted, it seems fairly obvious that the machinery of narration, with its multiple sources of information and opinion, poses no problem at all; in fact, given the importance of Marlow's role of co-ordinator and interpreter of this information, a variety of sources and a fairly complex system of retrieval seems absolutely essential to the structure of the novel. It may even be the case, though this would be more difficult to prove, that the affective quality of *Chance* is further heightened by both the quirks and idiosyncrasies of Marlow and the complicated machinery of narration, since, as the lesson of Bertolt Brecht's plays suggests, such 'alienating' devices in art often serve to increase emotional identification as much as they redirect attention to intellectual content.

This is certainly the case with the imagery of drama or, more generally, theatre, which plays a significant role in such later novels as *Chance*, *The Rescue*, and *The Arrow of Gold*. As if he expected his readers to have difficulty comprehending genre and tone in *Chance*, Conrad very early in the novel has Marlow playfully address Fyne on the subject of Flora's disappearance in the following terms: 'I begged sarcastically to know whether he could tell me if we were engaged in a farce or a tragedy. I wanted to regulate my feelings which, I told him, were in an unbecoming state of confusion' (55). Fyne's behaviour suggests something tragic; but Marlow quickly dismisses the possibility: 'Nobody ever got up at six o'clock in the morning to commit suicide. . . . It's unheard of! This is a farce' (55). His next utterance denies both possibilities: 'As a matter of fact it was neither farce nor tragedy' (56). Fyne, too, concurs: 'Farce be hanged! She has bolted with my wife's brother, Captain Anthony' (65). Later, when we learn the details of Powell's experience on the *Ferndale*, he is described as having been thrown by chance on 'the floating stage of that tragi-comedy' (272). As Powell relates the events on board ship, Marlow continues to see it all in theatrical terms: 'The girl's life had presented itself to me as a tragicomical adventure, the saddest thing on earth, slipping between frank laughter and unabashed tears. Yes, the saddest facts and the most common, perhaps the most worthy of our pity' (310).

As the novel progresses, the theatrical imagery becomes more and more pervasive. De Barral's trial is described at first as a 'sinister farce, bursts of laughter in a setting of mute anguish—that of the depositors; hundreds of thousands of them' (81). The court proceedings become increasingly absurd, because the public and prosecutors cannot decide how to react:

> As the grotesque details of these incredible transactions came out one by one ripples of laughter ran over the closely packed court—each one a little louder than the other. The audience ended by fairly roaring under the cumulative effect of absurdity. The Registrar laughed, the barristers laughed, the reporters laughed, the serried ranks of the miserable depositors watching anxiously every word, laughed like one man. They laughed hysterically— the poor wretches—on the verge of tears.
>
> (81–82)

The scene is worthy of being staged as it stands and easily calls to mind those post-Conradian experiences of Absurdist drama with which we are all familiar.

All of Marlow's encounters with the Fynes have a theatrical quality and produce in him an impulse to play-act. A discussion becomes so solemn that he refers to it as a 'sublunary comedy' (148). He remarks to Mrs. Fyne that the visit of de Barral's cousin 'would have been horrible even on stage' (171). Mrs. Fyne cannot fathom the look which this visit produces on Flora's face, which was suddenly 'horribly merry' (171); however, Marlow quickly assures her that Flora is 'no comedian' (177) and observes to himself that 'the vision of Mrs. Fyne dressed for a rather special afternoon function, engaged in wrestling with a wild-eyed, white-faced girl, had a certain dramatic fascination' (177). In relation to Mrs. Fyne's brother, cooped up with Flora on the floating stage of the *Ferndale*, Marlow says: 'There are on earth no actors too humble and obscure not to have a gallery, that gallery which envenoms the play by stealthy jeers, counsels of anger, amused comments or words of perfidious compassion. However, the Anthonys were free from all demoralizing influences. At sea, you know, there is no gallery' (326). Of course this proves to be incorrect, as the crew first, then Powell, observe, pronounce upon, and become involved in the tragicomedy.

Conrad intended these images to exert an influence on the overall structure and comprehensibility of the novel. He was aware that he was composing a work which would, to a considerable degree, defy the usual categories of description; and it is obvious from the mixed critical responses to *Chance* that he was right. Some critics read the novel as Flora's tragedy; others dismiss it as a sentimental romance; no one, as far as I know, has called it a comedy, though that is the direction pointed by the surface events, in particular the marriage. I believe that Conrad wanted to draw attention to matters of form here, but that he also needed the theatrical imagery, like the mysogyny, to help Marlow distance himself from the materials which he is analysing. By having recourse to such distancing, or alienating, images, Marlow is able, in the opposite direction, to resort on occasion to impassioned outbursts and diatribes. The effect for the reader is a greater degree of involvement in the process of imaginative reconstruction or understanding.

Much of the interest in *Chance*, as I have tried to suggest, resides in the language itself, in the fine discriminations of meanings, the word-play, the conversational tone, and the use of a wide range of English idiom and colloquial expression. Marlow enjoys Powell, who 'seemed wonderfully amenable to verbal suggestion' (36). He delights in gently mocking Fyne, a prodigious walker and an authority on footpaths, who has written a book called *Tramp's Itinerary*. Marlow refers to him as 'the pedestrian Fyne' (39), who possesses 'high pedestrian faculties' (48), and who is moved by the 'force of pedestrian genius' (53). He is less sympathetic to Mrs. Fyne and her use of words:

> I had always wondered how she occupied her time. It was in writing. Like her husband, she too published a little book. It had nothing to do with pedestrianism. It was a sort of handbook for women with grievances (and all women had them), a sort of compendious theory and practice of feminine free morality. . . . I marvelled to myself at her complete ignorance of the world, of her own sex, and of the other kind of sinners. . . . But, then, as she had set up for a guide and teacher, there was nothing surprising for me in the discovery that she was blind.
>
> (66)

More than any other Conrad narrator, the Marlow of *Chance* dwells on the meaning and significance of individual words. One such moment occurs in chapter six, where Marlow relates the details of the cardboard-box manufacturer's visit to retrieve the runaway Flora. When this bully refers to the reason for her flight as a 'tiff', Marlow observes:

> Tiff—was the sort of definition to take one's breath away, having regard to the fact that both the word convict and the word pauper had been used a moment before Flora de Barral ran away from the quarrel about the lace trimmings. Yes, these very words! So at least the girl had told Mrs. Fyne the evening before. The word tiff in connection with her tale had a peculiar savour, a paralysing effect.
>
> (167)

So often in *Chance* a single word—fool, non-entity, adventuress—will serve to wound, mortify, or devastate a character. When Anthony hears his interest in Flora described by
Fyne as 'abominably selfish' (251), the same action which
Flora considered to be generous, he is thrown off track. The
word 'unusual' uttered by the 'suddenly articulate' (293) de
Barral puts Powell out of gear mentally: 'The strange words,
the cautious tone, the whole person left a strange uneasiness
in the mind of Mr. Powell. . . . He felt all adrift. This was
funny talk and no mistake' (294).

Once he is sensitized to his environment by exposure to
the word 'unusual', Powell becomes aware of the difference
between true and false sentiment. He recognizes in Franklin
'the expression of a true sentiment' (303) which Marlow calls
'a thing so rare in this world where there are so many mutes
and so many excellent reasons even at sea for an articulate
man not to give himself away' (303). Perhaps this quotation
offers the proper note to end on, with its reference to mute-
ness and its caution about giving too much away. The characters in *Chance* move between chatter and silence, 'lofty
words' (309), and base sentiments. Flora, who used to chatter
on her walks with her father, chatters no more on board the
Ferndale. Silence claims her, for a time. She is paralysed by
her position with Anthony, who she feels 'caught her words
in the air, never letting her finish her thought' (333). He waits
for a word of denial of his accusations, but prefers to accept
her silence as consent, finally blurting out 'No! Don't speak. I
can't bear to think of it. . . . Say nothing. Don't move' (338).
The words which Flora utters to her father on his release
from prison are, ironically, identical to those words of vanity
and appropriation that Anthony has spoken to her: 'I won't
let you go. Not after all I went through. I won't' (369).

Fortunately, Conrad was in less doubt than his critics concerning the uniqueness of his achievement in *Chance*. As he
suggested in a letter to his agent J. B. Pinker: 'It is the biggest
piece of work I've done since *Lord Jim*. As to what *it is*
I am very confident. As to what will happen to it when
launched—I am much less confident. And it's a pity. One
doesn't do a trick like that twice—and I'm not growing
younger—alas! It will vanish in the ruck' (*LL*, II, 146). In
making this assertion Conrad has not forgotten his epic

struggles with *Nostromo*; he is simply aware of having faced very different technical difficulties in *Chance*. Writing to Alfred Knopf, then a representative of Doubleday, Conrad recommended *Chance*: 'I recommend to you that book very specially for, *of its kind*, it isn't a thing that one does twice in a lifetime' (*LL*, II, 149). Now that the range and scope of criticism of the novel is expanding, the nature of Conrad's 'trick' and the degree of his achievement in *Chance* should become increasingly apparent. As Flora de Barral says in one of the more ambivalent and ironic comments at the end of the novel: 'Truth will out, Mr. Marlow' (444).

2 Victory
The Aesthetics of Rejection

I

The characters and themes of a novel are by no means laid to
rest when their author completes his manuscript, puts it in a
drawer for a nine-year period, or ships it off to a publisher.
Most often, they go on pestering him, remonstrating, de-
manding more attention and, certainly, more justice. Precisely at the moment he thinks himself committed to an entirely new entourage and set of problems, he notices some
unexpected movement behind a bale of silk in the fiction
warehouse. *Hey! You! Come out from behind that container.
Haven't I seen you somewhere . . . no, it can't be. Well, I'll be
buggered. I thought I'd finished you off in Macao.* Alternative-
ly, while Flora's and Anthony's fictive destinies are being
worked out, just as the two of them are looking forward to a
season of peace and unemployment, their creator is saying to
himself, consciously or subliminally: *Now, suppose I were to
put Captain Anthony on an island called, let's say, Samburan, with
a young woman and the emotional legacy of a warped philosopher
father? And suppose his vision were a slight distortion of Marlow's,
a mixture of detachment and sympathy . . .*

The seeds of a novel are frequently planted in one of its
predecessors. Anyone who doubts these creative logistics has
only to think of the similarities between *Lord Jim* and *Victory*
or to turn for a moment back to *Chance* and to note that Marlow is described as being in possession of 'a turn of mind
composed of innocence and scepticism . . . with the addition
of an unexpected insight into motives, as of disinterested
lookers-on at a game' (*C*, 34). Change the game and the set-

ting and you could just as easily be reading about Axel Heyst, a somewhat unsuccessful looker-on who finds himself being constantly pulled into the action.

It's crucial to see *Victory* as a continuing exploration of the aesthetic and philosophical concerns given shape in *Chance*; otherwise, one is likely to misread not only *Victory*, but also the whole of the later fiction. In the *Metaphysics of Darkness*, Royal Roussel argues that Marlow's failure to establish the ground-rules for human interaction in *Chance* marks the end of Conrad's search and that, thereafter, his fiction is simply a reworking of the vision of *Under Western Eyes*. 'No matter how practised Marlow's eye becomes,' he says, 'it would seem that, because vision is tied to chance in this way, the future will always be the product of accident rather than design.'[1] Or, stated more strongly: 'Chance is thus the expression of the chaotic principle which determines human life. It is important to see that, for Conrad, this is not simply a question of man's being an essentially free agent acting in a limited situation. It is rather that the very structure of an individual's awareness, the source of his supposedly free action, is being determined by forces over which he has no control.'[2] In my view, in order to suit the needs of his convenient thesis, Roussel misreads the later fiction. Marlow does give poor advice to Fyne, as a result of his then limited understanding of the characters of Flora and Anthony. However, it must be remembered that his presence of mind combined with the chance barking of a dog result in his saving Flora from suicide. Similarly, his understanding of Flora's situation and Powell's real sentiments, in conjunction with the chance sighting of Powell's boat turning into a creek off the Thames for his rendezvous, results in Marlow seizing the opportunity to bring Powell and Flora more fully together. The epigraph by Sir Thomas Browne—'Those that hold all things are governed by fortune had not erred, had they not persisted there'— is not misapplied here. One of the great strengths and ironies of *Chance*, given the superficial affirmation of the romance pattern, is that Conrad does not skirt the issue of chaos and irrationality in human affairs, but, facing it squarely, holds up for our attention the ideal of imaginative sympathy.

He brings the same penetration and the same awareness of the complexity of human motivation to bear on the writing of *Victory*. Indeed, the images of dynamite and imminent dissolution in *Chance* and the apocalyptic imagery of *Victory* recall that remarkable passage in Conrad's essay on Henry James, in which he tries to express his convictions about language and silence, will and chance, action and detachment. He speaks of art, the writing of fiction, as a supreme form of action, one that is, if not impossible, precarious, but also more lasting because it is concerned with the matter of human consciousness. Then he describes a hypothetical final moment when, against all odds, against reason, the human voice makes itself heard:

When the last aqueduct shall have crumbled to pieces, the last airship fallen to the ground, the last blade of grass have died upon a dying earth, man, indomitable by his training in resistance to misery and pain, shall set this undiminished light of his eyes against the feeble glow of the sun. The artistic faculty, of which each of us has a minute grain, may find its voice in some individual of that last group, gifted with a power of expression and courageous enough to interpret the ultimate experience of mankind in terms of his temperament, in terms of art. I do not mean to say that he would attempt to beguile the last moments of humanity by an ingenious tale. It would be too much to expect—from humanity. I doubt the heroism of the hearers. As to the heroism of the artist, no doubt is necessary. There would be on his part no heroism. The artist in his calling of interpreter creates (the clearest form of demonstration) because he must. He is so much of a voice that, for him, silence is like death; and the postulate was, that there is a group alive, clustered on the threshold to watch the last flicker of light on a black sky, to hear the last word uttered in the still workshop of the earth. It is safe to affirm that, if anybody, it will be the imaginative man who would be moved to speak on the eve of that day without to-morrow—whether in austere exhortation or in a phrase of sardonic comment, who can guess?

For my own part, from a short and cursory acquaintance with my kind, I am inclined to think that the last utterance will formulate, strange as it may appear, some hope now to us utterly inconceivable. For mankind is delightful in its pride, its assurance, and its indomitable tenacity. It will sleep on the battlefield among its own dead, in the manner of an army having won a barren victory. It will not know when it is beaten. And perhaps it is the right quality. The victories are not, perhaps, so barren as it may appear from a purely strategical, utilitarian point of view.

(*NLL*, 13–14)

The writing of fiction may be, at best, a barren activity; the later Conrad may, according to some critics, not have known when he was beaten. However, I believe that his voice continued to be heard because there were things he had yet to say, notions of victory or defeat notwithstanding.

II

When the infernal trio of Jones, Ricardo, and Pedro arrive on the island of Samburan to lay waste to his world, Axel Heyst comes to a partial understanding of the nature of experience that seems, also, to sum up the critical situation with regard to *Victory*, Conrad's most controversial novel: 'There is a quality in events which is apprehended differently by different minds or even by the same minds at different times. Any man living at all consciously knows that embarrassing truth' (248). No other novel of Conrad has elicited such extreme and contradictory responses from his critics. Albert Guerard describes this colourful and controversial book as 'one of the worst novels for which high claims have been made by critics of standing'; he argues that 'the gross overvaluation of *Victory* is of such long-standing that it will not be easily corrected. *Victory* is Conrad for the high schools and motion pictures, the easiest and generically the most popular of the novels. And the easiest, incidentally, for the teacher or the critic blocking out themes, plot lines, symbols. The time has come', Guerard concludes, 'to drop *Victory* from the Conrad canon.'[3]

Victory's admirers, including F. R. Leavis, R. W. Stallman, Muriel Bradbrook, and John Palmer, are equally insistent. Bradbrook considers *Victory* the last novel of the middle period, 'and if not the greatest, it is the most firmly modelled, the most boldly wrought'.[4] John Palmer argues that '*Victory* is the high point of Conrad's third period' because it is Conrad's most 'successful allegorizing of his beliefs'.[5] One need not review the vast body of criticism of this novel in its entirety to be struck by the distance which separates the praisers from the detractors. Even Conrad himself seems to have been given to the use of superlatives in his remarks on *Victory*, describing it as 'a book in which I have tried to grasp at more "life-stuff" than perhaps in any other of my works, and the one of which the appreciation of the public has given me the most pleasure' (*LL*, II, 342). The gulf separating the critics suggests that there is still much to be said about the life-stuff and, more importantly, about the art-stuff in *Victory*.

Much of the disagreement concerning the meaning and success of *Victory* stems from an unwillingness to accommodate the mixing of fictional modes; or perhaps it would be more accurate to say, from a mystification as to how such a mixture should be handled critically. John Palmer states the problem succinctly:

> But the issue is confused, in *Victory*, by Conrad's unusual structural methods. At the beginning of the novel, the reader is confronted by what looks like conventional realistic narrative—experience seen from the normative public point of view. But gradually the symbolic overtones accumulate, as the book moves toward its inner core of allegory; and the reader must shift his stance, undergoing a process from one kind of pleasure at the beginning to another at the end; a gradual penetration through externals to the essential truths of Heyst's metaphysico-moral situation, much on the order of Marlow's meditative journeys. As the allegory becomes firmer, the need of fictional realism lessens; and Conrad has the additional advantage of having begun in a reasonably straightforward way, so that the reader carries his assent with him into the heightened experience of Samburan.[6]

Certainly, much of the criticism of *Victory* is characterized by an over-emphasis on either the realistic or the symbolic aspects at the expense of the totality of the novel as a structure of meaning. Moser and Hewitt are clearly committed on the side of fictional realism, though they profess not to be. Indeed, Hewitt's preface to the 1969 edition of *Conrad: A Reassessment* (1952) tries to hold its ground by arguing, not without some justification, that symbolic interpretations of Conrad have gone too far. Hewitt's long-standing objection to the characters in *Victory* is that they are stereotyped, not real enough. Lena is unbelievably flawless; Ricardo it seems, doesn't speak convincingly (Hewitt 'cannot take seriously a character who speaks thus').[7] His objection boils down to strictly realistic-naturalistic criteria: Ricardo does not even 'give a greater impression of reality when he is making love'.[8]

In the other direction, a great deal has been written about the mythic dimension of *Victory*—the Genesis myth, with its dramatization of the fall and prophecy of the redemption of man; the psychological myth of the integrated personality, represented by persona and shadow in harmony; the medieval psychodrama, in which the forces of good and evil battle for the soul of Everyman. These elements represent important threads in the rich tapestry of the novel, to be sure, but they have often been allowed by critics to obscure less obvious but very important formal considerations. Because of its pervading irony, *Victory* stops short of allegory; that is why strictly symbolic interpretations of the novel seem so hopelessly strained and reductive. John Palmer speaks wisely of *Victory*'s 'allegorical impulse', which recalls R. W. B. Lewis's phrase 'allegorical swelling'.[9] Indeed, Lewis is a useful indicator of how such matters should be viewed, especially in his remarks on the relation between Heyst and Jones: 'The strength of each often appears as an extension of the other's weakness and vice-versa; which is one reason why the conflict between them, as it assumes its form, seems to extend endlessly, to enlarge almost beyond the reach of human reckoning. It brushes the edge of allegory and touches briefly on the outskirts of myth—one "of those myths, current in Polynesia, of amazing strangers . . . gods or demons".'[10]

Lewis's attitude to *Victory*, which is that myth and symbol should be regarded as suggestive rather than conclusive components, not only encourages a more balanced reading of the novel, but also is in accord with Conrad's own remarks about *Victory* in a letter to Barrett Clark:

> Coming now to the subject of your inquiry, I wish at first to put before you a general proposition: that a work of art is very seldom limited to one exclusive meaning and not necessarily tending to a definite conclusion. And this for the reason that the nearer it approaches art, the more it acquires a symbolic character. This statement may sur-

prise you, who may imagine that I am alluding to the Symbolist School of poets or prose writers. Theirs, however, is only a literary proceeding against which I have nothing to say. I am concerned here with something much larger. But no doubt you have meditated on this and kindred questions yourself.

So I will only call your attention to the fact that the symbolic conception of a work of art has this advantage, that it makes a triple appeal covering the whole field of life. All the great creations of literature have been symbolic, and in that way have gained in complexity, in power, in depth, and in beauty.

(*LL*, II, 204–5)

What distinguishes *Victory* from conventional allegory is the kind, and degree, of irony operative throughout the novel, though this is a feature that critics have continually ignored. Guerard, whose comprehension of fictional modes and techniques in Conrad's early work is superb, allows for no irony in *Victory*, no possibilities for meaning and significance beneath the surfaces of plot, character, and speech; consequently, he finds the language 'flat and unenergized', the characters 'unfortunately one-dimensional', and the plot 'melodramatic'.[11] Even Muriel Bradbrook, who claims to understand and admire the novel, insists that 'The story is simply told, there is no narrator's perspective, there is neither irony, humour, nor comment in the telling; the irony, the humour and comments, such as they are, belong to Heyst.'[12]

Irony is, in fact, everywhere present in *Victory*. Structurally, as an ironic romance, *Victory* has a built-in antidote or counterweight to its allegorizing tendencies. It shares with its predecessor, *Chance*, a variation of the romance pattern of the rescue of the distressed individual, which includes Heyst's 'rescue' of Morrison from the Portuguese officials, the 'rescue' of Lena from captivity in Zangiacomo's Women's Orchestra, and the potential 'rescue' of Heyst from his life-denying philosophy. Beyond that, of course, there is always the rescue of the attentive reader who has perceived the folly of Heyst and Lena and Schomberg and who has assimilated certain lessons, consciously or otherwise, into his thinking. Similarly, the mixed modes and the shifting point of view, which are themselves a function of the ironic vision at work in *Vic-*

tory, serve to legislate against both a strictly realistic and a strictly allegorical interpretation. Even at the level of words on the page, dialogue, phrases, statements about language, Conrad has loaded every rift with irony, making it impossible to slip away comfortable in the assurance that one has fully understood the novel, in whole or in part. That is why no one can agree about Lena's 'sacrifice' or the meaning of Heyst's final words: 'Ah, Davidson, woe to the man whose heart has not learned while young to hope, to love—and to put its trust in life' (410).

According to Northrop Frye, 'Ironic literature begins with realism and tends towards myth, its mythical patterns being as a rule more suggestive of the demonic than of the apocalyptic, though sometimes it simply continues the romantic pattern of stylization.' [13] What Frye says of ironic literature in general accords with my own understanding of form in *Victory*, not only in terms of the modal shift and the demonic character of the mythical patterns, but also in terms of the emphasis on stylization. *Victory* is Conrad's most highly stylized and formalistic fictional work. Why it should have been so has to do, I believe, with the philosophical content with which he was dealing, the quasi-Schopenhauerian doctrine of detachment and withdrawal. When he insisted that 'the more a work approaches art the more it takes on a symbolic character', Conrad was also saying that the farther a work is removed from 'life' the less it is subject to the formal demands of realism-naturalism. Put another way, he is arguing that there is a significant distinction to be made between art and life and that art, in a very important sense, is a rejection and reconstruction of 'life as it is'.

III

The rejectivist aesthetic informing *Victory* might best be approached by way of Camus' chapter, 'Rebellion and Art', in *The Rebel*. Art, according to Camus, is a disputation of reality, a form of transcendence, the creation of a substitute world which has unity, design. The writing of fiction apparently serves a metaphysical need in man, since it is concerned with a 'rectification of the actual world—a world where suffering can, if it wishes, continue until death, where passions are never distracted, where people are prey to obsessions and are always present to one another. Man is finally able to give himself the alleviating form and limits which he pursues in vain in his own life.'[14] 'The novel', he says, 'creates destiny to suit eventuality. In this way it competes with creation and, provisionally, conquers death.'[15] There is a passage in *The Rebel* which explains this impulse more fully and which seems especially appropriate to the yearnings expressed in *Victory*, by Heyst, by Lena, and by the author:

The desire for possession is only another form of the desire to endure; it is this that comprises the impotent delirium of love. No human being, even the most passionately loved and passionately loving, is ever in our possession. On the pitiless earth where lovers are often separated in death and are always born divided, the total possession of another human being and absolute communion throughout an entire lifetime are impossible dreams. The desire for possession is insatiable, to such a point that it can survive even love itself. To love, therefore, is to sterilize the person one loves. The shamefaced suffering of the abandoned lover is not so much due to being no longer loved as to knowing that the other partner can and must love again. In the final analysis, every man devoured by the overpowering desire to endure and possess wishes that those whom he has loved were either sterile or dead. This is real rebellion. Those who have not insisted, at least once, on the absolute virginity of human beings and of the world, who have not trembled with longing and impotence at the fact that it is impossible, and have then not been destroyed by trying to love halfheartedly, perpetually forced back upon their longing for the absolute, cannot understand the realities of rebellion and its ravening desire for destruction. But the lives of others always escape us, and we escape them too; they have no firm outline. Life from this point of view is without style. It is only an impulse that endlessly pursues its form without ever finding it. Man, tortured by this, tries in vain to find the form that will impose certain limits between which he can be king. If only one single living thing had definite form, he would be reconciled![16]

Heyst's struggle, and Lena's too, is to find a style, a form for their lives, their fantasies. Each is trying to write the novel of the other, to find or create unity where it is not. Heyst cannot tolerate the senselessness or the randomness evident in the lives of Morrison and Lena; therefore, he imposes his own form on their lives, gives them his style. So, too, does Lena despair at not being in full possession of her mysterious and troubled lover; thus she constructs a myth that will embody her terribly destructive impulses, give them a more pleasant and comprehensible colouration. Heyst draws Lena into his magic circle, his web—not without good reason is one of his nicknames Spider Heyst. He succeeds for a time being king of his own small island, but the remorseless movement of time brings changes. Schomberg knows as well as any character in *Victory* the terror of unstructured space; that is why he totally reconstructs reality, by way of gossip, in terms that suit his limited understanding of human needs and motivations. Inevitably, the kingdom of his influence invades and overruns that of Heyst.

The most extreme case of possession, or domination, in *Victory* is that inflicted upon Heyst by his father, a philosophical rebel of the first order. Like Flora de Barral, Heyst is the victim of a perfidy enacted upon him at an impressionable age; he has been saddled with a philosophy of scepticism and withdrawal which leaves him unequipped for both the love and the crime that come his way. Where Flora has had her conception of herself shattered by the outburst of an enraged and unthinking governess, Heyst has had his vision of the world carefully and systematically warped by the teachings of his philosopher-father. I have tried to illustrate in the previous chapter the degree to which form and content were allied in *Chance*. The form of *Victory* is even more noticeably allied to its intellectual content, which Conrad describes briefly but not inaccurately in the Author's Note to the novel:

> Besides, Heyst in his fine detachment had lost the habit of asserting himself. I don't mean the courage of self-assertion, either moral or physical, but the mere way of it, the trick of the thing, the readiness to mind and the turn of the hand that come without reflection and lead the man to excellence in life, in art, in crime, in virtue, and for that matter, even in love. Thinking is the great enemy of perfection. The habit of profound reflection, I am compelled

to say, is the most pernicious of all habits formed by civilized man.

(*C*, xi)

The emphasis here, of course, is on the word perfection, for it is the desire for perfection that drives the lover or artist or criminal in man to rebel.

Victory, then, is an enquiry into the metaphysics of style. In Camus' words, 'This correction which the artist imposes by his language and by a redistribution of elements derived from reality is called style and gives the re-created universe its unity and boundaries.' [17] Not surprisingly, then, considerable emphasis is placed in the novel upon establishing the geographical and intellectual boundaries of the action, to setting the scene, as it were, for the various re-creations of reality with which the novel is concerned. As I mentioned, the most complete re-creation is inflicted upon Heyst, after which he is set adrift by his father with only indifference and scepticism to sustain him. Perhaps set adrift is not the right phrase, since Heyst has been advised by his father to avoid the stream of life, to 'Look on—make no sound' (175); but it does suggest an appropriate lack of control and direction. Although he underlines Heyst's problem in the Author's Note, Conrad shows remarkable skill in the novel by delaying any detailed explanation of the nature and origins of Heyst's scepticism until the main action—the affair with Lena and the confrontation with the infernal trio—is under way. In the first chapter we learn only that Heyst got a few books from his late father; in the fourth chapter, that his father, who was somewhat of a crank philosopher, has written some of these books; and, in the seventh and final chapter of Part I, that Heyst has somehow become a 'looker-on' (60). Then, in Part II, after the essential impressions of Heyst have been conveyed through the offices of the narrator and after the crucial events leading to Heyst's 'elopement' with Lena have been orchestrated, Conrad devotes several pages to an analysis of the present state of Heyst's mind: his disenchantment with life, his guilt over the death of Morrison, and his sense of the loneliness and isolation of his hermit's existence. This information is perfectly timed to render more credible the state of awakened sympathy which prompts Heyst to steal Lena from

Zangiacomo's orchestra and from the clutches of the lecherous Schomberg. Finally, the spectral figure of the elder Heyst surfaces in the third chapter of Part II, replete with disenchantment and blue silk dressing-gown: 'Three years of such companionship at that plastic and impressionable age were bound to leave in the boy a profound distrust of life. The young man learned to reflect, which is a destructive process, a reckoning with the past' (91–92).

Heyst's father, then, becomes a haunting presence in the novel. The essence of his legacy to his son is most fully revealed in Part III, as Heyst meditates upon the significance and probable outcome of his involvement with Lena on Samburan. In the first chapter we discover that Heyst's father bequeathed him 'his contemptuous, inflexible negation of all effort' (173); both father and son regard action as 'a barbed hook, baited with the illusion of progress, to bring out of the lightless void the shoals of unnumbered generations!' (174). The old cynic suggests that a 'full and equable contempt' (174) would soon do away with his son's lingering belief in flesh and blood. Although the old man is a 'destroyer of systems, of hopes, of beliefs' and a 'bitter condemner of life' (175), Heyst nevertheless reveres him, holds him in a sort of religious awe; and, when eventually he has his father's effects shipped out to Samburan, after his first lapse into the traps of pity and financial enterprise, Heyst, the narrator informs us, 'must have felt like a remorseful apostate before those relics' (177). Heyst lives the life of a saintly hermit on his island, plunged into 'an abyss of meditation over books' (180), while Wang, his Chinese servant, goes about 'in obedience to his instincts' (181), tending to job, family, and the necessities of physical survival. Religious images of this sort recur throughout the novel, in connection with Heyst's father, until we see Heyst seemingly in a position to renounce the false god of his scepticism and to transfer his allegiance to the sacrificial humanity of Lena. He burns the offending relics— books, furniture, portrait of his father—but he also burns himself, in a final, enigmatic act of suicide.

Heyst's reaction to his father's death is important to note, at this point in the novel, as an indicator of his future behaviour. In the same chapter we find Heyst meditating on his failure to live up to his philosophy of non-involvement; and we learn that he 'was hurt by the sight of his own life, which ought to have been a masterpiece of aloofness' (174), the word 'masterpiece' aptly recalling Camus' conception of art as recreation. This sober thought ushers him back in time to the funeral of his father, where he had read the abusive death-notices with 'mournful detachment' (175). The contradiction implicit in this description of his feelings characterizes Heyst's life, his *imperfect* detachment; his compassion or sympathy is the Achilles heel that will bring him down, that will make it impossible for him ever to achieve the detachment necessary if he is to survive intact his travels along 'the broad path of human involvement' (177). Heyst, to use Davidson's phrase, will be always in danger of 'spiritual starvation' (177); his is 'a spirit which had renounced all outside nourishment, and was sustaining itself proudly on its own contempt of the usual aliments which life offers to the common appetites of men' (177). This remark is followed in the novel by a clever shift to Wang's garden and his role as provider; the numerous images of nourishment also link up, ironically, with Schomberg the hotel-keeper, who is concerned not with the state of Heyst's soul, but only with discovering where the Swede gets his food to eat on the island. Schomberg, apart in the world of men, is a deceitful host, who seasons his hospitality with treachery and violence, and who starves his wretched wife emotionally.

The most extensive and suggestive account of the Heyst philosophy occurs when Heyst returns from his walk with Lena and is prompted, by the sense of her presence and the momentous nature of events, to talk of his life. Enervated, and in love among the 'ruins' (195) of the Tropical Belt Coal Company, he tries to explain to Lena the cause of his solitary confinement, of his incarceration in the void. Pointing to the painting of his father on the wall, he says:

> Primarily the man with the quill pen in his hand that you so often look at is responsible for my existence. He is also responsible for what my existence is, or rather has been. He was a great man in his way. I don't know much of his history. I suppose he began like other people; took fine words for good ringing coin and noble ideas for valuable banknotes. He was a great master of both, himself, by the way. Later he discovered—how am I to explain it to you? Suppose the world were a factory and all mankind work-

men in it. Well, he discovered that the wages were not good enough. That they were paid in counterfeit money.
(195–96)

This passage is fascinating for what it reveals about Heyst's sensitivity concerning his choice of words; he recognizes, as my initial quotation from *Victory* suggests, that every person perceives things differently and that the utmost care must be taken with words if one hopes to reduce the gap that ultimately exists between the sentiment and the language chosen to express it. It is interesting, too, that he chooses to explain his father's disaffection with life in terms of a commercial or monetary image, in view of Lena's background among the commercial outposts of empire, his own financial collapse in the coal business with Morrison, and the imminent arrival of the world, in the persons of Jones, Ricardo, and Pedro, to collect its dues from the aristocratic Swede.

In the course of this visitation Heyst will learn much of the wages of detachment, of the cost of his father's alternative career of avoidance and indifference. As he continues with his autobiographical comments to Lena, Heyst's language bristles with ironies and religious allusions. 'It wasn't a new discovery,' he admits, still speaking of life's false coin and inadequate wages,

> but he brought his capacity for scorn to bear on it. It was immense. It ought to have withered this globe. I don't know how many minds he convinced. But my mind was very young then, and youth can be easily seduced—even by a negation. He was very ruthless, and yet he was not without pity. He dominated me without difficulty. A heartless man could not have done so. Even to fools he was not utterly merciless. He could be indignant, but he was too great for flouts and jeers. What he said was not meant for the crowd; it could not be; and I was flattered to find myself among the elect. They read his books, but I have heard his living word. It was irresistible. It was as if that mind were taking me into its confidence, giving me a special insight into its mastery of despair. Mistake, no doubt. There is something of my father in every man who lives long enough. But they don't say anything. They can't. They wouldn't know how, or perhaps, they

wouldn't speak if they could. Man on this earth is an unforeseen accident which does not stand close investiga-
tion. However, that particular man died as quietly as a
child goes to sleep. But after listening to him, I could not
take my soul down into the street to fight there. I started
off to wander about, an independent spectator—if that's
possible.

(196)

This beautifully evocative language, with its religious allusions to 'the elect' and the 'living word', recalls the language
of Conrad's intimate correspondence and suggests that there
was more than a good deal of Heyst's father in the author of
Victory as well.

To understand the importance of such matters to Conrad,
one has only to glance briefly at the early fiction, such as *An
Outcast of the Islands*, or examine the correspondence, both of
which bear striking resemblances, in terms of both rhetoric
and sentiment, to the preceding quotations about detachment
and scepticism.

In the letters, Conrad described the universe as a tragic accident, a vast inhuman machine: 'It knits us in and it knits us
out. It has knitted time, space, pain, death, corruption, despair and all the illusions—and nothing matters' (*LL*, I, 215–
16). He spoke of human values as mere illusions: theory was
'a cold lying tombstone of departed truth' (*LL*, I, 174); hope
was 'the best and worst of life. Half of it comes from God and
half from the devil, but it behooves men to take gifts and
curses with a steady hand and an equable mind—because of
such is made up Fate, the blind, the Invincible' (*LL*, I, 176);
truth was the most evasive of all illusions: 'And suppose truth
is just around the corner, like the elusive and useless loafer it
is? I can't tell. No one can know. It is impossible to know
anything' (*LL*, I, 208). 'All is illusion,' Conrad wrote to
his friend and literary acquaintance Edward Garnett, '—the
words written, the mind at which they are aimed, the truth
they are intended to express, the hands that will hold the paper, the eyes that will glance at their lines. Every image floats
in a sea of doubt—and the doubt itself is lost in an unexplored
universe of incertitudes.'[18]

Conrad's most extreme statement touching on the meaninglessness of life is to be found in a letter to R. B. Cun-

ninghame Graham, a friend to whom he could frankly and
honestly express his darkest thoughts:

> 'Put out the tongue', why not? One ought to really and
> the machine will run all the same. The question is
> whether the fatigue of the muscular exertion is worth the
> transient pleasure of indulgent scorn. On the other hand
> one may ask whether scorn, love or hate are justified in
> the face of such shadowy illusions.
> The machine is thinner than air and as evanescent as a
> flash of lightning. The attitude of cold unconcern is the
> only reasonable one. Of course reason is hateful,—but
> why? Because it demonstrates (to those who have the
> courage) that we, living, are out of life, —utterly out of
> it. The mysteries of a universe made up of drops of fire
> and clods of mud do not concern us in the least. The fate
> of a humanity condemned ultimately to perish from cold
> is not worth troubling about. If you take it to heart it
> becomes an unendurable tragedy. . . .
> Life knows us not and we do not know life,—we don't
> even know our own thoughts. Half the words we use
> have no meaning whatever and of the other half each man
> understands each word after the fashion of his own folly
> and conceit. Faith is a myth and beliefs shift like mists on
> the shore: thoughts vanish: words once pronounced, die:
> and the memory of yesterday is as shadowy as the hope of
> tomorrow, —only the string of my platitudes seems to
> have no end. As our peasants say: 'Pray, brother, forgive
> me for the love of God.' And we don't know what for-
> giveness is, nor what is love, nor where God is. *Assez*!
>
> (*LL*, I, 222–23)

Conrad did take it all seriously and suffered terribly as a result, but he could not put out his tongue at the universe for
long; that gesture was confined to such fictional characters as
Decoud in *Nostromo* and Kayerts in the short story 'An Outpost of Progress'.

It hardly seems necessary to underline those phrases that
relate most clearly to a reading of *Victory*: 'indulgent scorn',
'cold unconcern', 'humanity not worth troubling about'.
These words might have been lifted directly from the writings of Heyst's father. The point to be made here is that the

intellectual content is important to a genuine understanding of the novel, that it is by no means a cosmetic.

There is an important encounter in the final pages of *Victory* between Heyst and his major adversary Mr. Jones, which further emphasizes the centrality of these philosophical elements in the novel, and which seems to have been overlooked by the critics. Plain Mr. Jones remarks to Heyst that they are living in a peculiar time, a soft age: 'This, Mr. Heyst, is a soft age. It is also an age without prejudices. I've heard that you are free of them yourself. You mustn't be shocked if I tell you that we are after your money' (379). The irony here is partly situational, partly cumulative. Mr. Jones has been working on Heyst's nerves, trying his patience, jabbing him where he is most vulnerable, with references to Heyst's 'subtler weapons of intelligence' (377), to the 'originality' (377) of Heyst's ideas and tastes. Jones says these things, of course, with 'languid irony' (378), because Heyst is his unarmed prisoner, a victim of the grosser, more worldly devices of a fellow-gentleman. Mr. Jones has a revolver, whereas Heyst has not even the presence of mind with which to defend himself. When Jones describes himself as an outcast, or outlaw, he makes a point of defining the term especially for Heyst, in language he is certain Heyst will understand: 'If you prefer a less materialistic view, I am a sort of fate—the retribution that waits its time' (379).

It would be easy to miss the ironies and echoes in this passage, while attending to the more obvious fictional technique of doubling. The key word here is 'materialistic'. Heyst, too, is an outcast, or to use Camus' term for the romantic, a rebel, but one whose adopted ideas have separated him from life to the point that he has neither the resourcefulness nor the cunning to protect himself and Lena. Material reality astounds and distresses him. Wang, who functions literally as Heyst's servant/provider and symbolically as his body, recognizes his master's ineffectuality and makes off with the only revolver. Like Anthony in *Chance*, who is also compared to Othello, Heyst is disarmed and paralysed even by a bit of gossip; he has been too long out of touch with the real world of thieves and lovers and prevaricators to have any perspective on the gossip and innuendo that follow him to Samburan and to recognize the evil that confronts him in the persons of his deadly visitors. Thus Jones' facetious remark is all the more signifi-

cant because it points ironically to Heyst's dangerous separation from material reality, just as his remark about being free
from prejudices serves to undermine the idea of ethical indifference or relativity about which Heyst and his father have
conversed.

I mention this incident because it brings into focus the relation which Conrad saw between the world of *Victory* and the
larger context of post-Enlightenment Europe. Like another
Shakespearean character, Hamlet, Heyst suffers from the
curse of consciousness; he cannot bring himself to act and is
consequently a prey to destructive forces within himself and
at large in the world. I have already quoted the passage from
the Author's Note, in which Conrad speaks of Heyst's 'fine
detachment' (xi) and resultant volitional problems. Conrad
also mentions in his preface the 'unchanging Man of history'
(ix), whose 'power of endurance' and 'capacity for detachment' (ix) have continually brought down on his head the
'trump of the Last Judgment' and the 'lightning of wrath' (x).
The writing of *Victory*, Conrad reminds us, was 'finished in
1914 before the murder of an Austrian Archduke sounded the
first note for a world already full of doubts and fears' (ix).
Detachment, as Conrad so clearly understood, was very
much a European malaise, a romantic sickness unto death
that would sooner or later take by the throat the whole of
western civilization, as Heyst's detachment brought down on
his head the revenge of the pompous and half-mad German
hotel-keeper, Schomberg. The distance from Samburan to
Europe should not blind readers to the relevance for Conrad's
contemporaries of the issues that he dramatizes in *Victory*: the
sickness that eats away at the human heart.

IV

It's tempting but wrong-headed to use the philosophical content in *Victory* as a means of pigeon-holing Conrad as a humanist or an existentialist. The novel is too rich and too complex to allow such reductive thinking. Besides, as I have
indicated by my quotation from his essay on Henry James,
Conrad distinguished between the man who suffers and the
writer who creates. Having argued that *Victory* is an enquiry
into the metaphysics of style, I would like to show how Conrad once again takes his cues from the content he is exploring.
Victory is formalistic; and the many formal elements—the

transition from a realistic to a symbolic mode, the shifting point of view, the romance pattern, the multi-dimensional rhetoric, the symbolism bordering on allegory, the dialectical configurations into which the characters often fall—reflect the intensity of Heyst's and, to a certain extent, his creator's rejection of things as they are. If the style of *Victory* is difficult, it is a function of the vision embodied therein, which is more complex than has been admitted.

The shift from first-person to omniscient narration and from a realistic to a symbolic mode corresponds almost exactly to the gradual elaborating in Part II of the philosophical basis for the action. The transition from a chatty, conjecturing narrator in Part I to a relatively transparent omniscient narration thereafter makes perfect sense aesthetically, although it is regarded with dismay by critics, especially those who have come to associate Conrad, as a result of his success with *Lord Jim*, *Heart of Darkness*, *Chance*, and *The Shadow Line*, exclusively with notions about the superiority of ironic first-person narration. Objectionable by the same standard is the presence at the end of *Victory* of Heyst's friend, Davidson, from whom most of the information about Heyst's enigmatic career presumably derives. Rather than assume that the shift in point of view indicates a softening in Conrad, a lessening of interest in technique, the critical challenge is to determine precisely what is achieved by the first-person narration.

Part I of *Victory* stands out from the rest of the novel by the presence of this talkative narrator, who is given to making fine distinctions about the meanings of words, to punning, and to such quirky habits as providing an interpretation of Heyst's career and then casting doubts about the reliability of his interpretation or about the appropriateness of his terminology. The novel begins with a rather peculiar observation that there is 'as every schoolboy knows in this scientific age, a very close chemical relation between coal and diamonds' (3). The narrator then proceeds with his 'unnatural physics' (3) to make a joke about the relation of 'evaporation' to 'liquidation' in the world of finance, informing us, by the by, of Heyst's failure in the coal business. This liquidation, we are told, was 'forced' but not 'forcible', in the sense of expeditious, because of the slowness of such proceedings. However off-handed these remarks appear to be at first, they gather in retrospect considerable meaning and significance, giving the

events that follow a distinctly ironic colouring. The fact that
Heyst is *queer* but not mad is an important distinction which
recurs throughout the novel. When Davidson hears that
Heyst has eloped with Lena he thinks to himself that Heyst
has gone mad but quickly dismisses 'the notion of common
crude lunacy' (54); and, in the final pages of the novel, he says
to the unnamed Excellency that Heyst 'was a queer chap. I
doubt if he himself knew how queer he was' (408). One of
the main functions of the narrator and his method, it seems,
is to establish in these early pages an interesting but thoroughly ambiguous portrait of Heyst.

The portrait of Heyst which emerges from the first chapter
is amusing and ironic: he is an inert idealist, obsessed with
facts, whose only visitors are clouds and whose nearest
neighbour is a volcano with identical smoking habits; he is
becomingly bald, nobly bewhiskered, resembles Charles XII,
but is himself definitely not a fighting man. This last point is
extremely interesting for the way in which it connects with
Heyst's dilemma on Samburan. Heyst, like Hamlet and that
much-reduced Hamlet of the twentieth-century, Prufrock,
suffers from indecision; he cannot bring himself to act, especially to act violently when violence is needed. Eliot's Prufrock at least fantasizes that there will be 'time to murder and
create', but Heyst has an aversion to violence: 'There is a
strain in me which lays me under an insensate obligation to
avoid even the appearance of murder' (329).[19] Heyst doubts
his capacity to shoot the intruders even if he were armed; he
admits to having refined everything away except disgust. As
he says to Lena, 'To slay, to love—the greatest enterprises of
life upon a man! And I have no experience of either' (212).
Heyst remains to the end, even in his inability to speak the
words of love to Lena on her deathbed, an enigma within an
enigma.

What this facetious and analytical narrator offers us is essentially a number of *views* of Heyst—views that derive from
plain gossip. The whole of the first part of *Victory* resembles
an elaborate piece of gossip or scandal. We learn, in short
space, all of Heyst's nicknames: Enchanted Heyst, who is at
first spellbound by the islands and then disenchanted with his
own inadequate detachment from life; Hard Facts Heyst,
who for a time believes that there is 'nothing worth knowing
but facts' (7), but who soon learns to have done even with

them; Utopist Heyst, whose faith in the 'great stride forward' (6) is shattered by the collapse of the Tropical Belt Coal Company; Angel Heyst, who ministers to Morrison's financial needs and indirectly brings about the man's death; Spider Heyst, who is accused by Schomberg of having intentionally lured Morrison into his web; Heyst the Enemy, whose financial dealings and speculations render him vulnerable to the envy and suspicion of the inhabitants of the islands; Hermit Heyst, who retires from all forms of human involvement only to learn that 'He had not the hermit's vocation' (31); and 'Mr. Blasted Heyst' (340), Ricardo's hated foe and rival. Most of the information about Heyst and his checkered career emanates from local sources: the manager of the Oriental Banking Corporation in Malacca, Mr. Tesman, McNab the drinker, Morrison, Davidson, Schomberg, and Mrs. Schomberg. Schomberg's role in unfolding the truth of Heyst's situation is extremely interesting because it emerges so appropriately from the gossipy, conjectural beginnings of the novel.

Our first encounter with Schomberg comes at the end of the second chapter in Part I, after we have learned something of Heyst's 'complex' (10) relationship with Morrison. Significantly, he is introduced in terms of his function in the novel, spreading gossip and murdering reputations:

> And for a time the conspiracy was successful in so far that we all concluded that Heyst was boarding with the good-natured—some said: sponging on the imbecile— Morrison, in his brig. But you know how it is with all such mysteries. There is always a leak somewhere. Morrison himself, not a perfect vessel by any means, was bursting with gratitude, and under the stress he must have let out something vague—enough to give the island gossip a chance. And you know how kindly the world is in its comments on what it does not understand. A rumour sprang out that Heyst, having obtained some mysterious hold on Morrison, had fastened himself on him and was sucking him dry. Those who had traced these matters back to their origin were very careful not to believe them. The originator, it seems, was a certain Schomberg, a big, manly, bearded creature of the Teutonic persuasion, with an ungovernable tongue which surely must have worked

on a pivot. . . . He was a noxious ass, and he satisfied his
lust for silly gossip at the cost of his customers.

(19–20)

Interestingly enough, only Schomberg keeps alive the memory of Heyst by continually slandering and inquiring after
him among the clientele of his establishment. This habit is
expressed by the narrator in terms of a perversely ironic alteration of the words of Christ in the New Testament: 'Whenever three people came together in his hotel, he took good
care that Heyst should be with them' (26). Until the elopement with Lena, Heyst's only sin appears to have been his ne-
glect of Schomberg's *table d'hôte*; yet this is apparently enough
to bring upon his head the inn-keeper's unlimited malice. After
Heyst has bested him in love, Schomberg himself undergoes
a form of madness, fuming and raging against the terrible
Swede, Spider Heyst. He becomes so demoralized, so disturbed morally and emotionally, that he is only too ready for
the arrival of those perfect instruments of revenge, Jones,
Ricardo, and Pedro: 'It seemed to him that he could never be
himself again till he had got even with that artful Swede. He
was ready to swear that Heyst had ruined his life' (96).

Schomberg does swear precisely that; but before the agents
of his revenge can reach Heyst, Schomberg's gossip, his version of reality which is described as 'the Schombergian theory of Heyst' (264), travels across the shallow sea to Samburan with Lena, preparing the way so to speak. Heyst first
learns that he is the subject of gossip when he is telling Lena
of his business with Morrison. She reacts to the mention of
that name with dismay, having heard Schomberg's version of
the story bandied about amongst the tables at his hotel in
Sourabaya. At first her disclosure merely surprises the detached Heyst: 'The idea of being talked about was always
novel to Heyst's simplified conception of himself. For a moment he was as much surprised as if he had believed himself
to be a mere gliding shadow among men. Besides, he had in
him a half-unconscious notion that he was above the level of
island gossip' (206). The surprise soon turns to distress and
then to curiosity. Heyst admits to feeling hurt and to having
been 'as much of a fool as those everybodies who know the
story' (208). 'I've often heard of the moral advantages of
seeing oneself as others see one. Let us investigate further.

Can't you recall something else that everybody knows?'
(208). Heyst laughs (for only the second time in the novel),
but he is clearly quite disturbed by the information.

In the pages that follow this scene, Heyst and Lena are back
in the bungalow after their love-making, she resting and he
reading his father's writings, which seem to suit the bad taste
he has in his mouth from the 'abominable calumny' that has
'crept back into his recollection' (218). The elder Heyst's
words in *Storm and Dust* describe the nothingness of life, and
love as a cruel stratagem and dream; and they bear directly on
Heyst's condition, his sense of having lost his liberty: 'Clairvoyance or no clairvoyance, men love their captivity. To the
unknown force of negation they prefer the miserably tum-
bled bed of their servitude. Man alone can give one the disgust of pity; yet I find it easier to believe in the misfortune of
mankind than in its wickedness' (220). The passage is slightly
ironic, slightly enigmatic, but it does contain some suggestion of the source of Heyst's dismay, his failure to take into
account the *whole* of life, including the calumny of Schomberg and, eventually, the evil that confronts him in the visitors from Sourabaya. In the presence of these visitors, Heyst
feels stagnant and inert; he feels separated from Lena and
from the growing sense of reality that her presence on the island has given him. Contemplating the situation of the missing revolver, the unwelcome visitors, and his own sense of
uneasiness, Heyst cannot help but relate them to the matter of
the gossip: 'He felt contemptuously irritated with the situation. The outer world had broken upon him; and he did not
know what wrong he had done to bring this upon himself,
any more than he knew what he had done to provoke the
horrible calumny about his treatment of poor Morrison'
(258). Eventually, Heyst concludes that 'the power of calumny grows with time. It's insidious and penetrating. It can
even destroy one's faith in oneself—dry-rot the soul' (362).
And, finally, when plain Mr. Jones mentions Schomberg as
the source of his information that there is money to be had on
Samburan, Heyst thinks: 'This diabolical calumny will end in
actually and literally taking my life from me' (381).

The matter of gossip, then, which has been firmly established by the narrative technique in Part I, serves as a unifying
element in the novel, linking Heyst's weakness in the face of
evil with his debilitating scepticism. It also serves to give a

realistic colouring to the strange events that follow. As Mary McCarthy suggests in 'The Fact in Fiction', 'there is one thing that most novelists have in common: a deep love of fact, of the empiric element in experience.'[20] She insists that gossip is one of the essential ingredients of the realistic novel: 'Even when it is more serious, the novel's characteristic tone is one of gossip and tittle-tattle . . . if the breath of scandal has not touched it, the book is not a novel. That is the trouble with the art-novel (most of Virginia Woolf, for instance); it does not stoop to gossip.'[21] Whatever one may think of McCarthy's thesis, particularly her cursory dismissal of Virginia Woolf, there is in these remarks a clue to one of the moderating aspects of *Victory*'s technique. In *Victory* Conrad does stoop to gossip; he uses gossip and hearsay to establish an illusion of reality in Part I, to give the novel a basis in actuality, in the quirks and habits of a narrator with an itchy ear. And this gossipy quality provides a balance for the symbolic dimension that predominates as the novel winds its way deeper into the forest of Heyst's psyche.

The empiric elements and the first-person narration provide a realistic and ironic frame through which to view Heyst's confrontation with his shadow self and his experience of the potentially redemptive powers of human love through Lena's symbolic triumph over the powers of darkness, as prophesied in Genesis and fulfilled in the New Testament story of the crucifixion. And these events must be examined in the light of the realistic beginnings—the multiple views of Heyst and the heavy residue of irony. As the narrator informs us, concerning the Heyst-Morrison episode, 'the real truth of the matter was more complex' (10) than it appeared to be on the surface to the casual observer. At times the narrator identifies with collective opinion, but more often his sense of the complexity of Heyst's situation is reflected in his ironic description of events, such as his hilarious account of Heyst's rescue of Morrison in comic opera terms. In Part II, however, with two exceptions, the narrator disappears or becomes invisible; perhaps it would be more appropriate to say that he goes underground and lets the main action get under way. His last significant appearance is with these important words: 'That was how it began. How it was that it ended as we know it did end, is not so easy to state precisely' (77).

The narrator is not so inquisitive or sympathetic as Marlow in *Chance*; that role is left to the supplier of most of the information, Davidson, who utters the last words spoken in the novel. Davidson is a minor character in *Victory* but his role is extremely important; he serves as a sort of value centre for the novel. We learn that he has an 'innate curiosity' (33), that he 'was easily sorry for people' (39) as Heyst himself was, that he has a capacity for awe and wonder that is unusual. When he sees Samburan for the first time, Davidson decides that the desolate, elemental conditions there are 'incompatible with the frivolous comments of people who had not seen it' (42). Davidson's shock at Heyst's elopement is such that he wonders if Heyst has gone mad and addresses himself to the task of finding out what he can about the real nature of events. He makes numerous inquiries after Heyst when he finds him already departed from Sourabaya, even of Schomberg because 'he would fain have heard something more of Heyst's exploit from another point of view' (46). The narrator describes Davidson as 'poor, simple Davidson' (54), when he thinks of him confronted with the force of Heyst's negation, and suggests that Davidson views many of the events with as much incredulity as comprehension. But this is not to suggest, as Guerard does, that Davidson is thick: 'And *Victory*, before dispensing with a narrator altogether, offers a dullard within a dullard, Davidson within the "I".'[22] Davidson is no genius, but he is not stupid; he is 'imaginative under his invincible placidity' (45), 'sympathetic' (57), his 'silence concealed a good deal of thought' (62). He and the narrator concur in their interpretations of Heyst's elopement: 'Davidson shared my suspicion that this was in its essence the rescue of a distressed being. Not that we were two romantics, tingeing the world to the hue of our temperament, but that both of us had been acute enough to discover a long time ago that Heyst was' (51).

Davidson's interest in Heyst is sufficient to cause him to make a substantial detour around Samburan during each trip, on the off-chance that he might be of some assistance. While Schomberg is busy murdering Heyst's reputation, Davidson is quietly attentive to his friend's needs. We are told that he is 'delicate, humane and regular', a man 'with unwearied and punctual humanity' (52); when Heyst accepts Davidson's free

passage to Sourabaya and confides in him, he says to Davidson: 'I am touched by your humanity. . . . Believe me, I am
profoundly aware of having been an object of it' (33). This
quiet sea-captain is drawn by his humanity into Heyst's circle;
he gets caught up in the web of duplicities when he returns
Mrs. Schomberg's shawl without her husband's knowledge.
Next to the fact of Heyst's 'getting mixed up with petticoats'
(59), Mrs. Schomberg's duplicity comes as the greatest illumination to Davidson:

> Davidson was lost in admiration. He believed, now, that
> the woman had been putting it on for years. She never
> even winked. It was immense! The insight he had ob-
> tained almost frightened him; he couldn't get over his
> wonder at knowing more of the real Mrs. Schomberg
> than anybody in the Islands, including Schomberg him-
> self. She was a miracle of dissimulation.
>
> (59)

Conrad's decision to make Davidson's the last voice heard in
Victory is not, as some critics suggest, a clumsy but expedient
way to conclude a popular romance; rather, it is an ending
that has been carefully prepared for in Part I and that brings
into focus again all of the ironies and enigmas of Heyst's existence before his meeting with Lena and his psycho-moral
struggles on Samburan. Davidson is the one figure outside it
all who combines intelligence and intuition: his sympathy is
informed with much delicacy and tact, so much so, in fact,
that this very delicacy prevents him from interfering with
Heyst's destiny; his intelligence is tempered with a keen sense
of wonder and humility before the spectacle of an un-
fathomable mystery. In the world of literature he most resembles another sea-captain, the honest Portuguese Don
Pedro de Mendez who rescues Gulliver after his sojourn
among the Yahoos in *Gulliver's Travels*, a profoundly rejectivist document. There are many similarities between these
strikingly different books; most significantly, they are both
about the dangers of the fragmentation of human nature,
where the rational side of man is developed to the exclusion
of others and to the destruction or disintegration of the whole
individual. After the strange events in *Victory*, as after the
outrageous happenings in *Gulliver's Travels*, a normalizing

presence, a representative of balanced humanity, seems in order; and Davidson, who has been Heyst's only friend, seems ideally suited to write his obituary. He does not sentimentalize events or become didactic; he merely reports Heyst's last words and declares that, indeed, nothing else remains to be said.[23]

Of course much remains to be said beyond Davidson's brief account. That is the point of having him rather than the original narrator sum up the carnage on Samburan. The technique employed here recalls the ending of *Nostromo*, where Conrad chose to relate certain events through the limited consciousness of Captain Mitchell. In *Victory*, he quite deliberately abandons the mannered first-person narrator when he embarks upon the more symbolic part of his work; by calling again upon the assistance of Davidson, he is able effectively to recall both the ironies and sympathies of Part I without actually disturbing the omniscience he has adopted for the major portion of the novel. Davidson's abrupt and surprising re-entry in the middle of a paragraph, serves also to heighten the dream-like quality of the preceding events, giving that portion of the novel an even greater aura of fable or romance.

V

A good deal of what I have said concerning stylization and form in *Victory* has touched upon matters of language and character, especially as idiosyncrasies of speech and thought were used to render the first-person narrator and to bring into focus Schomberg and his kingdom of calumny. However, I would like to suggest some directions which I believe future criticism of the novel might profitably take.

Far from being flat and unenergized, as Guerard suggests, the prose in *Victory* seems to me very much alive and brimming with suggestion. There is a passage in Part III, for example, which, unless one is alerted to the possibilities of irony, might not surrender its full potential. At one moment Heyst is walking with Lena on Samburan, trying to reconcile his fears over his 'wrecked philosophy' (185) and his attraction to this quietly strong woman. Lena appears, on the surface level of dialogue, to be obtuse. She objects to the panoramic view which Heyst offers her because the sea seems to her abominably desolate, 'as if everything that there is had gone under' (191). She prefers the concrete, sensible world of people and feelings, the immediate and particular rather than the abstract and the general. Her comments make Heyst think of the Biblical story of the flood and 'the vision of a world destroyed' (191). Lena's response to this morbid association is that she would be 'sorry for the happy folk in it' (191). The simplicity of both replies intrigues Heyst and he recognizes in her a kind of sensitivity and intelligence that differs from and clearly challenges his own scepticism and habit of generalizing. This is a major discovery for Heyst; and the images that support that discovery gather meaning for the careful reader by their association with earlier images in the novel and by setting off verbal echoes which will be heard throughout the rest of *Victory*.

One of these echoes is associated with the sea, which we know from the initial pages of the novel is a 'tepid, shallow sea' (4), the same sea that, in a few hours, will spew forth Jones, Ricardo, and Pedro out of its 'flaming abyss of nothingness' (232). Thus the emptiness of the sea comes to be associated with its deadliness, as Heyst's own philosophy of nothingness proves to be his undoing. At this moment too Heyst begins to reflect on his past and mentions, off-handedly, that there was once a 'mud-shower' (192) on his island, as a result of a thunderstorm coming along at the precise moment that the neighbouring volcano had chosen to clear its 'red-hot gullet' (192). On the level of realistic dialogue, this anecdote is interesting enough, conveying as it does the underlying emotions which prompt Heyst to chatter uncharacteristically and which make Lena respond so cryptically and woefully. At a deeper level, however, the exchange seems almost inexhaustible in its possibilities of interpretation.

Heyst's attraction to Lena, his fascination with her peculiar kind of intelligence, lies in the fact that she is truly a creature of mud, of the earth. With her he is able to sense, and possibly recapture, the humanity and the will of which his philosophizing father has robbed him, to become again like the first Adam, a piece of mud into which has been breathed the breath of life. Later in the novel, when Lena is engaged in taking from Ricardo the knife, which has in it the sting of death, plain Mr. Jones, who witnesses the scene and cannot stomach the thought of its sexual import, pours his fears and loathing of humanity into Heyst's ear: 'Mud souls, obscene and cunning! Mud bodies, too—the mud of the gutter! I tell you, we are no match for the vile populace!' (392). In his dealings with Lena, which give him a profound sense of his own reality, Heyst begins to understand that he must soil his hands, must perhaps sacrifice his pride and sense of decorum, if he is to play well the rough game of life. Significantly, his story begins with a comparison between the red-hot ash of his cigar and the glow of the smoking volcano; and it ends with Davidson's account of poking in the ashes on Samburan for evidence that Baron Heyst has died in the fire which consumed his little world, the fire which has perhaps purified him of his deathly philosophy and returned him at last to his origins in ashes, in dust.

At times, Conrad's method in this ironic novel seems so rich that even the most insignificant word or phrase may be seen to assume dimensions that are quite unexpected. I am reminded in this context of the delight which Conrad always took in quoting to Ford Madox Ford a particular line that amused them both so much in *Romance*, their novel of collaboration: 'Still what I always said was the only immortal line in *Romance*: "Excellency, a few goats," survives,—esoteric, symbolic, profound and comic,—it survives' (*LL*, II, 169). So much of *Victory*'s language operates precisely at these levels; and critics who want to understand the kind of expression which interests Conrad in this complicated novel, and in much of the later fiction, will have to concern themselves not only with the surfaces of grammar and syntax and literal meaning, but also with the whole substratum of association and suggestibility of words. In *Victory*, the narrator's word-play, his fine discriminations of meaning, and his conviction that things 'are not so easy to state precisely' (77), recall *Chance* and *Heart of Darkness* and anticipate the distinction between what is stated and what is meant in human speech which Conrad makes in *The Rescue*. Here, too, the images of gossip acquire an added significance. Words, as rumour, assume a palpable reality of their own, capable of deceiving, debilitating, torturing and, ultimately, of murdering. And Heyst, who has been weaned on the 'living word' (196) of his father and damned by the lies and calumny of Schomberg, does not learn soon enough that language, not life, is the false coin.

Unless considerable emphasis is placed upon *Victory*'s aesthetic variety and complexity, including its ironic nature, not only will Conrad's subtle manipulation of effects at the linguistic and non-linguistic levels be ignored, but also a proper description and evaluation of the novel will be impossible. This is particularly the case in the matter of character and character relations. Obviously, in a narrative which moves from a realistic to a symbolic mode and which employs a romance pattern, there will be problems for the critic in assessing the various characters, or types, and their effectiveness within the novel. Conrad has been criticized, for example, for the apparent transparency of Lena and her relationship with Heyst, as well as for the stereotyping of Jones, Ricardo, and Pedro. Jocelyn Baines complains that the infernal trio are over-drawn, that they are abstractions, two-dimensional figures presented by way of imagery that is 'obvious and repetitive'; he admits, however, that 'The scenes in which they participate are intensely visualized' and that these figures have 'a certain glamour and even a ghoulish charm . . . which makes them more vivid than life'.[24] Baines' observations, to the effect that these characters are insufficiently life-like and more vivid than life, are as typical as they are unsatisfactory and contradictory. Like most critics, he reveals a rather strong bias towards the realistic and the representational, a bias which does little to shed light on the cast of strange figures that moves upon the stage of *Victory*.

The work of Robert Scholes and Robert Kellogg is useful in this connection.[25] They identify three primary dimensions, or thrusts, in fiction, each of which has its own unique kind of character or type—representative, illustrative, and aesthetic. The representative type is often highly individualized, with a certain psychological credibility, and is susceptible to change as a result of the introduction of new elements into the plot; the illustrative type, which is a unit of meaning within the intellectual configuration of the novel, illustrates an idea or essence and so expands the philosophical possibilities of the narrative; the aesthetic type, which is a construct designed to stimulate and satisfy certain emotional responses in the reader, contributes nothing to the meaning of the narrative because it is purely a creature of plot. All of these types may be present in a single work of fiction, even in a single character. Heyst is an aesthetic type, the hero, whose function in terms of plot is to rescue the heroine and to triumph over evil. But he is an odd hero: he 'rescues' Morrison

and Lena at the eventual cost of their lives and his own; and
he is himself a trapped soul, Enchanted Heyst, who needs to
be rescued from his intellectual bondage. Heyst cuts a peculiar figure as a knight errant who, as a result of putting a foot
in the forbidden stream of life, becomes bogged down in the
mundane world of business and domesticity. As an illustrative type, too, Heyst does not remain static. On one level, he
is an Everyman, at war with the destructive forces in his own
psyche; he illustrates the intellect subjugating the heart and
body. But even here we observe, ironically, that Heyst is less
typical than Davidson and the normative world of the narrator in Sourabaya; in fact, he is a romantic whose death is as
enigmatic and unacademic as his life. In other words, Heyst is
a fairly complex creation, whose illustrative and aesthetic
roles serve to deepen rather than violate his potential as a representative character.

Although *Victory* is cast somewhat in the light of an ironic
redemption parable or psychodrama, in which the various
types are projections of the hero's subconscious struggles,
secondary figures like Lena and Schomberg do progress
beyond the illustrative and aesthetic types with which they
begin. Schomberg, in particular, assumes considerable proportions as a character and as a force within the narrative. On
one level, he is simply the curious, gossipy host, familiar to
readers of Chaucer and fictional romances such as those of
Fielding. But Schomberg is deeply suspicious of the aristocratic Swede; he cannot understand and accept that it is
Heyst's reserve, and not his malice, that keeps him away
from the *table d'hôte*. Schomberg becomes obsessed with the
economic side of Heyst's existence, with his dealings with
Morrison in the Tropical Belt Coal Company. On another
level, Schomberg represents those appetites of the flesh
which Heyst in his intellectual orientation has eschewed; in
addition to his appetite for news and food, Schomberg reveals himself to be a lecher with a ravenous appetite for Lena's
body. Schomberg moves some distance beyond the general
types which he contains and becomes, as it were, a genuine
'character' within the narrative; in fact, he graduates from an
offensive though somewhat amusing gossip and humbug to
an accessory to murder, as he spreads false rumours of
Heyst's money and shady dealings throughout the archipelago.

Although Heyst and Schomberg cease to be merely functions of plot and become part of the whole process of characterization towards which the complex narrative is moving, the infernal trio, introduced after the novel has progressed some distance beyond its realistic frame, remain, for the most part, within the aesthetic and illustrative types of which they partake. Mr. Jones is important as a villain, as an embodiment of the destructiveness in Heyst's philosophy. His function is not to draw attention to himself as a character, but rather to draw attention to certain elements in Heyst's character. Within these limitations, however, Jones is not without interest. He does reveal a grim sense of humour, a potential for irony; and he does exhibit a capacity for such human emotions as anger, fear, and disgust. Also, he is an unusual villain, effeminate, squeamish to a fault, fussy and singularly inept; like Heyst, he is blind even to the real nature of his closest ally. Jones's henchman, Martin Ricardo, makes somewhat less progress beyond the aesthetic type, which is not surprising since he is the infernal counterpart of Lena, who is herself a rather shadowy figure in the narrative. Ricardo is the embodiment of instinct, of animal vitality; he is the deadly word of Mr. Jones made flesh. Nevertheless, Conrad labours to make even Ricardo a figure of some interest and amusement. His speeches to Schomberg concerning the origins and activities of himself and his colleagues are full of comical asides, as well as idiosyncrasies of speech and thought, that reveal more about his peculiar psychology (to say that Ricardo has a psychology at all is an important admission) than might be expected, given the emphasis placed on his animal-like movements and appearance. Ricardo's moments with Lena also contain a variety of colloquial delights that are of more than symbolic interest. He moralizes, ironically, about Heyst's treatment of Morrison, expresses disgust for that 'fat, tame slug of a gin-slinger, Schomberg' (296), and considers that Lena's willingness to deceive Heyst 'proved that she was no hypocrite' (299). Thus Ricardo's type, though not substantially elaborated or expanded, is at least concretely and engagingly rendered.

Many of the encounters in *Victory*, between Lena and Ricardo or between Heyst and his double, Jones, are highly stylized, almost dialectical in their configuration; they involve, primarily, the working out of a set of ideas. In the encounters between the two principal characters, Heyst and Lena, however, the real and the symbolic elements are more clearly in balance; seldom can the patterns of myth or romance be said to overrun the psychological demands of the situation. The conversations between Lena and Heyst, as I suggested earlier, are not so awkward or one-dimensional as they have been considered; before they can be dismissed as awkward, these encounters must be examined not only in terms of their aesthetic and illustrative functions, but also in terms of their representative qualities, particularly their underlying psychology.

Lena's reticence concerning Ricardo's visit is a case in point. Sharon Kaehele and Howard German, in their perceptive analysis of the use of doubles in *Victory*, argue that 'Lena has no justification for continuing to conceal the attack from Heyst once Ricardo has leaped through the window.' [26] They also suggest that Lena 'does change in a way that makes it difficult to regard her as the paragon of virtue which many critics consider her'. [27] Lena has no experience of the reflective, sceptical, generalizing mentality which Heyst represents, though she does know something of the ways of the male world as represented by the actions of men like Zangiacomo, Schomberg, and Ricardo. Nor has Heyst, living alone and without even the memory of a mother, had much useful experience of the opposite sex, let alone of the world in general. There can be little doubt that Lena senses immediately the kind and degree of danger which Ricardo represents for herself and Heyst. Her subsequent deception of Heyst is no different from his deception of her over the loss of the revolver; each is trying to protect the other from undue worry and stress. Recognizing that the knowledge of Ricardo's visit would precipitate Heyst into some sort of disastrous action, since he has no means, physical or psychological, with which to defend himself, Lena keeps the visit a secret and prepares to use her feminine attractiveness to disarm the deadly Ricardo. The whole complex relationship between Lena and Heyst, who cannot even cope with the knowledge that he is the object of local gossip, eddies back and forth in a veritable archipelago of fears, self-doubts, and misunderstandings.

The important question is not whether or not Lena is flawless—she is, by conventional standards of the time, living in sin; and she is caught up in and blinded by her dream of sacrifice—but whether, in making the decision to conceal the visit, she may be committing the very error of deadly generalizing which so bedevils Heyst. The ambiguity of this incident contributes to the representative aspect of Lena's character; she is subject to the influence of events, just as she has humanizing inconsistencies. It also adds to the strong undertow of irony which makes these final events on Samburan stranger and more complex than they appear to be on the surface level of romance. Scholes and Kellogg suggest that 'when aesthetic types are merged with illustrative types, and purely emotional situations or events are combined with allegorical situations or events, the tension between ethical and aesthetic impulses can become complex, working modifications in both story and meaning'.[28] Conrad's determination to satisfy certain realistic criteria and to establish an ironic framework in which to view events adds not only another source of tension, but also infinite possibilities for modifying the aesthetic and illustrative expectations in the novel.

Conrad is as fastidious in matters of language and character as he is in the more obvious matters of fictional modes and point of view. As if the novel itself were not sufficient indication of intention, there is evidence in the correspondence to show that he did not take lightly the psychological credibility of his characters in *Victory*. Writing to Christopher Sandeman about its adaptation for the stage, he said: 'The point of criticism you raise in *Victory* (the novel) is not so apparent in the play. Perhaps you are right. But I still think the psychology possible. My fault is that I haven't made Lena's reticence credible *enough*—since a mind like yours (after reflexion) remains unconvinced. I need not tell you that while I wrote, her silence seemed to me truth itself, a rigorous consequence of the character and situation. It was not invented for the sake of the "story"' (*LL*, II, 184). Given the concern for effects, for credibility, there is little wonder that, according to his biographers, Conrad delighted in discussing *Victory*'s characters and events with his friends (especially the fight between Schomberg and Zangiacomo) and that, on the occasion of his only public reading and lecture, he chose to read the whole chapter of Lena's death to his New York audience.

In addition to those elements which I have discussed, the short fiction of this period provides some interesting and largely unexplored perspectives on *Victory*. Conrad composed *Victory* between May 1912 and June 1914, during the final stages of which he paused to write 'Because of the Dollars' and 'The Planter of Malata'. These stories bear somewhat the same relation to *Victory* as 'An Outpost of Progress' bears to *Heart of Darkness*; they are obviously spin-offs from the writing of the novel, sharing certain thematic elements and employing a number of similar characters differently disguised. The slightest of the two, 'Because of the Dollars', is a cleverly turned short story about the wages of curiosity and whim. Captain Davidson, a tactful and delicate man who is really a version of Heyst, becomes the victim of his curiosity about, and concern for, a cast-off woman named Laughing Anne, adrift like Lena in a hostile male environment. Davidson wanders inadvertently into her sphere while collecting obsolete currency for the government, and becomes a prey to three shady characters who have a taste for his dollars. Fector and his 'precious couple' (*WT*, 186), one with hands and no brains and the other, called the Frenchman, with brains but no hands, are versions of Jones, Ricardo, and Pedro. Laughing Anne sacrifices herself to save Davidson from the three conspirators who are after his dollars, leaving Davidson with his guilt and the problem of caring for and explaining to his wife Laughing Anne's son.

'Because of the Dollars' is a bleakly ironic tale. Davidson, whose experience throws a grey pall over his life, eradicating his previously perpetual smile, is left an unhappy and lonely man at the end, deprived of his illusions, his bitchy wife, and even the company of Laughing Anne's son, who departs to take up the religious life. Conrad's superbly ironic touch is used to great advantage here: the handless murderer, whose physical deformity gives him a sinister, palpable reality that his counterpart in *Victory*, Mr. Jones, does not have; Laughing Anne's philosophy, 'Laugh or cry—what's the odds' (*WT*, 198), which strikes just the right note, considering the physical and moral carnage with which the story ends; and the obsolete currency, which resembles the false coin that Heyst's father perceives life to be, taking its terrible toll. Something of the bleakness and irony of this story pervades *Victory*'s pages, though subdued and modified by the romance pattern, the mythic thrust and the narrative perspective.

It is in 'The Planter of Malata', however, that Conrad experiments most significantly and successfully with themes and characters related to *Victory*. Renouard, the planter of Malata, is detached and isolated like Heyst, sensitive to a fault, a 'hermit on the sea shore' who does not particularly 'like mankind' (*WT*, 25). He is not, however, warped by a perverse, life-denying philosophy; that role belongs to Felicia Moorsom, a woman of epic beauty, anticipating Edith Travers in *The Rescue*, her head 'crowned' (9) with hair that suggests 'a helmet of burnished copper' (10). Her father resembles the elder Heyst somewhat; although he is 'the fashionable philosopher of the age' (14) and 'has made philosophy pay' (16), Professor Moorsom nevertheless scorns the world: 'But you don't know what it is to have moved, breathed, existed, and even triumphed in the mere smother and froth of life—the brilliant froth. These thoughts, sentiments, feelings, actions too, are nothing but agitation in empty space— to amuse life—a sort of superior debauchery, exciting and fatiguing, meaning nothing, leading nowhere' (40–41). Once again, the lives are moved, not by feeling and passion, but by perverse ideals: Felicia cannot respond to Renouard's love because she is engaged in the 'sentimental exercise of a declared love' (30). Renouard's suicide, like Heyst's, remains something of a mystery. He has been stricken by love, but his death takes place in the full awareness of the hollowness and vanity of his beloved; he sees that she cannot understand and respond to his passionate confession because 'she is so used to the forms of repression enveloping the crude impulses of old humanity' (77). He also perceives that he has 'nothing to offer her vanity' (80). His suicide represents an escape from the emptiness which her departure would bring; but more than that, it represents a repulsion from the vision of a vulgar reality which he cannot accommodate. Conrad's description of Renouard's collapse in the face of an overwhelming moral and emotional shock is interesting for the light it throws on the death of Heyst:

> This walk up the hill and down again was like the supreme effort of an explorer trying to penetrate the interior of an unknown country, the secret of which is too well defended by its cruel and barren nature. Decoyed by a mirage, he had gone too far—so far that there was no going back. His strength was at an end, and with a sort of de-

spairing self-possession he tried to understand the cause of his defeat.

(79–80)

In the face of his own ordeal, Heyst too is exhausted; he has gone too far to turn back, but also too far to carry on with the knowledge of his own folly and of Lena's illusion of a sacrificial death. His death, like his life, is at best enigmatic; and considering the pervading irony in the novel, it has, like Renouard's, more the cast of a defeat than a victory.

Renouard's predicament also has its origins in language, in gossip. He has his own Schomberg to contend with, this time in the form of an interfering newspaper editor. This 'meddlesome journalist' (55), 'confounded busybody' (56), and 'all-knowing one' (56) wreaks havoc in Renouard's life. He inhabits a 'temple of publicity' (28), where 'everything is known about everybody—including even a great deal of nobodies' (6); he controls the movement of information, is a sort of data-centre for the colonies; he makes his living 'talking about mankind's affairs' (25). Renouard, like Heyst, is unequipped for this facet of reality: 'Solitary life makes a man reticent in respect of anything in the nature of gossip, which those to whom chatting about their kind is an everyday exercise regard as the commonest use of speech' (5). The editor insists that Renouard is 'leading an unhealthy life. . . . Solitude works like a sort of poison' (5); he suggests that Renouard's isolation represents an 'immoral detachment from mankind' (26). Eventually, the editor's persistent harping and interference prompt Renouard to take on an assistant who, like Morrison in *Victory*, dies shortly after. This concession to public pressure involves Renouard fatally with the Moorsoms, who are looking for the dead man; and his passion for Felicia makes him plunge deeper and deeper into an inescapable deceit in order to detain her. As he tries to explain his motivation to Felicia, Renouard, like Heyst, feels himself strangled by his reputation as a man who would not count the cost:

> Ha! the legendary Renouard of sensitive idiots—the ruthless adventurer—the ogre with a future. That was a parrot cry, Miss Moorsom. I don't think that the greatest fool of

them all ever dared hint such a stupid thing of me that I
killed men for nothing. No, I had noticed this man in a
hotel. He had come from up-country I was told, and was
doing nothing. I saw him sitting there lonely in a corner
like a sick crow, and ı went over one evening to talk to
him. Just on impulse. He wasn't impressive. He was pitiful. My worst enemy could have told you he wasn't good
enough to be one of Renouard's victims.

(74)

These two stories provide another perspective from which
to view *Victory*, shifting critical attention to matters other
than myth and symbol and permitting the sensitive critic to
perceive elements of the novel which Conrad considered important, or unresolved, enough to explore further.

VI

Victory invites controversy and reassessment. It does not, as
Conrad suggested, necessarily tend towards a definite meaning or conclusion. I would recommend that the critic approach this novel like a dog worrying a bone, except that the
image is not particularly graceful and does not convey adequately an impression of the feast that is in store. One thing is
certain: *Victory* belongs in the Conrad canon as surely as do
any of his simpler, more accessible works. It sheds light on all
that he had previously written and anticipates the themes and
techniques which would preoccupy him until his death. It is
not only an essay on the dilemma of post-Enlightenment
man, but also an essay on the novel and what can be achieved
within its constantly shifting boundaries.

Victory is modern in terms of applied content, but moving
towards what critics have begun to call the post-modern in
terms of *achieved* content, that is, in terms of the vision embodied in its form. The difference between Conrad and
someone like Alain Robbe-Grillet is that, although he comprehends fully the contradictions inherent in the fictive act,
he refuses to dispense entirely with metaphor and the old
myth of depth of meaning implied by its use. *Chance* embodies the humanistic 'pledge of solidarity' that Robbe-Grillet eschews, especially Marlow's belief that it's worth putting two
and two together.[29] *Chance* is metaphorical to the core and

metaphor, as Robbe-Grillet argues, 'always introduces in fact a subterranean communication, a movement of sympathy—or of antipathy—which is its true *raison d'être*'.[30] It's as though, after exploring the sympathetic contract in *Chance*, Conrad was compelled to examine the origins and nature of antipathy in the human situation. But he does not leap wholeheartedly and uncritically into the anthropomorphic fallacy, lamenting the evidence of a fractured unity in the world. His stance is remarkably objective, considering the intensely personal nature of the materials; and his manner is controlled and ironic.

I mention Robbe-Grillet at this point because of his critique of Camus and because his terminology echoes Conrad at every turn. References to solidarity and sympathy recall my discussion of *Chance*; talk of purity and surfaces seems to belong to Heyst, who has been advised to avoid the hidden stream of life and be a good empiricist, but whose facade of aloofness and indifference is insufficient to protect him from compassion and curiosity, two of his obvious impurities. 'Everything is contaminated. Above all the novel,' says Robbe-Grillet. 'From women in love who become nuns to policemen who become gangsters . . . the typical "character" of the novel must be, above all, a double being.'[31] I think the point to be made here is that, although Heyst is a double being, his creator is a good deal more complicated. One senses that Conrad understands in his bones Heyst's predicament, but that, as author, he stands back from him critically. That is doubtless why the character is so engaging and mystifying to readers. Conrad also stands back from the ending of the novel, allowing the reader to struggle with the opposing forces of tragedy and romance at work there in terms of plot and character. Robbe-Grillet criticizes Camus for not keeping *L'Etranger* linguistically clean, or neutral; apparently, anthropomorphic metaphor keeps intruding, so that the concept of ' "absurdity" turns out to be a form of tragic Humanism. It is not a recognition of the separation between man and objects. It is a lover's quarrel between them.'[32] One might say about *Victory* as well that the struggle between the various sides of Conrad's psyche dramatized there is more of a quarrel than a final resolution.

There are many ways to murder the silence, as Conrad

knew so well. Words, in the form of negation, calumny, or illusion, are capable of driving a man to violence or to the paralysis that comes of despair. As novelist, Conrad could not escape the impurities of his medium. Words are contaminated; they have about them the stink of reality. However, although they cannot be purged of their impurities, neither can words be robbed of their power to move the human heart and mind to murder or creation. *Victory* goes as far as Conrad was willing to go in the direction of formalism and stylization without giving up his contract between author and reader. He knew, finally, to use Camus' words again, that the only real formalism is silence, the silence of a heap of ashes on Samburan.[33] For critics such as Moser and Guerard, he obviously went too far; for Robbe-Grillet, had he commented on the novel, Conrad would not have gone far enough. For my own part, *Victory* is a profound dramatization of the very problems of meaning and style which critics like Camus and Robbe-Grillet were to address, so many years later.

Victory belongs with *Tom Jones* and *Moby Dick* and *The French Lieutenant's Woman*, vast multi-dimensional novels written by authors whose philosophical reach may have exceeded their technical grasp, novels which make unusual, perhaps even outrageous, demands upon their readers. We rejoice at the range and diversity of such books even when we cannot fully comprehend them. Scholes' and Kellogg's observation about Fielding—that his 'great power as a novelist derives in part from his ability to hold the representative, illustrative and aesthetic aspects of his narrative in a fluid, homogenous suspension'—applies equally well to the Conrad of *Victory*; so does Malcolm Bradbury's remark about *The French Lieutenant's Woman*: 'The book actually succeeds, I suspect, on the level of its sheer impurity.'[34]

3 The Shadow Line
The Art of Work and the Work of Art

After the completion of *Victory*, the serial rights of which his agent sold for £1,000, Conrad accepted an invitation to visit Poland with his family. They set out on July 25, 1914, for Conrad's first visit in twenty-one years, less than a month after the assassination of Archduke Ferdinand of Austria. This return, as described in 'Poland Revisited' and 'First News', two essays collected in *Notes on Life and Letters*, released in Conrad an incredible flood of associations and memories. Everything about the trip contributed to its epic character. The long route by sea from Harwich to Hamburg brought freshly to mind his apprenticeship among the coastal seamen of Norfolk, as well as numerous experiences that must have lapped continually at the edges of his consciousness. As the essays suggest, he was full of thoughts of his childhood, made more poignant and significant by the company of his own sons on the trip; but uppermost in his mind were images of his father, Apollo Korzeniowski, whose slow death he had attended as a child in Cracow. There is a moving account in 'First News' of a visit with his eldest son to the library of the university where Conrad's own father's manuscripts were preserved; Conrad recounts handling a bundle of letters written by his father to an intimate friend, an incident more awesome in retrospect because the 'academical peace' (*NLL*, 176) of the library had not yet been troubled by the news of the German declaration of war on Russia which was on the winds in Poland at that very moment.

The shock of revisiting Poland, of immersing himself in a complex and difficult past, was multiplied for Conrad by the conditions of his visit—the impending threat of war and the

subsequent mobilization of Cracow. In 'Poland Revisited'
Conrad says that his youthful departure from Poland often
had for him the character of a betrayal; and now, in perhaps
its darkest hour, he had to forsake again the country of his
birth, fleeing first to Vienna and then to Milan, from where
he arrived safely in England by ship on November 3, 1914.
Once back in England Conrad was faced with the task of
picking up the threads of his writing. Although he was now
sufficiently successful and financially secure to relax, the conditions of his mind and the momentum of an active and com-
pulsive literary career would not permit Conrad to rest comfortably on his laurels.

What to say in the face of war, when writing of any sort
seemed an impossibly inadequate form of action? Age and ill-
health precluded a more active role in the war, though Conrad did spend time afloat and aloft for the Ministry of War on
several occasions. After writing *Victory*, which examines
obliquely but undeniably the deathly philosophical conditions of the late nineteenth and early twentieth centuries that
led to the war, and which signals, with uncanny prophecy,
the holocaust, the trial by fire (and air and water and land),
that was to descend upon Europe in World War I—after all
this, what could master-mariner Conrad offer as a naviga-
tional chart for the age? Writing to Mrs. Wedgwood on Janu-
ary 28, 1915, he said: 'It seems almost criminal levity to talk
at this time of books, stories, publication. This war attends
my uneasy pillow like a nightmare. I feel oppressed even in
my sleep and the moment of waking brings no relief—' (*LL*,
II, 168). Throughout the war, Conrad found 'work, properly
speaking, impossible' (*LL*, II, 168), as he said to his friend
Edward Garnett. However, as he was writing to Mrs. Wedgwood, he was also making a start on his next fiction, *The
Shadow Line*, which he was to complete the same year on December 18, 1915. In a letter to Sidney Colvin in 1917 about
that book, Conrad remarked: 'I discovered that this was what
I could write in my then moral and intellectual condition;
tho' even *that* cost me an effort I remember with a shudder.
To sit down and invent fairy tales was impossible then' (*LL*,
II, 182).

A brief glance at Conrad's non-fiction writings during and
immediately after the war confirms the feeling that *The*

Shadow Line is a temperamental composition, a book written directly out of the intellectual and emotional distress of the war and the return to Poland. In addition to the essays on Poland—'Poland Revisited', 'A Note on the Polish Problem', and 'First News'—Conrad wrote a number of pieces about the sea, particularly about responsibility and command in the Merchant Service, about jobs being well done, that bear directly on the concerns dramatized in *The Shadow Line*. In an essay entitled 'Well Done', he declares that 'A man is a worker. If he is not that he is nothing. Just nothing—like a mere adventurer' (*NLL*, 190); in 'Confidence', he praises those men who are fashioned by hard work and tradition; and in the essay 'Tradition', he commends the merchant seamen for their fidelity to the tasks at hand, beginning his appreciation with an approximate quotation from the note books of Leonardo da Vinci: 'Work is law. Like iron that lying idle degenerates into a mass of useless rust, like water that in an unruffled pool sickens into a stagnant and corrupt state, so without action the spirit of men turns to a dead thing, loses its force, ceases prompting us to leave some trace of ourselves on earth' (*NLL*, 194).

Conrad's preoccupation with the moral question of responsibility and with work as a technique of survival informs *The Shadow Line* at every level. After the bleakly ironic, aesthetically complex, and controversial *Victory*, Conrad composed what is, without doubt, his purest and most beautiful story. *The Shadow Line*, with its more personal analysis of the efforts of a young man to find meaning and significance in life, to discover how to be, or at least what to do, follows appropriately in the wake of *Victory* and on the heels of the emotionally charged return to Poland. In *Victory* Conrad relates the details of Heyst's efforts to be, after his education in scepticism and withdrawal; however, the reader is less certain at the end of that novel of how to be than he is of how not to be. On one level, Heyst's problem consists of never having found work, or employment, which might possibly give his life shape, if not meaning; he wanders, dabbles, interferes with the lives of Morrison and Lena. He learns nothing that will sustain him in the crunch, in the face of the invasion by Jones, Ricardo, and Pedro, or in the face of Lena's death. He does not, like Marlow in *Heart of Darkness* or Coleridge's Ancient Mariner, assume the educational role of a sadder and wiser man; he simply takes his own life, after which, in Davidson's words, nothing can be said.

This is the important thing to remember about *The Shadow Line*, in trying to assess its place amongst the later novels— Conrad did try to say something more on the subject. Faced with a war that would sink his birthplace in bloodshed and bondage, that would involve his adopted country in a long, costly, and horrific conflict, that would perhaps cost the life of one of his own sons, Conrad sat down to write what he could in a movingly personal, but aesthetically honest, manner about the art of work, the art of taking command of one's actions and thoughts, as he alone could know from the experience of gaining mastery in two professions.

The Shadow Line, which Conrad called a confession and dedicated to his son Borys and other young men thrown into the extreme trials of World War I, can hardly be described as a blueprint for social change. On turning to the last pages, the reader learns only that a ship has staggered into port, its crew desperately ill but alive; that the young captain, somewhat older and wiser than when he set out—certainly more tired— makes ready to depart immediately with a new crew, encounters an older captain who seems in some mysterious way implicated in the events that have transpired, and pays off his faithful, ailing steward. Also, the reader will encounter the following statements: 'The truth is that one must not make too much of anything in life, good or bad' (131); 'Yes, that's what it amounts to. . . . Precious little rest in life for anybody. Better not to think of it' (132). Not exactly a highly dramatic or affirmative ending: there are no paradisal promises of happiness ever after; nor does the novel conclude in conflagration or suicidal despair. Instead of high-blown rhetoric or effusions of sentiment, one finds a delicacy, evocativeness, and moral sympathy that are quite moving, especially in the description of the departing steward easing himself and his diseased heart up the companion stairs.

The question, How to be?, is central to the dilemma of the young hero in *The Shadow Line*, though it might be expressed as What to be? or To be or not to be? at different points in the narrative. Feeling the shades of the prisonhouse close around his late youth, he becomes disenchanted with his life and throws up his too secure job as mate. He drops out of the stream, not for political reasons, not in protest against any particular *way* of life, but in protest against the nature of life itself, its drabness, its sadness, its lack of interest and glamour. In the midst of his existential malaise, he views everything around him as part of 'the universal hollow conceit' (23); he perceives 'the sense of absurdity' (24) that informs the affairs of men on earth; he suffers from a 'feeling of life-emptiness' (49); he considers his own life a 'dreary, prosaic waste of days' (7). The sudden disappearance of all mystery and excitement from the young man's life, producing what he calls 'this stale, unprofitable world of my discontent' (28), is accompanied by a vision of the world as a vast, inhuman machine. He resents the emergence of the internal combustion engine as a means of marine propulsion; he cannot endure the 'prosaic agencies of the commercial world' (36). In the harbour office he observes that the 'atmosphere of officialdom would kill anything that breathes the air of human endeavour, would extinguish hope and fear alike in the supremacy of paper and ink' (29). His own 'powers of locomotion' have been suspended and news of a command available puts him 'out of gear mentally' (28). During the trial by water, the ship's slow progress and his own helplessness madden him to the point that he has to keep a diary to retain a hold on his sanity, or some semblance of sanity: 'the effect is curiously mechanical', he observes, 'the sun climbs and descends, the night swings over our heads as if somebody below the horizon were turning a crank' (97). At his darkest moment, he has a vision of his own death and the end of all things, in which 'all our hearts would cease to beat like run-down clocks' (108).

The mechanical images that describe the young man's conception of life bear a remarkable resemblance to the images that abound in Conrad's letters, some of which I have mentioned already in my chapter on *Victory*. Conrad conceived of the universe as a vast knitting machine, that knits the crazy fabric of each man's destiny (*LL*, I, 176); and as an inhuman machine, 'thinner than air and as evanescent as a flash of lightning' (*LL*, II, 223), that rolls on heedless of the laughter and tears of men. His vision of life, like Heyst's and like the young captain's in *The Shadow Line*, was dark indeed—so

dark that it elicited once a severe reprimand from his uncle
Thaddeus Bobrowski. 'My dear boy,' he wrote to Conrad,

> I begin as I always do but I ought to address you as 'my
> dear pessimist'; for judging from your letters that descrip-
> tion would fit you best. I cannot say that I am pleased by
> your state of mind, or that I am without apprehension
> about your future. . . . Thinking over the causes of your
> melancholy most carefully I cannot attribute it either to
> youth or to age. In the case of one who is thirty-four and
> has had as full a life as you have had, I am forced to at-
> tribute it to ill-health, to your wretched sufferings on the
> African adventure, to your illness which resulted from
> them, and to the fact that you have had lately plenty of
> time to give yourself up to the habit of reverie which I
> have observed to be part of your character. It is inherited;
> it has always been there, in spite of your active life.
>   I may be mistaken but I think this tendency to pessi-
> mism was already in you as long ago as the days when
> you were at Marseilles, but it was then part of youth. I am
> sure that with your melancholy temperament you ought
> to avoid all meditations which lead to pessimistic con-
> clusions. I advise you to lead a more active life than ever
> and to cultivate some cheerful habits.[1]

Obviously the shadow-line can come at different moments
and, perhaps, extend over a number of years, if not over an
entire life, as in the case of Heyst. Although Uncle Thaddeus
was probably correct in his diagnosis, his remedy must have
seemed of scant use to a young man determined to get to the
truth of his own sensations as a novelist.

Like the Conrad of Uncle Thaddeus' letter, the young cap-
tain-to-be is what might be called manic-depressive. When
the colour drains from his life, his spirits plunge; when the
offer of a command materializes, he recovers miraculously, if
only briefly. Images of air and flight and dream abound. Life
is again 'an enchanted garden' (3), full of marvels and mysteries. His disgust and scorn give way to boyish and buoyant
expectancy; in fact, he is so buoyant that he feels himself
floating down the street from the harbour office. His world
takes on the aspect of a dream; Ellis, the harbour master, appears to him as 'a fierce sort of fairy' (40). He sees his new

ship as 'disengaged from the material conditions of her being' (50), as a living thing—an Arab steed, a rare woman—in contrast to the teak-wood cargo, which is mere 'lifeless matter' (50) suspended over the hold. He admits to having been so caught up in the 'ideal completeness of that emotional experience which came to me without the preliminary toil and disenchantment of an obscure career' (50), that the 'life-emptiness which had made me so restless for the last few months lost its bitter plausibility, its evil influence, dissolved in a flow of joyous emotion' (49). He burns with such intense heat that he is in danger of disappearing from the text completely. However, he still has much to learn about the nature of reality, about his capacities for error and weakness and irresponsibility; he is a poor judge of character and motive, his own as well as that of others. In other words, he has not yet achieved that loss of ego, that restraint, which, as Conrad advised his aunt Marguerite Poradowska, comes with experience: 'The fact is, however, that one becomes useful only on realizing the utter insignificance of the individual in the scheme of the universe.'[2] He makes a similar point in another letter to his literary friend, Edward Garnett: 'If one looks at life in its true aspect then everything becomes cleared of what are only unimportant mists that drift in imposing shapes. When once the truth is grasped that one's own personality is only a ridiculous masquerade of something hopelessly unknown, the attainment of serenity is not very far off' (*LL*, I, 186).

The destructive element to which this Conradian hero submits is work itself, and the responsibilities and opportunities for failure or success that go with it. *The Shadow Line* follows on the heels of *Victory* and shares with that novel a preoccupation with the nature of involvement or commitment. Like Heyst, the young captain is a sensitive, inward-looking romantic; although both intellectually and temperamentally aloof from certain conditions of the physical world, he is nevertheless not satisfied to look on and make no sound, to remain a mere passenger in life, which is exactly what he will be if he books passage home. He contemplates the offer of a command somewhat hesitantly at first; then, as the idea throws him into gear and hooks itself firmly in the fabric of his ego, he jumps at it enthusiastically. The job promises not only to restore his 'feeling of wonder' (36), but also to help him in his search for meaning by giving 'opportunities to find out about oneself' (23). Echoes may be heard here coming from *Heart of Darkness*, where Marlow admits: 'No, I don't like work. I had rather laze about and think of all the fine things that can be done. I don't like work—no man does—but I like what is in the work, —the chance to find yourself' (*HD*, 85). So the vocational drop-out drops back in, naturally at a higher rank and in seemingly improved circumstances.

I do not mean to suggest that *The Shadow Line* is a treatise for departments of manpower; it is nothing of the sort. However, Conrad does think of work as an alternative, if not an antidote, to paralysing despair and cynicism; he followed his own chosen vocation with relentless energy and insisted that his writing saved him from that 'madness which, after a certain point in life is reached, awaits those who refuse to master their sensations and bring into coherent form the mysteries of their lives'.[3] Work, for Conrad, is something that stands between man and the vast indifference of things: it is, at least, a sustaining occupation; at best, it becomes a revealing pursuit. 'For the great mass of mankind,' Conrad observed, 'the only saving grace that is needed is fidelity to what is nearest to hand and heart in the short moment of each human effort' (*NLL*, 107). Even the man of imagination, with whom Conrad is primarily concerned in his novels, is not exempt from the benefits of work; he requires contact with the everyday realities and the ordering quality of work as a counterbalance to the chaotic nature of his own sensations. For both groups Conrad lists the positive results of work: 'From the hard work of men are born the sympathetic consciousness of a common destiny, the sense of right conduct which we may call honour, the devotion to our calling and the idealism which is not a misty, winged angel without eyes, but a divine figure of terrestrial aspect with a clear glance and with its feet resting firmly on the earth of which it was born' (*NLL*, 194).

The attitude to work that permeates *The Shadow Line* seems to be best expressed in Conrad's comments on the writing of Anatole France. He speaks of France's knowledge of the unrealizability of hope and the unavoidable sense of littleness that plagues all men: 'He knows this well because he is an artist and a master; but he knows, too, that only in the continuity of effort is there a refuge for minds less clear-seeing and philosophic than his own' (*NLL*, 33–34). The

young captain senses the force and significance of such continuity as he inspects the captain's quarters on his new ship:

> I sat down in the arm-chair at the head of the table—the
> captain's chair, with a small tell-tale compass swung
> above it—a mute reminder of unremitting vigilance.
>
> A succession of men had sat in that chair. I became
> aware of that thought suddenly, vividly, as though each
> had left a little of himself between the four walls of these
> ornate bulkheads; as if a sort of composite soul, the soul
> of command, had whispered suddenly to mine of long
> days at sea and of anxious moments.
>
> 'You, too!' it seemed to say, 'you, too, shall taste of
> that peace and that unrest in a searching intimacy with
> your own self—obscure as we were and as supreme in the
> face of all the winds and all the seas, in an immensity that
> receives no impress, preserves no memories, and keeps no
> reckoning of lives.'
>
> Deep within the tarnished ormolu frame, in the hot
> half-light sifted through the awning, I saw my own face
> propped between my hands. And I stared back at myself
> with the perfect detachment of distance, rather with curi-
> osity than with any other feeling, except of some sympa-
> thy for this latest representative of what for all intents and
> purposes was a dynasty; continuous not in blood, indeed,
> but in its experience, in its training, in its conception of
> duty, and in the blessed simplicity of its traditional point
> of view on life.
>
> It struck me that this quietly staring man whom I was
> watching, both as if he were myself and somebody else,
> was not exactly a lonely figure. He had his place in a line
> of men whom he did not know, of whom he had never
> heard, but who were fashioned by the same influences,
> whose souls in relation to their humble life's work had no
> secrets for him.
>
> (52–53)

In a Europe being progressively torn apart by hatred, treachery, and less abstract forms of artillery, such a tribute to tradition and continuity must have struck a powerful note.

One of Conrad's ways of giving shape to this young cap-

tain's education is through the grouping, in particular the
character relations, having him encounter a series of captains,
members of the dynasty of command, from whom he can
learn something about the continuity of effort, about the secrets and responsibilities of his chosen work.

Captain Giles is drawn with subtlety and economy. We are
told that he resembles a 'church warden' and an 'architect'
(12), a sort of benevolent god surveying his 'handiwork' (27)
with considerable satisfaction and complacency; that, in the
eyes of the young man who has chucked his job, he is a
friendly, interfering old duffer who is given to significant
pauses and to the use of understatement. His appearance is
sketched briefly but precisely: 'His smouldering black pipe
was very noticeable in his big, paternal fist. So, too, was the
glitter of his heavy gold watch-chain across the breast of his
white tunic. He exhaled an atmosphere of virtuous sagacity
thick enough for any innocent soul to fly to confidently' (26–
27). Initially, the young man finds that Giles' presence and
manner rankle him; he resents the air of experience and stability in the older man because it is a constant reminder of his
own erratic behaviour and psychological turmoil. Consequently, he tends to misinterpret Giles' interference and to
underestimate his intelligence. But there is much to be learned
from Giles: he comprehends the steward's real motives for
trying to get the command for the layabout Hamilton; and he
counters the young man's description of the steward as crazy
by saying: 'As to that, I believe that everybody is a little mad'
(42). Later, the young captain will have to learn to look beneath the surface behaviour and appearance of certain members of his crew, in order to ascertain properly their motives
and sentiments, to distinguish between mental distress and
vindictiveness, between the slouchers and the faithful stewards; he will also discover his own potential for funking out,
for behaving in a crazy fashion. Giles, who appears 'pathetic'
(42) as he hurries along to see his young friend off, anticipates
exactly the state of affairs on board; he also realizes that getting the ship into the Indian Ocean will be no small matter.
Giles describes the Gulf of Siam as 'A funny piece of water'
(44) and advises the new captain to 'keep to the east side of it'
(44), the wisdom of which advice eventually comes home to
its recipient.

After the trial by water they meet again, Giles radiating benevolence and paternal interest and exhibiting a ' "kind uncle" smile' (131) as he inquires about the troubled voyage. Giles seems to listen 'sagely' and 'condescendingly', to look 'insufferably exemplary' (131), but gradually the young man's conception alters as he perceives the wisdom in Giles' advice about not making 'too much of anything in life, good or bad' (131) and the welcome moodiness of his admission that life holds little rest for anyone: 'It was as if a ponderous curtain had rolled up disclosing an unexpected Captain Giles' (131). The two captains part company just as the young man realizes that 'he began to interest me for the first time in our intercourse' (132).

In addition to Giles there are four other captains with whom the young man has dealings. Captain Kent, the master of the ship from which he is signing off, is the first. Kent is disappointed to lose a good mate and considers the resignation rather crazy, but he fully understands the young man's motives: 'As I was going out of the chartroom he added suddenly, in a peculiar, wistful tone, that he hoped I would find what I was so anxious to go and look for' (6). The young man perceives in his captain's remark, which is 'a soft, cryptic utterance which seemed to reach deeper than any diamond-hard tool could have done' (6), reserves of sympathy and understanding. Later, when he must give leave to his faithful steward Ransome, it is with the same strained reluctance that he must shake the man's hand and wish him well. The second captain is Ellis, the harbour master, whom the young man describes satirically as 'deputy-Neptune for the circumambient seas' (30) and tends to consider a self-important ogre, a god-like being who wields his pen like a trident as he shapes at random the destinies of mariners. Ellis' gruff exterior masks compassion and generosity; the shrewdly aggressive manner with which he interviews the young appointee drops as soon as the official business has been transacted and we learn that 'A subtle change in Captain Ellis' manner became perceptible as though he had laid aside the trident of deputy-Neptune' (32). Not until his ship staggers into port does the newly initiated captain realize that Ellis has retired and gone home to live on a pension and that the appointment must have been 'the last act, outside the daily routine, of his official life' (130).

Conrad's attention to such small details is no less evident in

the case of the third captain, master of the *Melita*, 'a white,
ghostly steamer' (45). This man sets his passenger on edge
immediately by berating him for being three hours late. The
young man, in the full pride of his recent appointment, indulges his scorn for steamers and associates the *Melita*'s captain
and his bad manners with the 'modern spirit of haste' (45); he
takes the captain's abusiveness or hostility personally, considers the man an 'imbecile' (48), 'the ridiculous victim of jealousy' (48). Later, of course, he will understand the importance of haste, of punctual departures, as his own ship and
crew languish in the fever-infested port of Bankok. As his illusions about the romance of command drop away one by
one in the face of countless unexpected complications and de-
lays, the narrator says 'A mankind which has invented the
proverb, "Time is money", will understand my vexation.
The word "Delay" entered the secret chamber of my brain,
resounded there like a tolling bell which maddens the ear, affected my senses, took on a black colouring, a bitter taste, a
deadly meaning' (66). He describes the captain of the *Melita*
as 'the first really unsympathetic man I had ever come in contact with. My education was far from being finished, though
I didn't know it' (47). Although he cannot decide what the
captain's tone signifies and he suspects him of being mali-
cious, the young man has a moment of doubt concerning his
own hasty judgment of the captain; as the *Melita*'s engines are
stopped so that the young man may glimpse the object of his
command, a high-class sailing-ship, he wonders if perhaps
the ship itself could inspire in this cantankerous skeleton a
streak of 'unselfish delight' (49). Still, he does not fully ap-
preciate the extent to which he might have imposed on the
other man; this understanding must wait until he himself
feels profoundly imposed upon by the irresponsibilities of his
predecessor.

Naturally, or perhaps I should say unnaturally, it is the
ghost of the late captain with whom the young captain must
eventually come to terms, as his presence haunts the efforts to
get under way, troubles the fevered brain of the first-mate
Mr. Burns, and makes itself felt at sea in the empty quinine
bottles. The former captain is a marine version of Nero, a
one-man Zangiacomo orchestra, fiddling in his stateroom as
the ship's rigging blows away. He not only neglects his own
duties, but also keeps the first and second mates from sleep-

ing as a result of his infernal noise. His replacement considers
this behaviour strange when he hears of it from Burns, but
discovers that he 'has to hear stranger things yet. It came out
that this stern, grim, wind-tanned, rough, sea-salted, taciturn
sailor of sixty-five was not only an artist, but a lover as well'
(58). The mystery woman with whom he consorts on shore
is described as a 'professional sorceress from the slums' (59).
Once he heads out to sea, the old man can barely keep clear of
rocks and manages to bump a reef; then he decides to head for
the dry-docks in Hong-Kong, in the face of a monsoon and
without an adequate supply of water or sufficient ballast. The
old man's behaviour is as absurd and outrageous as that of
Marlow's predecessor, Fresleven, in *Heart of Darkness*, who
gets himself killed in a squabble over a few chickens; his madness, his complete breach of the dynastic code, can be seen in
his remarks to Mr. Burns: 'If I had my wish, neither this ship
nor any of you would ever reach a port. And I hope you
won't' (61). Interestingly enough, the description of his activities sounds vaguely like the young man's behaviour and
frame of mind at the beginning of the story: 'He had a mind
to cut adrift from everything. That's what it was. He didn't
care for business, or freights, or for making a passage—or
anything. He meant to have gone wandering about the world
till he lost her with all hands' (62). The young man will learn
shortly that he himself is capable of strange sensations and
very unorthodox behaviour for a captain, but at the moment
he finds that he is profoundly shocked with this member of
the dynasty: 'That man had been in all essentials but his age
just such another man as myself. Yet the end of his life was a
complete act of treason, the betrayal of a tradition which
seemed to me as imperative as any guide on earth could be'
(62).

From his encounters with these members of the dynasty,
the young captain learns something about himself and about
the nature of command. The ideal of leadership which emerges closely resembles the image of Conrad's most exemplary
ship's master, Captain Allistoun of the *Narcissus*. Like Giles,
Allistoun has matured by busying his hands about the work
of this earth; in his alertness and control, he exemplifies the
concept of self-discovery through work. As his long, sleep-
less vigil indicates, he has exceptional powers of endurance;
his expert handling of Donkin, Wait, and the remainder of

the ship's company, reveals not only his strength and decisiveness but also his depth of insight into human nature. When the ordeal is past, Captain Allistoun, in contrast with his harassed officers, is neither dismayed nor discouraged nor angry. 'He was one of those commanders who speak little, seem to hear nothing, look at no one—and know everything, hear every whisper, see every fleeting shadow of ship's life . . . the quiet little man seemed to have found his taciturn serenity in the profound depths of a larger experience' (_NN_, 125).

The one other character worth mentioning at this point, in connection with the images of responsibility and work that abound in _The Shadow Line_, is Ransome, from whom the narrator learns much about courage and steadfastness. Ransome's name, like Burns', is a clue to his character—his willingness, if necessary in the line of duty, to lay down his life. When the steward dies of fever, Ransome takes over as cook-steward, even ministering to the sick, hauling at the rigging, and taking his turn at the helm. He is first seen with his arms folded across his chest, looking 'well-proportioned' and 'thoroughly sailor-like in his poise' (67). The young captain notices Ransome's 'intelligent eyes, a well-bred face, the disciplined independence of his manner' (68). The fact that Ransome has a bad heart and may drop dead with too much exertion gives his performance on board a heroic cast. Ransome does not succumb to either depression or disease; and this for the reason that, 'carrying a deadly enemy in his breast, he had schooled himself into a systematic control of feelings and movements' (68). Ransome, we are told, moves as carefully and gracefully as a man carrying explosives; he radiates confidence and strength, so much so that at one point when he leaves the captain's presence the latter feels 'as if some support had been withdrawn' (112). Ransome brings to mind Podmore of the _Narcissus_ and the cook described in Conrad's essay 'Tradition'. The latter is commended for 'the manner in which he made the little food they had last, the cheery spirit he manifested, and the great help he was to the captain by keeping the men in good humour. That trusty man had "his hands cruelly chafed with the rowing, but it never damped his spirits"' (_NLL_, 200). At the height of the storm, when morale on board the _Narcissus_ is at its lowest, Podmore ventures aft to prepare something to drink for the wretched crew. As graceful as a milk-cow, he rushes to a probable death, muttering, 'Galley! . . . my business . . . As long as she swims I will cook! I will get you coffee' (*NN*, 81). Somehow Podmore returns bearing the fruit of his single, well-employed talent—hot coffee. In spite of the offensiveness of his claims to divine help, the crew pronounces Podmore's feat 'meeraculous' (83). Podmore's devotion to duty brings him close to canonization by the crew: 'He remained heroic. His saying—*the* saying of his life—became proverbial in the mouths of men as are the sayings of conquerors and sages. Later, whenever one of us was puzzled by a task and advised to relinquish it, he would express his determination to persevere and to succeed by the words: —"As long as she swims I will cook!"' (84). Ransome, who has given everything short of his life and is in danger of losing that too, refuses to acknowledge the captain's tribute and suggestion of the ship's great debt to its cook: 'He made as though he had not heard me, and steered in silence till I was ready to relieve him' (123). Like Podmore and all faithful servants in Conrad's fictional world, his commitment to the task at hand precludes any considerations of reward or congratulation.

The young captain must himself learn this lesson embodied in his remarkable cook. He is very dependent upon the approval and good-will of those with whom he associates for the maintenance of his self-respect and mental ease. The conniving steward in the Officer's Home and the unsympathetic captain of the *Melita* rock the poorly ballasted vessel of his equilibrium; and the friendliness and praise of the ministering doctor in Bankok buoy up his spirits immensely. This is where the images of illness on board ship link up with the images of psychic malaise in the young captain. A parallel begins to be apparent between the illness that besets the ship's crew, caused by the former captain's irresponsible lingering in an infested port, and the young captain's sickness of spirit. He is overwhelmed at the uncritical reaction of the men to his announcement concerning the empty quinine bottles and at their pluck and endurance: 'I ask myself whether it was the temper of their souls or the sympathy of their imagination that made them so wonderful, so worthy of my undying regard' (100). This last phrase serves also as part of the subtitle to *The Shadow Line*, which gives it additional weight. Like the crew and Ransome, the young man must learn to temper his soul, to school his emotions, if he is to achieve the full stature of his dynastic, or his human, inheritance.

I mentioned earlier that the young captain might be described as manic-depressive. Perhaps a more satisfactory way of viewing his situation would be to say simply that he is, like so many of Conrad's heroes, a romantic, and that his pessimism is but the reverse side of his romantic idealism. I think that Albert Guerard misreads *The Shadow Line* when he describes its theme as the 'passage from ignorant and untested confidence to the very different confidence of mature command', and when he criticizes Conrad for not having made the early pages of the novel reflect 'a naive and buoyant optimism'.[4] The movement of the novel begins, as I have suggested, from the young man's feelings, not of immature confidence but rather of genuine youthful pessimism, of indirection and life-emptiness. The issue is stated clearly in the first pages: 'Yes. One goes on. And the time, too, goes on— till one perceives ahead a shadow-line warning one that the region of early youth, too, must be left behind. This is the period of life in which such moments of which I have spoken are likely to come. What moments? Why, moments of boredom, of weariness, of dissatisfaction. Rash moments. I mean when the still young are inclined to commit rash actions . . .' (3–4). The young man described here is not exactly the 'naive and buoyant' figure Guerard imagines him to be; he is, rather, the meditative and melancholy pessimist of Uncle Thaddeus' letter. He has glimpsed the emptiness in the future and the vision offends him, threatens the very foundations of his being—his romantic conception of himself and life. Tossing over his job is simply an act of rebellion, a refusal to submit to a grey dismal existence. Rescued from his ennui by the challenge of a command, he slides easily and comfortably back into the womb of his romantic illusions. Once again life seems bright; the sea, pure and safe and friendly; his self-confidence, unshakeable. But the grim spectre of the shadow-line cannot be ignored: his hope is defeated in the face of an 'impenetrable blackness' (108); the sea assumes a deadly calm; and confidence gives way to rankling doubt and insecurity. In the demoralizing conditions of darkness and calm, he becomes preoccupied with death and sees the emaciated first-mate Burns as an 'Enviable man! So near extinction' (92).

Like the fog-bound Congo River in *Heart of Darkness*, the
Placid Gulf in *Nostromo*, and the still sea of the *Patna* in *Lord
Jim*, the calm in the Gulf of Siam is antecedent to the young
captain's moment of truth in *The Shadow Line*. The terror of
the calm, which is more terrible than the boredom of an
obscure job, is reflected in the epigraph from Baudelaire with
which the novel begins: '*D'autre fois, calme plat, grand miroir /
De mon désespoir.*' In the depths of his anguish and self-doubt
the young captain scribbles in his diary:

> . . . I have nothing to do to keep my imagination from
> running wild amongst the disastrous images of the worst
> that may befall us. . . . It seems to me that all my life be-
> fore that momentous day is infinitely remote, a fading
> memory of light-hearted youth, something on the other
> side of a shadow. . . . It's like being bound hand and foot
> preparatory to having one's throat cut. And what appalls
> me most of all is that I shrink from going on deck to face
> it. It's due to the ship, it's due to the men who are there
> on deck—some of them, ready to put out the last rem-
> nant of their strength at a word from me. And I am
> shrinking from it. From the mere vision. My first com-
> mand. Now I understand that strange sense of insecurity
> in my past. I always suspected that I might be no good.
> And here is proof positive, I am shirking it, I am no
> good.
>
> (106–7)

Earlier he had diagnosed his own illness acutely: 'My form of
sickness was indifference. The creeping paralysis of a hopeless
outlook' (93). His indifference may be different in origin and
in the degree of its sophistication from that of Heyst in *Victory*, or of Decoud in *Nostromo*, but it culminates also in debilitating self-doubt, in paralysis. All his illusions of gran-
deur, self-importance, and power are lost in 'the blackness
which had swallowed up our world' (110). When he goes on
deck at the prompting of the faithful Ransome, he has lost all
concern for himself; the darkness itself seems a comfort to
him: 'When the time came the blackness would overwhelm
silently the bit of starlight falling upon the ship, and the end
of all things would come without a sigh, stir, or murmur of
any kind, and all our hearts would cease. . . . The quietness

that came over me was like a foretaste of annihilation. It gave
a sort of comfort, as though my soul had become suddenly
reconciled to an eternity of blind stillness' (108). In the moment of quietness and reconciliation, he is able to recognize
and to accept the difficult truth of human littleness and isolation; and the image with which Conrad portrays his arrival
at this difficult psychological awareness is perhaps the most
beautiful and evocative passage in all of his novels: 'At once
an uneasiness possessed me, as if some support had been
withdrawn. I moved forward too, outside the circle of light,
into the darkness that stood in front of me like a wall. In one
stride I penetrated it. Such must have been the darkness before creation. It had closed behind me. I knew I was invisible
to the man at the helm. Neither could I see anything. He was
alone, I was alone, every man was alone where he stood'
(112–13).

As this passage and others that I have quoted suggest, in no
other novel does Conrad use to such good advantage his
imagistic technique, which he speaks of variously as *cultivat-
ing the poetic faculty* (*LL*, I, 183) or *concreting*. His comment on
the work of Maupassant, where this second term appears, is
particularly instructive: 'The work of Maupassant is honest.
He thinks sufficiently to concrete his fearless conclusions
in illuminative instances. He renders them with that exact
knowledge of the means and that absolute devotion to the
aim of creating a true effect—which is art' (*NLL*, 31). Conrad's use of the moral term 'honest' in connection with the
technique of rendering thought and feeling into appropriate
images recalls the Preface to *The Nigger of the 'Narcissus'*,
where he insists that art must make its appeal through the
senses; it is also a useful reminder to the critic that the Conrad
of the later fiction believed that the only morality of art lay in
its technique, in its expression. Readers of Conrad will recall
many illuminative instances throughout his work, even after
the details of plot and character have been forgotten: the
drifting tree rushing seaward down the debris-swollen river
in *Almayer's Folly*, which concretely renders Almayer's fantasies of freedom and escape; the collapse of Lingard's house
of cards in *An Outcast of the Islands*; the French man-of-war
shelling the jungle, the overturned railway car with its wheels
turned upward, and numerous other images of insanity and
waste in *Heart of Darkness*; Zangiacomo's orchestra murder-

ing the silence of Sourabaya in *Victory*; Peyrol's flight at sea
and his death on the tartane in the final pages of *The Rover*.

In *The Shadow Line* this technique has been brought to perfection, not only in the more obvious cases such as the image
of the composite soul of command, immersion in the darkness before creation, and Ransome's departure with his
diseased and overworked heart, but also in many less spectacular instances. One illuminative instance, which seems
inconspicuous at first reading but which gathers meaning to
itself as the novel unfolds, will serve to illustrate the extent to
which Conrad uses every detail for effect in this short novel.
The image occurs just as the young rebel steps into the office
of Captain Ellis, the harbour-master and deputy-Neptune:

> Three lofty windows gave on the harbour. There was
> nothing in them but the dark-blue sea and the paler lumi-
> nous blue of the sky. My eye caught in the depths and
> distances of these blue tones the white speck of some big
> ship just arrived and about to anchor in the outer road-
> stead. A ship from home—after perhaps ninety days at
> sea. There is something touching about a ship coming in
> from sea and folding her white wings for a rest.
>
> (30)

This image serves several distinct functions. First, at the level
of plot, it serves to place or locate the office of Captain Ellis,
with its command of the sea, both visually and, as we are to
learn, figuratively, since he has the power to direct the 'fate of
mortals whose lives were cast upon the waters' (30). Also, the
image of the ship as a bird coming home to rest, framed by
Ellis' window, serves as a reminder of the young man's own
sense of dislocation, having cast himself adrift from his connections with the sea; and it reminds us of his romantic, or
poetic, nature, which at times is submerged in the details of
his crankiness and lack of sociability. Barely half an hour
later, after the interview with Ellis and the miracle of his appointment, the young captain feels as if 'all of a sudden a pair
of wings had grown on my shoulders' (33). Seen in retrospect, of course, the image expands even further: if the white
ship is the same ghostly steamer, *Melita*, which is ordered to
take the new captain to Bankok, then the reference to the
ninety-day passage from home would explain the steamer

captain's tenseness and irritation with his unexpected and un-
wanted guest; it might also prefigure the young captain's own
return from his ordeal at sea for a much-earned but short-
lived rest at the end of the novel.

Much of the success of *The Shadow Line* may be attributed
to Conrad's subtle blending of plot, character relations, and
concreting. The progressive stages in the young captain's education are revealed through encounters (engineered with extreme precision and economy) with other characters until he
finally encounters himself. However a good deal of the emotional power and poignancy of the novel derives from the
narrative point of view. In the early pages of *The Shadow
Line*, as in *Victory*, an ironic tone is established which is designed to colour our interpretation of the events that follow.
In *Victory* the tone is more ironic than sympathetic, and at
times clearly sarcastic; in *The Shadow Line*, however, the
irony might be described as sympathetic, or indulgent, because it is self-directed, coloured, as Conrad admits in the
Author's Note, 'by that affection one can't help feeling for
such events of one's life as one has no reason to be ashamed
of' (vii). The narrator begins by establishing an appropriate
distance, by distinguishing between himself, the young, and
the very young:

> Only the young have such moments. I don't mean the
> very young. No. The very young have, properly speak-
> ing, no moments. It is the privilege of early youth to live
> in advance of its days in all the beautiful continuity of
> hope which knows no pauses and no introspection.
>
> One closes behind one the little gate of mere boyish-
> ness—and enters an enchanted garden. Its very shades
> glow with promise. Every turn of the path has its seduc-
> tion. And it isn't because it is an undiscovered country.
> One knows well enough that all mankind had steamed
> that way. It is the charm of universal experience from
> which one expects an uncommon or personal sensation—
> a bit of one's own.
>
> One goes on recognizing the landmarks of the pred-
> ecessors, excited, amused, taking the hard luck and the
> good luck together—the kicks and the halfpence, as the
> saying is—the picturesque common lot that holds so

many possibilities for the deserving or perhaps for the lucky. Yes. One goes on. And the time, too, goes on—till one perceives ahead a shadow-line warning one that the region of early youth, too, must be left behind.

(3)

The narrator then goes on to speak of marriage and resigning from a job as examples of the rash behaviour which the young are capable of when they see ahead the spectre of the shadow-line. He plays with the word 'marriage', suggesting that his youthful action of signing off his ship 'had more the character of a divorce—almost desertion' (4). He describes the state of mind which prompted this action humorously: 'The green sickness of late youth descended on me and carried me off. Carried me off that ship, I mean' (5). Then he calls his action 'my case' (6) and explains the various interpretations given to it by his former shipmates. The misogynist engineer remarks bitterly that he had been expecting him 'to run away home and get married to some silly girl' (6); the chief engineer attributes the action to a 'deranged liver' (6) and offers to prescribe a suitable elixir. The scene at the Harbour Office, where the young man must attend with his captain to collect his papers, assumes a very comic aspect, as the official's grin disappears in 'sudden solemnity' (7) and turns into 'a sorrowful expression' (7) over the young man's 'sad condition' (8).

This distance between the mature narrator, who is himself as experienced and as wise a navigator in psychic waters as Captain Giles, and his inexperienced self allows Conrad to imply a certain amount of dramatic irony in various situations, where the narrator and the reader are aware of implications of which the young man is ignorant. We know, for example, that Giles is no fool and that he is trying tactfully to suggest that a command is in the offing long before the young man is aware of these facts. Conrad is thus able to express the young man's feelings of discontent and irritability in seemingly exaggerated terms, while at the same time retaining our sympathies for him.[5] One might almost call this technique the achieving of a willing suspension of disdain, for the young man is often unbearable, both in his cranky indifference and in his romantic exuberance. One finds a similar

distance and humour in the pages of *Moby Dick*, where a
wiser and more seasoned Ishmael describes in comic terms
the funereal states of mind that drove him periodically from
teaching to the sea.[6]

The narrator's linguistic peculiarities give the reader not
only a sense of the speaking voice, but also a sense of being
both within and without the narrative. His use of understatement and his tendency to play down the potentially melodramatic or theatrical elements, making his point obliquely
through the image, are superb. The quinine incident, which
is central to the young narrator's moral growth, illustrates the
kind of restraint that I am referring to. It does not take place
until page 88 in the text, well after the ship has been becalmed
and the crew devastated by fever. The narrator speaks of his
faith in humorously exaggerated terms, employing such
words as 'believed', 'faith', 'virtue', 'precious', 'gold', 'pan-
acea'. The discovery itself is understated: 'But why record all
the swift steps of the appalling discovery. You have guessed it
already' (89). Then he discusses his reaction in rather clinical
terms, the very coolness of which add to the impact: 'It is a
fact that the very greatness of a mental shock helps one to
bear up against it, by producing a sort of temporary insen-
sibility' (89). The narrator explains that he suddenly felt an
urge to be on deck, since that is where a ship's problems are
best met: 'To this fact, as it were of nature, I responded instinctively, which may be taken as proof that for a moment I
must have been robbed of my reason' (89). However, the real
nature of his reaction is only fully understood in the description of his encounter with Burns, who appears to the distracted young captain to be trying to cut his throat:

> I was to a certain extent horrified; but it was rather a sec-
> ondary sort of effect, not really strong enough to make
> me yell at him in such a manner as: 'Stop!' . . . 'Heavens!'
> . . . 'What are you doing?'
> In reality he was simply overtaxing his returning
> strength in a shaky attempt to clip off the thick growth of
> his red beard. A large towel was spread over his lap, and
> a shower of stiff hairs, like bits of copper wire, was de-
> scending on it at every snip of the scissors.
> He turned to me his face grotesque beyond the fantasies
> of mad dreams, one cheek all bushy as if with a swollen

flame, the other denuded and shrunken, with the untouched long moustache on that side asserting itself,
lonely and fierce. And while he stared thunderstruck,
with the gaping scissors on his fingers, I shouted my discovery at him fiendishly, in six words, without comment.
(90)

The excruciating attention to such minute details suggests a
degree of psychological disturbance that could not have been
so satisfactorily rendered without introducing another character; and the restraining phrases, such as 'a secondary sort of
effect', 'to a certain extent', and 'In reality he was simply
overtaxing', serve only to heighten the impact of the descriptive details that follow.

Scholes and Kellogg, to whose work I referred in my chapter on *Victory*, attribute this kind of perspective and irony to
Rousseau:

> One of the many lessons that Rousseau taught subse-
> quent novelists was that even with the literal identity of
> subject and narrator, the mere span of time separating the
> two provides sufficient distance to allow for all the poten-
> tially ironical divergence in point of view between charac-
> ter and narrator that a novelist could require. Time
> became a significant dimension in the conception of char-
> acter. It wrought all the changes necessary for a genuine
> multiplicity of points of view toward the same facts and
> underlined the importance of defining the knower in
> order to interpret his telling.[7]

Obviously, the nature of the materials and the greater distance in time give *The Shadow Line* a more personal, human
dimension than is to be found even in the autobiographical
Heart of Darkness. Whether or not one gives the credit to Rousseau, however, it is evident that the unique relation between
narrator and subject produces in *The Shadow Line* a degree of
directness and intimacy that Conrad's other first-person nar-
ratives simply do not have; furthermore, the comparison
with Rousseau is useful because it raises the related and
equally interesting question of autobiographical fiction.

A simple explanation for the success of *The Shadow Line* is
to say that the story has a greater basis in actuality than the

rest of Conrad's fiction. Conrad encouraged this view on several occasions: he first described the novel to Pinker as 'not a story really but exact autobiography' (*LL*, II, 181); then, in a letter to Helen Sanderson after its publication, he referred to *The Shadow Line* as a 'piece of as strict autobiography as the form allowed, —I mean, the need of slight dramatization to make the thing actual. Very slight. For the rest, not a fact or sensation is "invented"' (*LL*, II, 195). Conrad often complained of not having had enough varied experience, of having had to invent too much. As he explains in his fictional autobiography *A Personal Record*: 'Only in men's minds does every truth find an effective and undeniable existence. Imagination, not invention, is the supreme master of art as of life. An imaginative and exact rendering of authentic memories may serve worthily that spirit of piety towards all things human which sanctions the conception of a writer of tales, and the emotions of a man reviewing his own experience' (*PR*, 25). These comments, though useful in understanding Conrad's attraction to hearsay, memoirs, and first-hand experience, have encouraged critics to dwell unduly on biography rather than technique in *The Shadow Line*.

Although it has fascinated many critics, the autobiographical aspect of *The Shadow Line* has become something of a red herring in Conrad criticism. Edward Said's thesis in *Joseph Conrad and the Fiction of Autobiography* is that all of Conrad's fiction is a kind of spiritual autobiography that charts, either directly or obliquely, his progress through a personal heart of darkness towards the (possibly dim) light of reconciliation and self-acceptance. Said's argument is intriguing but, I think, misguided in its attempt to force a complex and multi-faceted body of work into a suit of psycho-critical clothing that simply does not fit. It is true that Conrad's major works are temperamental creations—that is, that they reflect their author's vision of reality at the time of composition—but it is misleading to look too closely for analogies between the fictional plot and events of Conrad's personal life or contemporary European history. Although the doctrine of work and the notion of taking command of one's life and psychic resources in *The Shadow Line* reflects Conrad's wartime feelings, it seems perverse to view the story of his first command as an allegory of the war in Europe. Said is constrained to argue, for example, that Conrad's confusion in his Author's Note concerning the date of completion of *The Shadow Line* (which was finished late in 1915, rather than late in 1916) reflects, not a lapse of memory, but an unconscious equation of that book with his subsequent readings of Hartley Withers' *The War and Lombard Street*, an account of the general moratorium on credit imposed by the Treasury before the war in 1914; since, as Said speculates, *The Shadow Line* concerns a similar theme (the young captain's resolution somehow resembling the resourcefulness of the Bank of England in the face of political and economic crisis), the date of completing *The Shadow Line* may have merged in Conrad's mind with the date of reading Withers' book while he was on board H.M.S. *Ready* at the request of the British Admiralty a year later.[8]

This kind of speculation leads Said to make explicit analogies that serve only to distort our reading of *The Shadow Line*. He compares the secret enemy in Ransome's breast quite justifiably with the young captain's Achilles heel, his sense of insecurity and feelings of unworthiness; however, he goes on to suggest that Ransome's weak heart also represents the tortured past which Conrad must struggle to keep under control. If there is any analogy to be drawn here, it seems more likely that Conrad's secret enemy was his never fully conquered scepticism which could only be kept in check by an absolute commitment to the craft of fiction. Said also suggests that the young captain's recourse to Giles after his ordeal at sea signifies Conrad's 'belief in Europeanism' and that the war was a catharsis for Conrad, 'the public incarnation of his private struggles'.[9] Conrad's meagre fictional output during the war would indicate, not that his self-doubts and insecurities had been purged by the blood-letting in Europe, but rather that the war profoundly distressed and unsettled him; and a close examination of the novels written after *The Shadow Line*, particularly *The Rescue*, calls into question Said's view that Conrad's work subsequent to his analysis of the responsibilities of command was all sweetness and light:

> After that, until his death in 1924, Conrad returned in his fiction to episodes out of his past, now to complete stories he had once begun, now to idealize, almost always to elegize. The self-tormented characters undergoing radical experiences whose chronicler he had been were replaced either by strong old men like Peyrol in *The Rover*, or

troubled young people like Rita and George in *The Arrow of Gold*; young or old, Conrad allows them a final redemption, like a benign administrator, a Kurtz turned saint, who transmutes suffering into stillness and peace.[10]

Said's description applies reasonably well to the small world of Escampobar in *The Rover*, restored to equilibrium through the offices of ex-gunner Peyrol, but it certainly does not apply to the world of George and Rita in *The Arrow of Gold*— the one left heart-broken and alone, nursing physical and psychological wounds, the other left to be the endless prey of collectors and fortune-seekers. And the conclusion of *The Rescue*, which will be discussed in detail later in this study, provides no affirmations: the love of Edith and Lingard ends in moral death; the efforts to restore Hassim and Immada to their positions of power result in their annihilation; and the intrigues on the Shore of Refuge bring down on that little universe an unexpected holocaust.

Lawrence Graver, too, distorts *The Shadow Line* somewhat to fit his thesis that Conrad was almost always at his best in his short fiction. In his critical study, *Conrad's Short Fiction*, Graver accepts the autobiographical claims for *The Shadow Line*, praising the work highly and distinguishing it from the other novels of the later period. He suggests that Conrad set aside his experiments and returned to an earlier, simpler mode: 'The relief of being temporarily free from the obligations of comedy and romance can be seen on every page of "The Shadow-Line", one of the last and most memorable of his finest short fiction.'[11] There can be no doubt that, in comparison with such epic creations as *Nostromo* and *The Rescue* and such psychologically dense works as *Lord Jim* and *Under Western Eyes*, *The Shadow Line* seems pared to the bone: it has an extremely restricted place, a limited cast of characters (most of whom are conveniently sick or out of the way), and the most plain diction imaginable (except where the young captain's idiosyncrasies are exaggerated for comic or ironic effect). And the novel is much cleaner, by the same standards, than that other autobiographical fiction, *Heart of Darkness*, where image density is sometimes too great and where the exotic jungle setting and dramatic events often encourage a certain excess in the prose. Given these differences, *The Shadow Line* still belongs in the later period. All of the elements of romance can be found in its pages, particularly the romance pattern of the rescue of the individual in distress. With the assistance of godly Captain Giles and the good offices of deputy-Neptune Captain Ellis, the young captain is 'rescued' from his boredom and *ennui* and placed, ironically of course, in a situation that will test his mettle and bind him hand and foot to a life of routine and responsibility. The comic elements are there, too, as I have suggested throughout this discussion, in the exaggerated treatment of the young man's moods, the illuminative instances, and the dramatic irony which derives from the presence of the mature narrator. Conrad felt no obligation to either comedy or romance; he simply wished to experiment with various fictional components in different combinations, one of which was the combination of romance pattern and autobiographical first-person narration in *The Shadow Line*. If this short novel illustrates anything neatly, it is not that Conrad's short fiction was superior, but rather that he had a remarkable capacity to change pace, to employ the lessons which he had learned in his longer works on a substantially reduced scale.

Conrad may have anticipated a more sympathetic reception for his work by insisting initially on its autobiographical nature, but he was eventually obliged to admit that it was much more than a record of past events. When his literal-minded friend Sidney Colvin refused to review *The Shadow Line* on the grounds that he had no first-hand knowledge of its setting, Conrad insisted that 'The locality does not matter' (*LL*, II, 182) and that the story was really experience 'transposed into spiritual terms' (*LL*, II, 183). We know that Conrad did alter some of the facts of his first command in the *Otago*: the *Vidar*, the original of the ship which the young man leaves, was apparently a comfortable and satisfactory berth for Conrad; so, too, was John Snadden, former master of the *Otago*, not an irresponsible philanderer, but only a moody man who had the misfortune to die of a heart attack and who was buried at sea, far from the *Otago*'s later course through the Gulf of Siam. The portrait of Burns, with his premonition of disaster, also seems to have been considerably fictionalized.[12]

Conrad no doubt derived certain satisfactions from the use of personal materials—a pre-existing universe of things, events, and people, with an internal logic that attaches itself, however falsely and arbitrarily, to experience. Such materials, requiring only reflection and recall, rather than the invention of plot and character and setting, would leave the mind free to discover form, to attend to tone and colouring. This, at least, is the impression one receives from the prefaces and letters, especially a letter to his literary acquaintance Warrington Dawson. After reading Dawson's novel *The Grand Elixir*, Conrad questioned whether his friend had found the right mode for his particular talents:

> Thinking over all these matters it came into my mind whether it would not be rather good for you to throw your next fiction into the autobiographical form, which gives certain facilities and also imposes certain restraints. Your gift as raconteur will get full play while the necessity to keep your man *credibly convincing* will impose on you certain limitations from which your imagination will not suffer in the end. And then look at the advantage of *direct* expression for your thoughts and feelings. *Pensez-y mon cher.* You want something to steady you artistically.[13]

After the technical and intellectual struggles with *Chance* and *Victory*, as well as the shock of the war and the return to Poland, Conrad too may have needed steadying. His recognition that autobiography is a 'form', with very definite advantages and limitations, ought to indicate that he did not regard the writing of *The Shadow Line* as an artistic holiday.

What needs to be asserted here is not that *The Shadow Line* is substantially different and out of place by virtue of its autobiographical dimension, but rather that it belongs in the later period not only in terms of its formal characteristics, but also in terms of its vision. This point can be illustrated by referring briefly to 'The Secret Sharer', the short story which is usually mentioned in discussions of *The Shadow Line*. Conrad makes the connection too, in the Author's Note to *'Twixt Land and Sea*, the volume which contains 'The Secret Sharer'; but he links them only as stories about being becalmed at sea and claims that *The Shadow Line* is 'a book which belongs to a later period' (*TW*, ix). There is good reason to believe that this remark is neither gratuitous nor deceptive, but rather indicative of Conrad's sense of having conceived the later story under a very different inspiration and with quite different intentions.

Although the initial situation, the problem of first command, is similar, the two stories are quite distinct in terms of focus and perspective. 'The Secret Sharer' begins with a quick summary of the young captain's situation on board his new ship: 'But what I felt most was my being a stranger to the ship; and if all the truth must be told, I was somewhat of a stranger to myself' (*TW*, 93). He describes himself as the 'youngest man on board (barring the second mate), and untried as yet by a position of fullest command' (93). Through a generous and unthinking gesture, the young captain sets in motion a series of events involving the harbouring of a fugitive who has killed a fellow-seaman. Because of the exigencies of the short story, Conrad continually nudges the reader, both in the title and on every page of the text, so that the significance of the encounter between the young captain and his unexpected visitor is unmistakable. The young captain speaks of having been 'faced with my own reflection' (101), of seeing 'his own grey ghost' (103), his 'secret sharer' (114), 'my other self' (136); and, since the story falls into the tradition of the *doppelganger* tales, the word 'double' appears with great frequency.

The focus is quite different in *The Shadow Line* and the issues are more complex and interesting. First, the problem for the young man arises not from a situation of insecurity in the face of a new command, but rather from a state of disappointed idealism, of having to cope with feelings of rebelliousness and scepticism in late youth; and the development of his 'problem' is seen more in terms of establishing some sort of bridge between conduct and continuity in human affairs. The narrator in 'The Secret Sharer' suggests that the matter seemed quite clear-cut: 'it is only the young who are ever confronted by such clear issues' (99). Although there is room for irony here, in the distance between the narrator and his youthful self, that irony is missing and the short story ends with a note of extreme confidence, as if all the trials of life have been overcome in that one experience: 'Nothing! no one in the world should stand between us, throwing a shadow on the way of silent knowledge and mute affection, the perfect communion of a seaman with his first command' (143). And for his mysterious double, he sees freedom and a new destiny, a naively hopeful vision of the future for a man without home or friends or, possibly, even a habitable destination on the nearby island of Kohring.

The education of the young captain in *The Shadow Line* is, naturally, lengthier; in fact, when the story concludes one assumes that his education has just begun. His trials are also much more trying, physically and psychologically, as well as being less dramatic. Not for him the quick diagnosis and reckless resolution by way of a dangerous manoeuvre of his ship; his is a slower, more painful maturing, in keeping with the actualities of life at sea, and more realistic in human terms. As Conrad knew, faced with the panorama of his own life behind him and the spectacle of a war-torn Europe before him, there are no shortcuts through the shadow-line. Furthermore, the young captain in *The Shadow Line* cannot achieve any measure of maturity and control in isolation simply by locking himself away in his cabin; and this is what distinguishes *The Shadow Line* from the short story which had been written in 1909. The later work is informed by the vision of community, human community, where only the various human encounters, the illumination concerning the composite soul of command, and the unbelievable communal effort to get the ship into port can bring the young captain to a sense of his own worth and, equally important, a sense of his own insignificance in the scheme of the universe.

In *The Shadow Line* Conrad was reviewing his experience, not only in the literal sense of having struggled with the problems of first command on board a sailing ship, but also in the emotional sense of having had, throughout his life, to come to terms with the problems of self-control, with the dangers of self-doubt and indifference. The experience of the young captain in *The Shadow Line* is far from uncommon in his fiction. When Marlow learns of Jewel's traumatic experience in *Lord Jim*, for example, he says that the discovery 'had the power to drive me out of my conception of existence, out of the shelter each of us makes for himself to creep under in moments of danger, as a tortoise withdraws within its shell. For a moment I had a view of the world that seemed to wear a vast and dismal aspect of disorder. . . . I seemed to have lost all my words for a moment beyond the pale' (*LJ*, 13). The knowledge of his own insignificance and life's absurdity may drive a man to despair or it may free him for a creative existence. In Dr. Monygham in *Nostromo*, Conrad sums up the dangers precisely: 'he was well aware of the most dangerous element common to them all: of the crushing, paralyzing sense of human littleness, which is what really defeats a man struggling with natural forces, alone, far from the eyes of his fellows' (*N*, 433). The death of Decoud, the sceptical *boulevardier* in that novel, quite clearly demonstrates that Conrad had himself glimpsed the darkness that awaits any man who looks beyond the pale and that he knew the values of human community. The balance he recommends is, indeed, a precarious one, as he makes clear in his essay 'Books':

> It must not be supposed that I claim for the artist in fiction the freedom of moral Nihilism. I would require of him many acts of faith of which the first would be the cherishing of an undying hope; and hope, it will not be contested, implies all the piety of effort and renunciation. It is the God-sent form of trust in the magic force and inspiration belonging to the life of this earth. We are inclined to forget that the way of excellence is in intellectual, as distinguished from emotional, humility. What one feels so hopelessly barren in declared pessimism is just its arrogance. It seems as if the discovery made by many men at various times that there is much evil in the world were a source of proud and unholy joy unto some of the modern writers. That frame of mind is not the proper one in which to approach seriously the art of fiction. It gives an author—goodness only knows why—an elated sense of his own superiority. And there is nothing more dangerous than such an elation to that absolute loyalty towards his feelings and sensations an author should keep hold of in his most exalted moments of creation.
>
> To be hopeful in an artistic sense it is not necessary to think that the world is good. It is enough to believe that there is no impossibility of its being made so.
>
> (*NLL*, 8–9)

Writing, for Conrad, was a means of filling the void left by the clean sweep of his critical intellect over the half truths of life, a way of defying the delinquent gods and preserving the sanity which their absence threatens. The aim of art, like the aim of taking command of one's psychic resources in any form of work, is nothing less than survival. As Conrad suggests in the Preface to *The Nigger of the 'Narcissus'*, the artist must continually descend within himself and 'in that lonely region of stress and strife . . . find the terms of his appeal' (*NN*, vii). The truth that he finds there, Conrad continues, 'is not in the clear logic of a triumphant conclusion; it is not in the unveiling of one of those heartless secrets which are called Laws of Nature. It is not less great, but only more difficult' (xi–xii). The truth of the human situation is more than likely something simple but profound, in the nature of Captain Giles' departing comment to the young captain who has crossed, or is in the process of crossing, the shadow-line— 'Precious little rest in life for anybody' (132)—or in the words of Marlow in *Heart of Darkness*: 'Droll thing life is— that mysterious arrangement of merciless logic for a futile purpose. The most you can hope from it is some knowledge of yourself—that comes too late—a crop of unextinguishable regrets' (150).

What Conrad offers in *The Shadow Line* is not only a poetic interlude with important significance for England in time of war, but also a subtle and economical rendering of an important phase in his own emotional life, a phase which must have had to be relived again and again as he put down one completed manuscript and, without pausing to rest in port, set out again on the uncertain and exacting seas of literary creation.

'There's nothing like giving up one's life to an unselfish passion,' he wrote on behalf of the vagabond author of *Quiet Days in Spain*. 'No great passion can be barren. May a world of gracious and poignant images attend the lofty solitude of your renunciation' (*NLL*, 64–65). Similarly, in his essay on Henry James, Conrad defines in religious terms the necessary sacrifice that must attend the efforts of the serious artist:

> That a sacrifice must be made, that something has to be given up, is the truth engraved in the innermost recesses of the fair temple built for our edification by the masters of fiction. There is no other secret behind the curtain. All adventure, all love, every success is resumed in the supreme energy of an act of renunciation. It is the uttermost limit of our power; it is the most potent and effective

force at our disposal on which rest the labours of a solitary man in his study, the rock on which have been built commonwealths whose might casts a dwarfing shadow on the oceans. Like a natural force which is obscured as much as illuminated by the multiplicity of phenomena, the power of renunciation is obscured by the mass of weaknesses, vacillations, secondary motives and false steps and compromises which make up the sum of our activity.

(*NLL*, 15–16)

Like the young captain in *The Shadow Line*, Conrad continued to expand the range and depth of his experience. His own fidelity to the task bespeaks the importance he placed on his chosen form of work. And yet he had few illusions concerning the efficacy of his art, just as he had few illusions about the possibility of finding political cures for the world's ills. In 'Autocracy and War', he admits that 'The true peace of the world will be much less like a beleaguered fortress and more, let us hope, in the nature of an Inviolable Temple. It will be built on less perishable foundations than those of material interests. But it must be confessed that the architectural aspect of the universal city remains as yet inconceivable—that the very ground for its erection has not been cleared of the jungle' (*NLL*, 107). In the midst of war, which would play havoc with Poland and which would strain England's resources to the hilt, including the enlistment of his own son in battle, Conrad had no elaborate charts to offer. As he said in a letter to Edward Garnett years before the war (1907): 'You seem to forget that I am a Pole. You forget that we have been used to go to battle without illusions. It's you, Britishers, that "go in to win" only. We have been "going in" these last hundred years repeatedly, to be knocked on the head only' (*LL*, II, 59). Conrad did believe, however, that a passionate devotion to work was a possible means of clearing the jungle, which is in the human heart; and *The Shadow Line*, which renders this humble belief in illuminative instances, in terms of art, is an important step in that direction.

4 The Arrow of Gold
The Detailed Manner of a Study

The Arrow of Gold, like *The Rescue*, was long in the making. Conrad made various forays into the same materials off and on during his writing career: he touches briefly, but not very informatively, on the Marseilles experience in *A Personal Record*; in the '*Tremolino*' sketch in *The Mirror of the Sea*, he gives an impressionistic account of his gun-running experiences, including a description of the near capture and forced sinking of the *Tremolino* and introductions to several characters, including Rita, Dominic Cervoni, and J. M. K. Blunt, who would appear later in the novel; and he has left the fragments of an unfinished novel, *The Sisters*. In none of these pieces, however, does Conrad actually analyse the unusual social and psychological conditions of the Marseilles period, during which he appears to have fallen in love, drifted back and forth between the wharves and the wealthy Legitimist salons, engaged in smuggling guns, and attempted to take his own life.

Critics and biographers have indulged in considerable speculation concerning the details of Conrad's love affair and attempted suicide, as well as about the relation of the novel to the 'facts' of this period in his life. What seems more important to ask at this stage in Conrad studies is what, exactly, he achieved in *The Arrow of Gold* and, perhaps, how he came to write the novel at all, after having already exploited some of its possibilities and after a near silence of two years in the midst of the First World War.

It seems most likely that the writing of *The Shadow Line* prepared the way for *The Arrow*. The story of first command must have recalled those earlier days in Marseilles when the young Conrad had his first contact with the sea. More important, it hearkens back to his first and traumatic experience of being dangerously out of control of his feelings and actions. The war, too, and the insane character and proportions which it had assumed, no doubt commingled with Conrad's memories of his involvement in a rather bizarre, if not as violent and demented, struggle to restore the Pretender Don Carlos to the Spanish throne. The two stories which Conrad wrote in 1916 also contain a number of the seeds which were eventually to flower in *The Arrow*, although critics have failed to make the connection. The first of these stories, 'The Warrior's Soul', deserves considerable attention, not only for its powerful evocation of the horrors of war, but also for its relation to the novel which it precedes.

'The Warrior's Soul', which is the story of a crisis of conscience that takes place during Napoleon's terrible retreat from Moscow, derives mainly from Conrad's meditations on the nature of war and from his research for his great Napoleonic novel. However, its central character, Tomassov, and the woman with whom he has fallen in love, are precursors of George and Rita in *The Arrow*. Tomassov, forced on a point of honour to perform a mercy killing of the French officer who has helped him escape from Paris and who was his rival for the attentions of a beautiful, spirited *femme du monde*, is described in terms that anticipate M. George. He has 'lover's lips' (*TH*, 5), 'innocent, believing eyes' (5), and is forever rhapsodic about France, particularly about Paris: 'He considered himself a sort of privileged person, not because a woman had looked on him with favour, but simply because, how should I say it, he had had the wonderful illumination of his worship for her, as if it were heaven itself that had done this for him' (7). Like M. George, Tomassov has 'a lot of poetry in his nature' (17), but has fallen 'artlessly' (9) in love. The object of his affections is a distinguished widow, who appears to be as beautiful and captivating and recherchée as her counterpart Rita de Lastaola in *The Arrow*. 'She was a secret delight and a secret trouble. All the men when they looked at her fell to brooding as if struck by the thought that their lives had been wasted. She was the very joy and shudder of felicity and she brought only sadness and torment to the hearts of men' (9). The relationship between these two lovers assumes only a small portion of 'The Warrior's Soul', most of the space being devoted to moving descriptions of the wretched and bloody retreat of the remnants of the French army, with the Cossacks at their heels 'cutting down galvanized corpses that didn't care' (4), and to Tomassov's character and moral dilemma; but Tomassov and his exquisite confidant are unmistakably related to the two lovers around whom a very different, but equally deadly, struggle will ensue in *The Arrow*.

I will pass quickly over 'The Tale', which was written seven months later in October 1916, because it is a much slighter, less important piece, and because it possesses fewer points of comparison with *The Arrow*. The central incident of the story, a captain's decision in time of war which sends a ship full of possibly innocent men to their deaths, derives probably from a combination of wartime incidents with which Conrad was familiar and the memory of his own earlier shore connections with the coastal fishermen of England and the running aground of the *Tremolino* during his days as a gun-runner in the Mediterranean. What is most significant about this tale is the witty exchange between the man in uniform and his mistress, the ironic playfulness of their moments together in the shadowy room. They anticipate scenes between George and Rita in her private galleries and salons, with their constant shifting between embarrassment, confidence, caprice, irony, passion. The mistress, who acts as interlocutor and foil for the commanding officer, has something of the audaciousness of Rita de Lastaola and appears at times to be equally mysterious, 'a voice from the sofa' (67) which keeps interrupting the uniformed narrator with queries and asides. Together they play various games with words that are, of course, beyond George and Rita, in the sense that they are the games of seasoned and secure lovers: she asks for a story, claiming that he used to be quite professional at telling tales, that he had 'a sort of art' (*TH*, 60); for his part, he makes various pronouncements about his art, including the observations that 'comedy is but a matter of the visual angle' (62) and that 'My tales if often professional (as you remarked just now) have never been technical' (63). The point to be made here is not that this couple resemble George and Rita in anything more than slightest manner, but rather that Conrad seems to have written this cloistered tale with the scenes between George and Rita already in mind.

If the two short stories provided a testing ground for some

of Conrad's deliberations about the characters and events of
The Arrow, the visit of the American journalist Jane Anderson must have provided the necessary inspiration. Conrad
describes her in a letter to Sidney Colvin: 'We made the acquaintance of a new young woman. She comes from Arizona
and (strange to say!) has a European mind. She is seeking to
get herself adopted as our big daughter and is succeeding
fairly. To put it shortly she's quite yum-yum. But those matters can't interest a man of your austere character. So I hasten
away from these petty frivolities . . .'[1] Conrad appears to
have been somewhat smitten by his worldly and vivacious
visitor. When his son Borys decided to ask for leave from the
front to pay her a visit in Paris, Conrad sent the address and
the advice to 'take care not to make a damned fool of yourself'; when Borys went ahead and fell in love with Jane, as his
father might have done (and had done at a similar age with
Rita de Lastaola's original), Conrad wrote, according to
Borys, to say that he hoped 'the enemy would keep me
sufficiently pre-occupied to enable me to "get Jane out of my
system".'[2] To his agent Pinker, Conrad made a comment on
the subject that bears directly on *The Arrow*: 'If he must meet
a "Jane" it's better he should meet her at nineteen than at
twenty-four.'[3] This is clearly an allusion to the trauma he had
experienced as a young man in Marseilles, after which he shot
himself in the chest.

The Arrow has had a thorny critical history; no other novel
written by Conrad has received more abuse and less serious
critical attention. Achievement-and-decline critics point to it
as Exhibit A in their case against the later fiction. One member of this troupe, Neville Newhouse, calls *The Arrow* a 'romantically sentimental and over-dramatized treatment of a
young man's first love affair. It is best forgotten.'[4] Eloise
Knapp Hay says that this is Conrad's worst novel, which
'may have failed as it did because what he told about Monsieur George amounted to telling a lie about himself'.[5] Leo
Gurko describes *The Arrow* as 'an unreliable guide to Conrad's early life. As a work of art, it ranks near the bottom if
not the bottom of the novels.'[6] Even Conrad's contemporaries received the book with some hesitation and disappointment. The anonymous reviewer in the *New Statesman*, on
August 16, 1919, in what was perhaps the most favourable of
the reviews, expressed his hesitation by stressing Conrad's

debt to his earlier *Tremolino* sketch in *The Mirror of the Sea* and by complaining about the lack of gun-running incidents. 'The story is in itself a little unfortunate,' he said. Clearly, Conrad 'failed a little in the construction of his story'. A few days earlier, on August 7, 1919, the reviewer in the *Times Literary Supplement* had found *The Arrow* 'fragmentarily and insecurely told' and called the Second Note a 'chillingly dissipating douche to the story's illusion, to its romance'.

Conrad's own remarks about these views and about his aims in *The Arrow* are quite illuminating and worth paying close critical attention to. Writing to his agent, Pinker, Conrad admitted that the first reviews 'were very poor. Not inimical, you understand, but puzzled and hesitating. Just what I feared! An uncertain send-off' (*LL*, II, 225). Six days later he expanded his remarks to include several more recent reviews:

> I had this morning also a whole batch of cuttings, including a review by Holbrook Jackson in the *New Nation*, very enthusiastic, and another in *Everyman* by Beresford, who finds I am growing old, a rather sudden conclusion to arrive at on the evidence of only one book; because, as far as I can remember, nobody found traces of senile decay in *Victory* or *Shadow-Line*. . . .
>
> There is no denying the fact that there is a note of disappointment in·almost every review; but as far as I can judge it seems to arise more from the subject and its treatment, which somehow fail to satisfy the critical mind, than from any perception of failing powers in the writer. This is the penalty for having produced something unexpected, and I don't grumble at it. I only don't see why I should have *Lord Jim* thrown at my head at every turn. I couldn't go on writing *Lord Jim* all my life.
>
> (*LL*, II, 227)

Conrad then mentions the case of Anatole France's *Lys Rouge*, which had taken reviewers by surprise but which went on to a great popular success. What is important about these remarks is not the question of aging, but rather the question of critical expectation. Many novelists, including the American William T. Farrell, have disappeared from the public's attention because they did not continue to pursue the same subjects and techniques with which their reputations had been established; Conrad's refusal to keep on writing *Lord Jim*, like Farrell's refusal to resurrect the corpse of Studs Lonigan, seems to have cost him a number of admirers, in his own time and more recently.

Conrad was extremely sensitive concerning the personal nature of his materials in *The Arrow*, so much so that he admitted to John Galsworthy that 'Never before was the act of publication so distasteful to me as on this occasion. Not that I shrink from what may be said. I can form a pretty good guess as to what will be said' (*LL*, II, 226). To Sidney Colvin he confessed his inability to read the proofs of *The Arrow* 'in cold blood. Ridiculous! My dear (as D. Rita would have said) there are some of these 42-year-old episodes of which I cannot think now without a slight tightness of the chest—*un petit serrement de coeur*' (*LL*, II, 229). The more personal his writing was the more likely he seems to have been to speak of it in an off-handed or deprecatory fashion; however, this tendency should not blind readers to the value of his specific claims for *The Arrow*. Eight months previously, in a letter dated December 21, 1918, he had written to his American publisher F. N. Doubleday, explaining, among other things, that he had put off writing about this part of his life for eighteen years: 'But having found the mood, I didn't tarry much on my way, having finished the novel in about ten months. This for a piece of creation depending so much for its truth on actual brush-strokes, one may say, is rather a short time; especially as it was also an essay, I won't say in a new technique (there is nothing new under the sun) but in a method of presentation which was a new departure in J. C.'s art—if such a thing as J. C.'s art exists. I wouldn't like to have to demonstrate this in set terms; but some people say that it does exist' (*LL*, II, 213). This remark seems almost identical to the claim he made in his letter to Pinker about having aimed in *The Arrow* for 'something unexpected'.

In what sense does Conrad actually achieve 'a new departure' in *The Arrow*? I am not interested in committing the intentional fallacy and accepting his claims of newness as proof that *The Arrow* is ultimately successful as an imaginative creation, but there are in the letters a number of clues about technique that are extremely useful to any discussion of Conrad's method in this relatively unpopular novel. One such clue may be found in the preceding quotation in the letter to Doubleday. The phrase 'brush-strokes' does not appear haphazardly at this point in the letter; Conrad picks up the painting image again a few sentences later, when he says: 'I feel a particular interest in that book, which is so much of a portraiture of vanished years, of feelings that had once their actuating power, and of people who probably are all at rest by now' (*LL*, II, 214). In another letter, written ten months earlier, Conrad says to S. A. Everitt that *The Arrow* 'is really an episode, related dramatically and in the detailed manner of a study' (*LL*, II, 201). The three words—'brush-strokes', 'portraiture', and 'study'—which Conrad uses to describe his method in *The Arrow* are too similar to be either unimportant or coincidental. Conrad gives few clues to the artistic secrets of his novels, but when he does offer some assistance to the critic he usually does so deliberately; and, considering the reception he expected and which *The Arrow* actually received, it is not surprising that Conrad should have felt tempted to hint at the fundamentals of form in the novel.

Art, or more specifically painting, is one of the working metaphors with which Conrad gives imaginative shape to these materials from his romantic past. This metaphor touches upon all aspects of technique—character, incident, point of view—and is everywhere present in the pages of *The Arrow*, as a few quotations chosen at random will indicate. Blunt's first glimpse of Rita, which is related to M. George, is like a picture: 'the charm, the brilliance, and force of her personality was adequately framed between those magnificently palladin-like attendants' (32); when M. George himself sees Rita for the first time, the effect is almost identical: 'And even then the visual impression was more of colour in a picture than of the forms of actual life' (66). The approach to characterization here is far more visually oriented than is usual for Conrad; and the seeing eye is obviously that of the painter or art-critic: 'the light blue of the dress made an effective combination of colour to set off the delicate carnation of that face . . .' (66). At this particular point in the novel, the occasion of the journalist's unannounced and unwelcome visit to Rita's salon, the text bristles with images from the visual arts; the room itself resembles a gallery and the dinner guests sit like 'deaf and dumb people', like 'a very superior lot of waxworks' (69). At other points in the novel we discover that

Therese looks like 'a face in a painting' (137), though 'an old, cracked, smoky painting' (139); that Ortega, the blight of Rita's early life among the sheep, has a face which has 'fallen into a brown study' (270).

Conrad's description of Rita de Lastaola and her situation in *The Arrow* suggests a rather perverse version of the Pygmalion myth, or of the recent rendering of that myth in the stage-play, *My Fair Lady*. In the letter to Everitt, he stresses the fact that the story centres on Rita; in fact, all of the titles which first suggested themselves to Conrad concern Rita and her various roles in the novel: *L'Amie du Roi*, *The Goatherd*, *Two Sisters*, *Mme de Lastaola*, and *The Heiress*:

> As you see, the above are all connected with a woman. And indeed the novel may be best described as the Study of a Woman who might have been a very brilliant phenomenon but has remained obscure, playing her little part in the Carlist war of '75 and then going as completely out of the very special world which knew her as though she had returned in despair to the goats of her childhood in some lonely valley on the south slope of the Pyrenees. The book, however, is but slightly concerned with her public (so to speak) activity, which was really of a secret nature. What it deals with is her private life; her sense of her own position, her sentiments and her fears.
>
> (*LL*, II, 201)

Rita's position is only superficially enviable; her fears and her desperation are related not only to the fact that she has a sort of timeless beauty that men find irresistible, but also to the fact that she has inherited the wealth of the famous art-collector, Henri Allègre. In other words, she is doubly cursed with possessions that make her prey to a seemingly endless host of lesser, but equally disturbed and dangerous collectors.

When Rita wanders by chance into Allègre's garden, she does not find the happiness which his name promises, but rather falls into a sort of spell or enchantment. Allègre sees in Rita some quality of timelessness, something that compels both admiration and possession. He transforms Rita with his Midas-touch, his Zeus-like power, into an *objet d'art*, into an artifact for his collection. He is described by Mills as a 'collector of fine things' (22), of which Rita is 'the most admira-

ble find amongst all those priceless items he had accumulated
in that house' (23). Rita is 'like an object of art from some
unknown period' (36). Her experience with Allègre is disastrous, destroying or paralysing the life in her, causing her to
suffer 'from a sense of unreality' (55). Like Flora de Barral in
Chance, she finds that her conception of herself is shattered by
her experience with Allègre. His death seems to have the
character of a 'heartless desertion':

> It gave one a glimpse of amazing egoism in a sentiment to
> which one could hardly give a name, a mysterious appro-
> priation of one human being by another as if in defiance
> of unexpressed things and for an unheard-of satisfaction
> of an inconceivable pride. If he had hated her he could not
> have flung that enormous fortune more brutally at her
> head. And this unrepentant death seemed to lift for a mo-
> ment the curtain on something lofty and sinister like an
> Olympian's caprice.
>
> (108)

The appropriation of Rita, like the rape of Leda, makes her
less and more than human; and this dehumanization is reflected in the descriptions of her person. Not only does she
have a 'head so fine in modelling' and a neck 'round like the
shaft of a column' (92), but also her appearance gives the impression of something 'inanimate', with 'enamel' eyes, suggesting 'a creation of a distant past: immortal art, not tran-
sient life' (93). To Don Juan Blunt, who would also like to
appropriate her, Rita says that her experience with Mills and
the world of culture had 'all but killed me morally' (147); and
she explains to Mills that he and Don Carlos de Bourbon
'were the only people who didn't approach me as if I had been
a precious object in a collection, an ivory carving or a piece of
Chinese porcelain' (84).

Allègre has effectively thrown Rita to the dogs, the 'intellectual dogs' (56) of French society. One of her 'admirers'
from the world of art is a journalist, whose hair is 'artistically
arranged' (71), but whose passions and manners resemble
those of a wild beast; he devours his cutlets and his acquain-
tances in a single, undiscriminating gulp. He cannot believe
that Rita is capable of passionate devotion to a cause like the
restoration of Don Carlos to the throne of Spain, because he

himself is incapable of decent emotion; he is interested only in the Allègre fortune and seems prepared to cut off heads to get it. Mrs. Blunt, too, wants to annex Rita and her fortune; she is an American import to the sham world of art-appreciators and life-destroyers in Europe. She hides her greed and hypocrisy behind the robes of art; she spouts clichés about aesthetic truth and describes Rita in terms that she has adopted from the Allègre circle: 'the image of her has come into my life, into that part of it where art and letters reign undisputed like a sort of religion of beauty to which I have been faithful through all the vicissitudes of my existence' (181). The inner narrator (the mature M. George), who remembers having listened to this lady display the blunt edge of her intellect, remarks ironically in retrospect: 'I just let myself go admiring her as though I had been a mere slave of aesthetics' (182). When Mrs. Blunt's real purpose of annexing Rita is exposed, the narrator explains that 'her well-bred ease appeared sinister, her aristocratic repose a treacherous device, her venerable graciousness a mask of unbounded contempt for all human beings whatever. She was a terrible old woman with those straight white, wolfish eyebrows' (184). Later, Rita asks her devoted M. George what they are doing in a world with people such as the Blunts, 'in this world which is eaten up with charlatanism of all sorts so that even we, the simple, don't know any longer how to trust each other' (199).

Against this corrupt world of collectors, appropriators, and annexers, stand the simple life of Dominic, the rustic simplicity of Rita's origins, and the genuinely artistic sensitivity and devotion of M. George. They are all three committed to the furthering of an absurd illusion, the reinstating of Don Carlos de Bourbon to the throne of Spain; but, in comparison with the false world of culture, their political adventure seems pure and innocent, positively Arcadian. While Rita's commitment to the Legitimist Principle stems from friendship, from her affair with Don Carlos, M. George's commitment stems from his love for her. He refuses to be 'merged in the Legitimist Principle. Mine was an act of independent assertion,' he confesses. 'Never before had I felt so intensely aware of my personality' (89). Like Heyst and the young captain in *The Shadow Line*, he is of a sensitive, romantic nature and is most fully himself when the call of love

and/or duty is strongest. He is, according to his youthful ac-
quaintances in the Bohemian circles of Marseilles,

> . . . a primitive nature, but he may be an artist in a sense.
> He had broken away from his conventions. He is trying
> to put a special vibration and his own notion of colour
> into his life; and perhaps even to give it a modelling ac-
> cording to his own ideas. And for all you know he may
> be on the track of a masterpiece; but observe: if it happens
> to be one nobody will see it. It can only be for himself.
> And even he won't be able to see it in its completeness
> except on his death-bed. There is something fine in that.
>
> (166)

Heyst, too, had been an imperfect masterpiece until he had
found, perhaps, an original colouring for his own life; M.
George, however, insists upon his own colours from the beginning of his young adulthood. His view of life is essentially
poetic; and Rita, on various occasions, praises or teases him
for his 'poetical expressions' (199). In the midst of his romantic fantasies about the possibilities of dying for her during the
Carlist intrigues, he thinks of writing her a unique and moving letter and confesses to his childhood friend, to whom the
account of these events is addressed, that 'I regretted I was
not a poet' (264).

M. George's sensitivity and simplicity, the naturalness of
his affection and the roughness of his exchanges with Rita,
are set against the so-called refinement and aristocratic breed-
ing of the Blunts. M. George describes Don Juan Blunt's appearance in one delightfully ironic and economical passage:

> Blunt came towards me in all the elegance of his slimness
> and affirming in every line of his face and body, in the
> correct set of his shoulders and the careless freedom of his
> movements, the superiority, the inexpressible superiority,
> the unconscious, the unmarked, the not-to-be-described,
> and even not-to-be-caught, superiority of the naturally
> born and the perfectly finished man of the world, over the
> simple young man. He was smiling, easy, correct, per-
> fectly delightful, fit to kill.
>
> (169)

Considering the rapaciousness that all of Blunt's clothing and
manners are designed to mask, and the treachery of his shoot-
ing of M. George, the phrase 'fit to kill' serves perfectly as a
summing up of his character. Blunt is, of course, the child of
his mother. This lady, scandalized by M. George's reminder
that Rita was once a goatherd, eloquently denounces everything common in women, after which M. George observes:
'The implication of scorn in her tranquil manner was immense. It seemed to condemn all those that were not born in
the Blunt connection. It was the perfect pride of Republican
aristocracy, which has no gradations and knows no limit,
and, as if created by the grace of God, thinks it ennobles everything it touches: people, ideas, even passing tastes!' (185).

The reference to tastes brings the discussion full circle again
to the art-life, or culture-nature, polarity that is set up in *The
Arrow*. Dominic, M. George's partner in the gun-running,
remarks wisely that 'there is not a woman that wouldn't at
some time or other get down from her pillar for no bigger
bribe perhaps than just a flower which is fresh today and
withered tomorrow' (127). Dominic, whose 'general scorn
for the beliefs, and activities, and abilities of upper-class people covered the Principle of Legitimacy itself' (90), enlists his
services in Rita's cause because 'he could not resist the opportunity to exercise his special faculties in a field he knew of old'
(90). What he and M. George have to offer Rita is, in comparison with the wealth and position of the Blunts, as fragile
and impermanent as a flower in the world's terms. Ironically,
Conrad puts the most important summation of the beautiful
absurdity of events in *The Arrow* in the mouth of this old
smuggler who, like Peyrol in *The Rover*, cannot resist the sea
and the challenge of adventure. Addressing M. George, as
the two of them carry out conscientiously their mission of
'deadly foolishness' (129), he tries to answer the question that
is paramount in both of their minds:

> '*Prenez mon bras, Monsieur*. Take a firm hold, or I will
> have you stumbling again and falling into one of those
> beastly holes, with a good chance to crack your head.
> And there is no need to take offence. For, speaking with
> all respect, why should you, and I with you, be here on
> this lonely spot, barking our shins in the dark on the way

to a confounded flickering light where there will be no
other supper but a piece of a stale sausage and a draught of
leathery wine out of a stinking skin. Pah!'
    I had a good hold of his arm. Suddenly he dropped the
formal French and pronounced in his inflexible voice:
    'For a pair of white arms, Señor. *Bueno.*'

(130)

They are both artists in the purest sense, natural men whose
sensitivity enables them to perceive the form and the beauty
that may underlie the commonest experience or enterprise,
and whose romantic natures endow them with the will to
serve a worthy contradiction. In other words, they are both
essentially mad, a characteristic which Conrad associates
with sailors and artists and lovers, all those capable of absurd
fidelity to an illusion. As he said in a letter to Mme. Alvar, in
response to her comments about *The Arrow*: 'Nothing could
have been more flattering to my *amour-propre* than your saying that "I knew how to lose my head and how to keep it."
The "Divine Madness" was so strong that I would have
walked into a precipice, deliberately, with my eyes open, for
its sake. And now it seems incredible; and yet it is the same
old heart—for even at that distance of time I can't smile at it'
(*LL*, II, 232).
    When he calls *The Arrow* 'an episode, related dramatically
and in the detailed manner of a study' and describes Rita as
'playing her little part' in the Carlist war (*LL*, II, 210) in his
letter to Everitt, Conrad draws attention to yet another
working metaphor that helps to give imaginative shape to his
subject: the theatre or the stage. Theatrical images abound in
The Arrow, either as specific references or as a manner of
drawing a scene or creating a dramatic effect, through juxtaposition, montage, tableaux, and so on. In the first chapter,
while M. George and Mills and Blunt are talking in the cafe,
George's friend Prax enters 'theatrically', dressed in the fashion of an operatic Faust, addresses his friend, and swaggers
'off the stage' (14). George refers later to part of Blunt's story
of Rita as the 'second act' (41); and he admits that 'I sat there
staring and listening like a yokel at a play' (58). Rita tells
George that Henri Allègre 'masked' (80) his greatness from
the world; and she herself is compared by Mills to 'an actress.

A great artist' (84). In the Second Note, with which the story ends, the outer narrator confesses to editing certain material because it 'lacks dramatic interest' (337); and he speaks of Rita's and George's affair and retreat to the Alps in terms of drama:

> I think there must always have been something childlike in their relation. In the unreserved and instant sharing of all thoughts, all impressions, all sensations, we see the na-iveness of a children's foolhardy adventure. This unre-serve expressed for him the whole truth of the situation. With her it may have been different. It might have been assumed; yet no-body is altogether a comedian; and even comedians themselves have got to believe in the part they play.
>
> (338)

The theatrical metaphor extends to the descriptions of char-acter and setting throughout *The Arrow*, as does the painting metaphor. Blunt is described in the second chapter of Part One as 'looking like the conventional conception of a fash-ionable reveller, with his opera-hat pushed off his forehead' (21). Many of the scenes seem to be tableaux that could ap-pear on stage or in a painting. While Rita speaks, George says: 'we three sat smoking to give ourselves a countenance (it was certainly no enjoyment) and wondering what we would hear next' (75). During the rapacious journalist's intru-sion at the dinner-party, George observes that 'The others, including Mills, sat like a lot of deaf and dumb people. No. It was even something more detached. They sat rather like a very superior lot of wax-works, with the fixed but deter-mined facial expression and with that odd air wax figures have of being aware of their existence being but a sham' (69). There are numerous scenes where Rita is described as having assumed a fixed pose like a figure in a painting or a piece of sculpture; and, of course, the gallery-like, highly decorated quality of the drawing-rooms and salons in *The Arrow* resem-bles nothing so much as sets for the stage:

> I knew that room. When Henri Allègre gave the house to Rita in the early days (long before he made his will) he

had planned a complete renovation and this room had been meant for the drawing-room. Furniture had been made for it specially, upholstered in beautiful ribbed stuff, made to order, of dull gold colour with a pale blue tracery of arabesques and oval medallions enclosing Rita's monogram, repeated on the backs of chairs and sofas, and on the heavy curtains reaching from ceiling to floor. To the same time belonged the ebony and bronze doors, the silver statuette at the foot of the stairs, the forged iron balustrade reproducing right up the marble staircase Rita's decorative monogram in its complicated design.

(285)

The winged figures, the statuary, the patterning of the rooms serve not only to establish a richly symbolic texture for the novel, but also to accentuate the theatrical aspect of events.

Closely related to these theatrical images are the images of the carnival, with which the events of *The Arrow* begin and end. There is a 'touch of bedlam' (7) surrounding the events. The Carlist affair itself is *London Illustrated* material, a farcical throwback to simpler times. Everyone except Mills is in some sense mad, or at least touched by various forms of insanity: Ortega, Blunt, George, Therese. Therese is mad with greed and righteousness; Ortega with a peculiar mixture of loneliness and lust. George finds himself caught in a 'strange wild faith' (140). He asks, 'Am I as crazy as Therese?' (164). 'I wasn't mad,' he admits. 'I was only convinced that I soon would be' (241). His diary, like that of the young captain in *The Shadow Line*, helps him to keep hold of the reality that he feels slipping through his fingers. In the midst of the 'Carnivalesque lunacy' (273) that surrounds him, M. George experiences 'a most horrible fellowship' (274) with the grotesque Ortega and has a sort of epiphany about the madness at the heart of the human condition:

My lucid thinking was, as it were, enveloped by the wide shouting of the consecrated Carnival gaiety. I have heard many noises since, but nothing gave me such an intimate impression of the savage instincts hidden in the breast of mankind; these yells of festivity suggested agonizing fear, rage of murder, ferocity of lust, and the irremediable

joylessness of the human condition; yet they were emitted
by people who were convinced that they were amusing
themselves supremely, traditionally, with the sanction of
ages, with the approval of their conscience—and no mistake about it whatever!

(272)

Unlike Heyst, whose detachment and indifference undermine
his will to act, M. George becomes mad enough to try to
murder Ortega. He comes face to face with his own potential for violence: 'The suddenness of this sinister conclusion
had in it something comic and unbelievable. It loosened my
grip on my mental processes. A Latin tag came into my head
about the facile descent into the abyss' (276).

Behind the scenes, significantly, and presiding over this
mad world of threats and masquerades, stands the mysterious figure of Don Carlos de Bourbon who, M. George
tells us, is 'attending to his business of Pretender' (8). Like
that of the lesser pretenders in *The Arrow*, his 'business' has
both a serious and a comic aspect. M. George's initial impression is that the business is commonplace: 'most of my friends
were legitimists and intensely interested in the events of the
frontier of Spain, for political, religious, or romantic reasons.
But I was not interested. Apparently I was not romantic
enough. Or was it that I was even more romantic than all
those good people? The affair seemed to me commonplace'
(8). In his letters Conrad expressed a similar view of these
events; in reply to critics who complained of a lack of gun-
running incidents, he said:

> I am sorry for the disappointment. Nothing would
> have been more dreary than a record of those adventures.
> All this gun-running was a very dull, if dangerous busi-
> ness. As to intrigues, if there were any, I didn't know
> anything of them. But in truth, the Carlist invasion was a
> very straightforward adventure conducted with incon-
> ceivable stupidity from the first. There was indeed noth-
> ing great there worthy of anybody's passionate devotion.
> (*LL*, II, 228)

But passionate devotion there is, for whatever reasons; and
M. George finds himself before long launched in a series of

desperate and dangerous missions on behalf of this commonplace business, for his own romantic reasons.

Considering these theatrical illusions, it is not surprising to
find Conrad writing to Pinker in 1922 about the possibility of
doing a dramatization of *The Arrow* to be staged by Benrimo,
who had produced the stage-play of *The Secret Agent*:

> I don't know, my dear, whether it ever struck you that
> there is a very possible play in the *Arrow*. I don't mean a
> play that could be cut out of the text as it stands in the
> book, but made of the tale itself and especially out of its
> atmosphere. I think if it ever came to it I could convey it
> into the writing and I am damned if I don't think that that
> man is quite capable to put it on the stage. Personally I
> feel that if that thing could be done at all I would sign an
> agreement with the Devil himself for the chance; and
> think the experiment worth trying. It's a fact that a
> woman like Rita has never been put on the stage, and
> there are many facts in her story which are merely indi-
> cated in the book (and some that are not in it at all) which
> could be used for the purposes of the action. I can almost
> see it all in seven scenes distributed amongst three acts. It
> is possible, of course, that I am labouring under a delu-
> sion. But I think you know me well enough not to be
> frightened by these confidences. Anyway you may take it
> that I am not likely to drop serious work to indulge in
> delusions. I got into this train of thought simply because
> you have brought me in contact with a man who, appar-
> ently, seems to understand my conception of stagecraft—
> at any rate, in this instance.
>
> (LL, II, 276)

It would be a difficult but perhaps extremely fruitful task to
try to describe Conrad's 'conception of stagecraft', especially
as it makes itself felt in the later fiction. Conrad seems to have
become more and more intrigued with the parallels between
fiction and stage, and fiction and cinema. One of his major
preoccupations during the interlude between *The Arrow of
Gold* and its successor was drama, the possible dramatization
of *Victory* and *Under Western Eyes*. When he began writing
The Arrow of Gold he informed Pinker that he wanted to
'launch out single-handed on the stage', 'the play won't be

easy. To put a *femme galante* (not exactly in that character
but as an ardent Royalist) and her peasant sister, very hard-
headed, very religious and very mercenary, on the stage will
not be an easy matter.'[7] On his trip to New York he pro-
posed to give a lecture 'on the (apparently) extravagant lines
of the imaginative literary art being based fundamentally on
scenic motion, like a cinema; with this addition that for certain purposes the artist is a much more subtle and complicated machine than a camera, and with a wider range, if in the
visual effects less precise' (*LL*, II, 302). There is certainly no
doubt that his awareness of other forms of art, including the
drama, informs every aspect of *The Arrow*.

The painting and theatrical images in *The Arrow* are part of
a richly woven tapestry that includes too many threads to discuss in these pages. Of these other threads, the most obvious
are the images of sculpture and the images from classical and
romance literatures. Rita, who is described as a 'captive'
(215), a victim of the cynical indifference of Henri Allègre,
acts 'as if turned to stone' (227); M. George calls her a
'woman of granite' (298). Under Allègre's spell she has, to
corrupt Milton's phrase, forgotten herself to marble—or granite; she is essentially a version of the sleeping beauty or enchanted princess who can be freed or awakened only by an
act of love. As a woman who is as old as the world, Rita
seems to be all things to all men. She is compared to
Cleopatra, to the slave-girl Theodosia; Blunt likens her to
Danaë, suggesting that Allègre has wooed her like Zeus, with
a shower of gold. 'Mythology may give us a hint' (37), he
says. Mills calls Rita 'Old Enchantress' (104); she calls him
'poor Magician' (105). The mythical allusions are not always
used consistently throughout *The Arrow*: for example, Allègre first appears to Rita in the garden, looking 'like Jove at a
mortal' (34); but Mills, too, is described as sitting 'unmoved,
like Jove in his cloud' (15). M. George has the nickname of
'Young Ulysses' (12) among his Bohemian friends; and Ortega seems to Rita to be a 'wretched little Prometheus with a
sparrow pecking at his miserable little liver' (111). Most of
these allusions, except for the ones connected with Rita and
Allègre, are significant locally, as part of the descriptive detail
at a given moment in the narrative, but not structurally.
Clearly, Rita's rape, or appropriation, by the gods of Culture,
by the 'intellectual dogs' (56), is the most central of the clas-

sical allusions; Conrad endeavours to keep that suggestion in the reader's mind, calling Allègre 'Heaven-sent' (82) and making the point repeatedly that Rita's furnishings have a 'Pompeiian' (214, 218, 225) quality. In this last instance, Conrad might well have used the word 'Olympian', though it might not have been quite as materially suggestive as its earthly equivalent in the Roman Empire.

These mythical allusions can be accounted for, in part, by their appropriateness to the characters and situation of *The Arrow*, which is a world of galleries and highly decorated salons that abounds with would-be artists and art-collectors; in other words, it would be unfair to say that Conrad has imposed these allusions on the text without some internal justification.[8] Obviously, he is aligning the story of Rita de Lastaola with traditional romance without wishing to sacrifice credibility on the level of realism. The mythical allusions are balanced, and complemented, by rather homely allusions to certain fairy-tale situations. Rita tells M. George and Mills of the results of Allègre's pouring his cynicism into her ears: 'If ever anybody was mankind stripped of its clothes as the child sees the king in the German Fairy tale, it's I. Into my ears! A child's! Too young to die of fright. Certainly not old enough to understand—or even to believe. But then his arm was about me. I used to laugh, sometimes. Laugh! At this destruction—at these ruins!' (96). Like Heyst at the feet of his philosopher father, Rita has been robbed of her comforting illusions; she has been too quickly matured. M. George has a vision of his affair with Rita that suggests a reclaiming of childhood and innocence: 'But the picture I had in my eye, coloured and simple like an illustration to a nursery-book tale of two venturesome children's escapade, was what fascinated me most. Indeed I felt that we were like two children under the gaze of a man of the world—who lived by his sword' (149). Mrs. Blunt has in mind a different nursery story which accommodates her ambitions for her son and Rita: 'In the fairy tale I believe the girl that marries the prince is—what is it?—a *gardeuse d'oies*' (185). To M. George, whose initiation into the life of passion is rather clumsy and naive, the romance has the cast of 'An unmannerly, Arcadian state of affairs' (217); he feels hopelessly young and inexperienced and afflicted with a 'nursery point of view' (144). George and Rita remain, to the end, star-crossed lovers, too innocent for their love to survive intact in a world of political intrigues and cultural caprice. As Mills says to the convalescing and remorseful M. George, after Rita has gone away:

> What's the good of being angry? . . . You know that
> this world is not for lovers, not even for such lovers as
> you two who have nothing to do with the world as it is.
> No, a world of lovers would be impossible. It would be a
> mere ruin of lives which seem to be meant for something
> else. What this something is, I don't know; and I am cer-
> tain . . . that she and you will never find out.
>
> (350)

Conrad's allusions to sculpture and to the spells or enchantments of romance literature are carefully interwoven with the images of painting and theatre in *The Arrow*. Failure to examine the novel in terms of its texture has resulted in certain critical judgments being made about its structure and point of view that can no longer be taken seriously. Frederick Karl has complained that *The Arrow* 'is concerned almost solely not with action but with personal relationships'.[9] Leo Gurko writes: 'The narrative is curiously rigid: the characters assume fixed positions; the incidents do not flow into one another but are static in the manner of still photographs; the story tends to freeze rather than move.'[10] Gurko comes unwittingly close to the essence of Conrad's method in *The Arrow*; his reference to photographic stills seems remarkably close to what I have shown to be the still-life, or tableaux, effect of Conrad's allusions to painting and theatre. And Gurko's references to the freezing or immobility of the characters corresponds exactly with my own comments about the romance structures at work in the novel, where Rita de Lastaola has been presented as the victim of the curse or spell of Henri Allègre's Olympian indifference. Conrad did not, as these critics and the previously mentioned reviewer in the *New Statesman* believe, 'fail a little in the construction of his story'. In his correspondence, he was concerned to justify his method in *The Arrow*; in a letter to Doubleday, for example, about the failure to serialize *The Arrow*, he tried to distinguish between action that is physical and action that is psychological:

The question of what is or is not fit for publication re-
duces itself, when all is said and done, to the single point
of 'suspended interest'. That, I judge, is the 'master-
quality' of a serial; and it is not always to be obtained by
the mere multiplicity of episodes. One single episode out
of a life, one single feeling combined with a certain form
of action (you'll notice I say *action* not analysis) may give
the quality of 'suspended interest' to the tale of one single
adventure in which the deepest sensations (and not only
the bodies) of the actors are involved.

(*LL*, II, 214)

He is concerned, as in all of his novels, with the underlying
psychology of his situation; as he said to Everitt, the story
was not about the Carlist war but about an episode in the
'private life' of Rita de Lastaola and an 'episode in the general
experience of the young narrator' which 'serves only to
round it off and give it a completeness as a novel' (*LL*, II,
201). I have already quoted his remark about the minimiza-
tion of the gun-running element; he claims to have had more
important concerns in *The Arrow*: 'But the undeserved appreciation of all those figures, which I have been moved to go
and seek in that deep shadow in which from now on they
shall rest undisturbed, is what touched me most' (*LL*, II,
228). Conrad is asking that his readers be touched by the atmosphere, the detail, the actual 'brush-strokes' and 'portraiture' of *The Arrow*; he is asking them to redefine dramatic action in psychological terms, to be moved by the inner
landscapes of feeling and emotion.

It seems as if the mere fact that events of the Carlist war are
so eminently 'do-able', in the light of Conrad's success with
the Latin American intrigues of *Nostromo*, has blinded some
critics to the directions in which the novel is moving. As
early as the Preface to *The Nigger of the 'Narcissus'*, Conrad
has made reference to the relation between fiction and the
other arts and had stressed his desire to make his work aspire
to the 'colour of painting' (ix):

To snatch in a moment of courage, from the remorseless rush of time, a passing phase of life, is only the beginning of the task. The task approached in tenderness and

faith is to hold up unquestioningly, without choice and without fear, the rescued fragment before all eyes in the light of a sincere mood. It is to show its vibrations, its colour, its form; and through its movement, its form, and its colour, reveal the substance of its truth—disclose its inspiring secret: the stress and passion within the core of each convincing moment.

(x)

Even for Conrad, working with a fragment from his own past, this was no easy task; as he admitted in a letter to Mrs. Thorne, whose appreciation of *The Arrow* he had gratefully received: 'You will easily understand that of this affair not everything could be set down. The inner truth of the scene in the locked room is only hinted at. And as to the whole who could have rendered its ominous glow, its atmosphere of exaltation and misery?' (*LL*, II, 232).

In order to hold up this rescued fragment before his readers, Conrad had not only to create a rich tapestry of images of his things, events, and people, but he had also to concern himself with the perspective, or angle of vision, from which these images should be viewed. A number of critics have expressed their dissatisfaction with the narrative frame in *The Arrow*. I have already mentioned the reviewer in the *Times Literary Supplement*, who considered the Second Note unsuccessful as a 'literary device and as an explanatory and tidying epilogue' and who described it as a 'chillingly dissipating douche to the story's illusion, to its romance'. From his remarks in the Author's Note to *The Arrow*, it appears that Conrad felt this criticism important enough to merit a reply:

But these notes are embodied in its very frame, belong to its texture, and their mission is to prepare and close the story. They are material to the comprehension of the experience related in the narrative and meant to determine the time and place together with certain historical circumstances conditioning the existence of the people concerned in the transactions of the twelve months covered by the narrative. It was the shortest way of getting over the preliminaries of a piece of work which could not have been of the nature of a chronicle.

(vii)

The words 'frame' and 'texture' suggest, at once, a connection between the point of view and the painting metaphor that is central to the novel. The notes in *The Arrow* serve, in a variety of ways, as a frame for the events of George's and Rita's initiation into the life of passion; in fact, the more one contemplates these notes the more they seem to be a genuine extension of the images of painting and theatre—as both a picture frame and a proscenium arch, or fourth wall, within which Conrad composes his portraits and tableaux, within which he paints his sets and choreographs his scenes. Perhaps 'choreographs' will seem inappropriate for an art that contains so many still-lifes, or stopped-frames, to use a term from the art of film-making; but it ought to be remembered that the author of *The Arrow* knew that one of the essences of a good painting or a good novel is that it has a quality of *caught* life, or life taken, as it were, on the wing. Rita herself is described as having this quality more than once in the novel; the point is also made in a letter to Sidney Colvin, in which Conrad calls *The Arrow* 'a study of a woman, *prise sur le vif*' (*LL*, II, 224). The French phrase, as nearly as I can determine, means 'very life-like' and is used in connection with pictures and descriptions of various sorts; literally, it would translate as 'taken alive' or 'caught on the quick'.

Anyone familiar with Conrad's work will recognize certain similarities between the narrative frame in *The Arrow* and that of the earlier fiction. Like *Heart of Darkness*, for example, *The Arrow* operates on three time levels and with three different points of view: it consists of the actual events, twelve turbulent months in the life of impressionable, romantic M. George in the Legitimist circles of Marseilles, far less shattering but only a little less sinister than Marlow's trip up the Congo; it consists of the relating of these events years later by an older, more mature M. George for the benefit of a childhood friend, who is perhaps more innocent than Marlow's listeners on board the *Nellie*; and finally, it consists of an outer narrator who edits the 'pile of manuscript' (3) in his possession and whose function is similar to but more important than that of the outer narrator in *Heart of Darkness*. No one level of narration will surrender the 'truth' of *The Arrow*; to read the inner narrative of George and Rita without the moderating effects of M. George's mature perspective would result in a serious misunderstanding of the novel. Like the young captain of *The Shadow Line*, M. George is erratic; his feelings alternate between passive indifference and passionate commitment and his exaggerated interpretation of, and reaction to, events brings them close to melodrama and sentimentality. However, Conrad does not let feelings or characters, with the notable exception of Mr. Burns and Ortega, run wild for long in his novels; instead, he maintains a distance, an ironic perspective, that varies the light in which we see the fumblings and intensities of his young heroes. If *The Arrow* is Conrad's portrait of the artist as a young man, it is clear that the story itself reveals more of the young man than of the artist, as did Joyce's *Portrait*. After his conversion in Part Two, chapter IV, M. George becomes (as does Stephen in the *Portrait*) more and more the object of combined sympathy and humour. The artist stands revealed in the manner in which he renders the events of this period in his life.

The mature M. George, whose manuscript eventually falls into other hands, resembles the narrator in *The Shadow Line* more than he resembles the mature Marlow in *Heart of Darkness*. Although his tale is less inconclusive than Marlow's, M. George shares with Conrad's earlier mouth-piece certain characteristics: we are told that he 'had not only a memory but that he also knew how to remember' (4); that he has a definite audience to whom he is speaking and an artist's desire: 'If I once start to tell you I would want you to feel you have been there yourself' (3); and that he is an analyst of emotions: 'You may think that I am subtilizing my impressions on purpose, but you may take it from a man who has lived a rough, a very rough life, that it is the subtleties of personalities, and contacts, and events, that count for interest and memory—and pretty well nothing else' (13). There is an important difference between the mature Marlow and the mature M. George in their attitude to their experience. Both narrators look back upon the arena of their youth without excesses of nostalgia and both have a capacity for irony and self-mockery; but there the resemblance ends. M. George takes himself less seriously than does Marlow; he is far enough removed to describe his twelve-month adventure as being characterized by a 'nursery point of view' (144) and to speak of it in terms that imply understanding and acceptance. His

employment of a theatrical metaphor also casts an additional
gauze of irony over events. Marlow, too, is aware of the il-
lusory nature of existence and of the moral ambiguity of his
experiences, but his response to that awareness is one of bitterness, sarcasm, anger. Like Coleridge's Ancient Mariner,
his eyes have seen strange and terrible things; consequently,
the humour of which he is capable is mostly black. The mature M. George is no Polyanna and his vision of the political
and cultural rapaciousness in Marseilles and Paris resembles
Marlow's vision of the nature of material interests and empire
in *Heart of Darkness*; but he is more concerned to render the
shades and vibrations for an interested friend than he is with
the moral dilemmas of meaning and communication. He
seems to share the perspective of the narrator in *The Shadow
Line*, who speaks affectionately of his 'case' in terms of the
'green sickness of late youth' (*TSL*, 5); and he shares with
this narrator a common source—the journals and notebooks
kept during the traumatic moments of young manhood—
and a common affection for the sense of romance that surrounds these moments of intense life.

The outer narrator in *The Arrow*, who extracts the essentials from, and provides some of the background to, M.
George's narrative resembles only superficially the outer narrator of *Heart of Darkness*. The latter, listening to Marlow tell
his tale on the deck of the *Nellie* in the Thames estuary, is little more than a filter, an additional consciousness through
which we are made more aware of Marlow's habits of mind
and speech and of the peculiar circumstances surrounding his
telling of the Congo story. His existence adds a further dimension to the novel, by throwing a slightly ironic light on
Marlow's account. The outer narrator in *The Arrow* serves a
different function. He does not intrude in the first-person
narrative, as Marlow's listener does; his editorial functions are
so transparent that we forget his existence entirely until he
reappears in the Second Note. His emendations, he informs
us in the First Note, consist mainly of pruning the 'minute
narration' (4) of the mature M. George: 'In the form in which
it is presented here it has been pruned of all allusions to their
common past, of all asides, disquisitions, and explanations
addressed directly to the friend of his childhood' (4). However, he does venture a few remarks about the motives of

Blunt and Mills in enlisting the services of M. George: 'two minds which did not give a single thought to his flesh and blood' (6). Thus he adds another brush-stroke to the allusions to fate, or Olympian caprice, with which M. George himself had described Allègre's appropriation of Rita. But the outer narrator considers that it is not his business to excuse or criticize Mills, since his youthful 'victim . . . has never harboured a single reproachful thought' (6).

There is certainly a significant contrast in tone between the story and the notes. The switch from the passionate first-person narrative to the relatively impersonal omniscient narration is quite striking; it has the effect of distancing the reader from the story proper, of preparing him emotionally for the ultimate separation of Rita and George. In this respect, the effect of the narrative frame is not unlike the effect achieved in *Victory* by describing the final events on Samburan in the words of Heyst's only surviving friend, Davidson; in *Victory*, too, the final pages are narrated omnisciently, but the effect is one of intimacy, of a return to the real world from the world of romance. In *The Arrow* we emerge from the claustrophobic, nightmarish atmosphere of the *Rue des Consuls* into the clear light of day; instead of a sentimental account of the six-month affair and a melodramatic account of its termination, we are given a brief but sympathetic description of its final days, before Rita goes into obscurity and George returns, wounded physically as well as emotionally, to his other love, the sea. After the passionate account of their initiation, even filtered as it is through the indulgent irony of maturity, we are offered a broader perspective, a wide-angle or panoramic view; stylistically, too, we discover a prose that is beautifully simple and restrained. Consider, for example, the outer narrator's highly controlled but moving account of the duel between George and Blunt:

> What happened was this. Monsieur George fired on the word and, whether luck or skill, managed to hit Captain Blunt in the upper part of the arm which was holding the pistol. That gentleman's arm dropped powerless by his side. But he did not drop his weapon. There was nothing equivocal about his determination. With the greatest deliberation he reached with his left hand for the pistol and

taking careful aim shot Monsieur George through the left side of his breast. One may imagine the consternation of the four seconds and the activity of the two surgeons in the confined, drowsy heat of that walled garden.

(346)

This passage, like the entire note, is a triumph of understatement; the excruciating concentration on detail and the air of detached observation are brilliantly juxtaposed with the deadly seriousness of the incident. So, also, Rita's final, single affirmation—'I am still alive' (339)—seems devastatingly affirmative when seen in the light of her captivity and near moral-death at the hands of Allègre and his dogs. In the light of such passages, the Second Note is no more a 'chilling dissipating douche' than it is a technical failure; it is, as Conrad suggested in the Author's Note, embodied in *The Arrow*'s frame and integral to its texture and detail. As the epigraph to the novel reminds us, '*Celui qui n'a connu que des hommes polis et raisonnables, ou ne connait pas l'homme, ne le connait que demi.*' Without the reasonable and restrained tone of the notes, the image of man, of human life, presented in the novel would be incomplete.

In the First Note, the outer narrator makes an observation about the nature of historians, that they are 'very much like other people' (4) in their moral pronouncements and their 'shame-faced regret for the departing romance' (4) of earlier, seemingly simpler and more heroic times. Then he remarks that 'History has nothing to do with this tale' (4). This remark is interesting, not only for the subsequent disclaimer of any 'moral justification or condemnation of conduct' (4), but also for its echo of something Conrad had written as early as 1905 in his essay on Henry James:

In one of his critical studies, published some fifteen years ago, Mr. Henry James claims for the novelist the standing of the historian as the only adequate one, as for himself and before his audience. I think that the claim cannot be contested, and that the position is unassailable. Fiction is history, human history, or it is nothing. But it is also more than that; it stands on firmer ground, being based on the reality of forms and the observation of social phenomena, whereas history is based on documents and the reading of print and hand-writing—on second-hand impression. Thus fiction is nearer truth.

(NNL, 16–17)

Herein lies one justification for his limited treatment of the Carlist war in *The Arrow*; the novel, as he said in his letters and as the mature M. George admitted to his childhood friend, is concerned first of all with the private lives of two people, with 'the subtleties of personalities, and contacts and events' (*AG*, 13). Conrad was, as he proclaimed Henry James to be, an 'historian of fine consciences', concerned ultimately with 'the nice discrimination of shades of conduct' (*NLL*, 17). And, significantly, of all Conrad's novels *The Arrow* most resembles the work of James, in its subject matter and in its form. This is not the place to explore such parallels, particularly with *The Ambassadors* which Conrad greatly admired and which he mentions in his essay on James, but the nature of his materials—drawing-rooms, art-collections, the polite society of the upper classes—as well as the narrative irony and literary allusiveness remind one continually of the novels and short stories of James. Conrad's tableaux, his portraits, his ear for the meaning that lurks between the words in human speech—all of these elements for which James is so often praised—give *The Arrow* a unique place among Conrad's novels.

The Arrow does represent, as Conrad suggested in his letters, a new departure: it follows *Chance* and *Victory* in its ironic treatment of the romance pattern of the damsel in distress, and it takes direction from *The Shadow Line*, and to a certain extent *Victory*, in its exploration of the events and emotions of Conrad's youth and young manhood; but it breaks new ground in terms of its employment of structurally significant metaphors, particularly those of painting and theatre. This technique is important to understand, not only for its role in *The Arrow* but also because it anticipates certain formal characteristics expanded and developed in Conrad's two final works, *The Rescue* and *The Rover*. The use of structural metaphors recalls Conrad's famous Preface to *The Nigger of the 'Narcissus'*, where he speaks of the need for fiction to 'aspire to the plasticity of sculpture, to the colour of painting, and to the magic suggestiveness of music' (*NN*, ix).

The Arrow takes its cue from the reference to painting; *The Rover*, from sculpture; and *The Rescue*, from a comment in the same paragraph about language, about 'the shape and ring of sentences . . . words, worn thin, defaced by ages of careless usage' (*NN*, ix).

Too little attention has been paid to such matters of form in *The Arrow*, though Paul Wiley did touch upon them in 1954 in his study, *Conrad's Measure of Man*. He describes *The Arrow* as Conrad's 'satire on aestheticism' and suggests that 'The novel is his one attempt to deal with the world of art, or at least with a level of society governed solely by aesthetic standards. . . . In no other book does Conrad work so steadily as a painter in prose; and one remembers *The Arrow* as in many respects a gallery of portraits and statues.' [11] Although Wiley does not expand these observations into an analysis of structure in *The Arrow*, he does perceive the fundamental polarities which give particular incidents their significance; as he says of the final scene with Ortega: 'This juxtaposing of the ultrarefined and the barbaric agrees, of course, with the fantastic tone of the novel; but it is also perhaps in keeping with a book which Conrad associated with "the darkest hour of the war" (I, viii) that the rattle of steel shaken by the hand of a homicidal madman can be heard outside the door of a room designed to represent the highest flowering of art and luxury.' [12]

Conrad believed with James and Ford and such moderns as Joyce and Pound that technique is the supreme test of an artist's sincerity. During the early, agonizing stages of composition, when his mind was often preoccupied with the war, with thoughts of Poland and of his son at the front in France, Conrad wrote to his friends Helen and Ted Sanderson a characteristically self-deprecating letter about *The Arrow*, claiming that his 'stuff' had 'No colour, no relief, no tonality; the thinnest possible squeaky bubble' (*LL*, II, 198). By the time he had finished *The Arrow*, however, Conrad had achieved a subtle blending of form and content, an alliance between the narrative point of view and the imagistic detail, that is quite remarkable. Those who cannot recognize his technical virtuosity in *The Arrow of Gold* are left with the King of Thule's question, with which the novel ends: 'But what else could he have done with it?' (352).

5 The Rescue
The Rhetoric of Diplomacy

In the final pages of *The Rescue*, Hassim's faithful messenger, Jaffir, wounded and dying, struggles through mud and the debris of wood and bodies, all that is left of Lingard's dream of the Shore of Refuge, to deliver his master's final words to King Tom. No thoughts of delay or failure enter his mind, for the simple reason that 'there is no rest for the messenger until the message is delivered' (447). Conrad, if we are to believe the record of agonies and setbacks revealed in his letters, must have felt something like this about the message that he hoped to deliver in *The Rescue*, that novel which took more than twenty years to complete. As early as 1896, Conrad wrote to Edward Garnett about his troubles with *The Rescue*, then known as *The Rescuer*. He claimed to have written only one page in over a week, pronouncing it a 'fine torture' to be 'able to think but unable to express' (*LL*, I, 192). With no end in sight, except to his patience, Conrad tried to assess his difficulties. 'Now I've got all my people together,' he explained, 'I don't know what to do with them. The progressive episodes *will* not emerge from the chaos of my sensations' (*LL*, I, 192). He complained of his lack of a framework, or peg, upon which to hang his ideas:

Other writers have some starting point. Something to catch hold of. They start from an anecdote—from a newspaper paragraph (a book may be suggested by a casual sentence in an old almanack), they lean on dialect—or on tradition—or on history—or on the prejudice or fad of the hour; they trade upon some tie or conviction of their time—or upon the absence of these things—which they

can abuse or praise. But at any rate they know something
to begin with—while I don't. I have had some impressions, some sensations—in my time;—impressions and
sensations of common things. And it's all faded—my very
being seems faded and thin like the ghost of a blonde and
sentimental woman, haunting romantic ruins pervaded by
rats. I am exceedingly miserable. My task seems to me as
sensible as lifting the world without that fulcrum which
even that conceited ass, Archimedes, admitted to be necessary.

(*LL*, I, 192)

Although he had written *The Nigger of the 'Narcissus'* while
still struggling with *The Rescuer*, Conrad felt that he was losing his creative powers whenever he took up the unfinished
work: 'I seem to have lost all *sense* of style and yet I am
haunted, mercilessly haunted, by the *necessity* of style. And
that story I can't write weaves itself into all I see. . . . My
story is there in a fluid—in an evading shape. I can't get hold
of it. It is all there—to bursting, yet I can't get hold of it, any
more than you can grasp a handful of water' (*LL*, I, 232). In
the midst of his frustration, of course, there is the determination to hang on: 'The fact however remains that this *Rescue*
makes me miserable—frightens me—and I shall not abandon
it—even temporarily. I must get on with it, and it will destroy my reputation. Sure!' (*LL*, I, 237).

Conrad did abandon *The Rescue* more than temporarily,
but when he took it up again he seems to have been temperamentally and artistically ready to see the job through to its
completion. In the Author's Note to *The Rescue*, he claims to
have had to wait for 'the proper formula of expression, the
only formula that would suit' (viii) before he could finish the
novel. This remark sounds too much like his earlier emphasis
on the need for an appropriate *style* to be ignored. As he had
said to Garnett: 'In the matter of *Rescue* I have lost all sense of
form and I can't see *images*. But what to write I *know*. I have
the action, only the hand is paralyzed when it comes to giving expression to that action' (*LL*, I, 237). It would be impossible to state precisely the source of this new formula of
expression, for which Conrad had to wait twenty years. Perhaps his emotional immersion in the political and diplomatic
intrigues of Europe during World War I and the rescue of

himself and his family from Poland at the outbreak of the war by the American Ambassador to Austria, Frederick Penfield, to whom the book is dedicated, helped Conrad to see afresh the psycho-political significance of those intrigues on the Shore of Refuge; perhaps also his experiments with an obviously symbolic fictional mode gave him a clearer sense of the *form* which lay submerged within his story of an obscure rescue in a distant land. Whatever truth there might be in such speculations, it seems clear that an examination of 'style' or 'expression' is most likely to provide a door into the densely populated and exotically coloured pages of *The Rescue*, to deliver the message so long pondered and so carefully composed.

In *The Rescue* there are a number of linguistic elements that are structurally important, that are fundamental to the patterning of the novel. I am referring to those words or phrases that, by virtue of being repeated often in related contexts, have assumed a special significance in my own understanding of *The Rescue*. This peculiar community of words, of which the key phrase is perhaps 'diplomacy', is associated with the field of human activity commonly called *manners*. *The Rescue* is not a comedy of manners at all; in fact, it might more accurately be called a tragedy of manners. In this novel Conrad is concerned to explore the relation between the sensible exterior of human behaviour—such elements as dress, gesture, speech, etiquette—and the psychology which underlies human action.

In the final chapter of *The Rescue* Edith Travers announces to her husband that she intends to meet Tom Lingard on the sandbank, even if it means paying the utmost farthing of her debt to her strange rescuer. Her husband dismisses the possibility as a matter of no consequence: 'Really it doesn't matter what you decide to do. All this is of so little importance' (456). Edith is shocked to discover that her husband can respond to this momentous decision in her life with such apparent indifference; then she realizes that he is using his illness as an excuse for taking no positive action, such as making a scene or forbidding her to go. 'He's making the most of it,' she finally concludes. 'It's a matter of diplomacy' (456). This awareness comes to Edith, who, except for her brief encounter with Lingard and his simple, heroic world, has spent all her life immersed in such diplomacy 'without irony, bitterness, or disgust' (456); it comes to her only with a certain sinking of the heart at the recognition that she is once again back in the artificial world of the *Hermit*, where honest speech and plain-dealing are not major considerations. Travers' diplomacy consists of bluffing, or face-saving; it is a mask for mere cowardice of dishonesty.

The word 'diplomatic' occurs frequently in *The Rescue*, but first in reference to Hassim and the qualities necessary to the successful Wajo trader: 'And with those people trading, which means also travelling afar, is a romantic and honourable occupation. The trader must possess an adventurous spirit and a keen understanding; he should have the fearlessness of youth and the sagacity of age; he should be diplomatic and courageous, so as to secure the favour of the great and inspire fear in evil-doers' (67). The ideal trader, the narrator says, carries 'important news as well as merchandise', 'secret messages and valuable goods', and so must be 'as ready to intrigue and fight as to buy and sell' (68). This description of one kind of diplomacy is followed by an account of the part played by the Wajo traders in 'all those national risings, religious disturbances, and also in the organized piratical movements on a large scale which, during the first half of the last century, affected the fate of more than one native dynasty and, for a few years at least, seriously endangered the Dutch rule in the East' (68). In the world of trade, as in the world of intimate human relationships, diplomacy seems a necessity; while Travers trades in favours and immunities, the Wajo traders use their diplomacy to secure supplies and markets.

In *The Rescue* there is a clear division between the diplomats and those whose dealings are direct and above board. The term 'diplomacy' occurs again during the infuriating initial exchange between Travers and Lingard, when the latter is rebuffed in his efforts to assist the stranded whites on the *Hermit*. Alluding to Lingard's efforts to communicate with Travers, one of the gentry, d'Alcacer, asks Edith Travers if she has 'ever seen a man dashing himself at a stone wall' (129). 'No,' she replies, 'I did not know it was ever done: men burrow under or slip round quietly while they look the other way' (130). D'Alcacer observes that Lingard has none of this kind of diplomacy; he is, rather, a direct, honest romantic who, as we eventually learn, has a 'singleminded brain' and a 'guileless breast' (282). In contrast, Travers is a politician in the worst sense. He suspects everyone; he projects his own low ambitions and methods on Lingard and accuses him of 'hectoring' (127), 'playing a dangerous game' (130), and applying the 'ethics of blackmail' (273). Travers is low enough to resort to intimidation, threatening to call his personal friend, Sir John. He cannot handle the unexpected straightforwardness of the situation. 'I don't know who you are,' he shouts in desperation; and King Tom, whose name does not appear in the European *Who's Who* or *Social Register*, can offer no other credentials than his word and his reputation in the Archipelago. With typical Conradian irony, we learn that Travers himself is 'not responsible. Like many men ambitious of directing the affairs of a nation, Mr. Travers disliked the sense of responsibility. He would not have been above evading it in case of need, but with perverse loftiness he really, in his heart, scorned it' (455).

There are some distinctions to be made between the *kinds* of diplomacy at work in *The Rescue*. Jorgenson, the pale ghost who resembles Lingard and who has seen the open grave yawning behind the affairs of men, understands when the time comes that 'his task was not diplomacy' (389); he has to act, and act promptly. In the native sphere the faithful Jaffir is set against Tengga's leering 'diplomatist' (421) with the forked tongue, who, when Jorgenson called him a liar, 'preserved a scandalized silence, though, of course, he had not expected to be believed for a moment' (420). Eventually, even local diplomacy wears thin; it impedes and crushes the efforts of Lingard to help his friends. Hassim's growing impatience with the praying and procrastinating Belarab is treated with superb irony:

> Belarab's hesitation had proved too much even for Hassim's hereditary patience in such matters. It is but becoming that weighty negotiations should be spread over many days, that the same requests and arguments should be repeated in the same words, at many successive interviews, and receive the same evasive answers. Matters of state demand the dignity and wisdom of rulers. Such are the proceedings of embassies and the dignified patience of envoys.
>
> (373)

Even Lingard is drawn into the sphere of diplomacy, by virtue of his split loyalties to the whites and to his native friends. Mrs. Travers explains to her husband that his and d'Alcacer's release was the result of Lingard's diplomacy:

> Matters of high policy and of local politics. Conflict of personal interests, mistrust between the parties, intrigues of individuals—you ought to know how that sort of thing works. His diplomacy made use of all that. The first thing to do was not to liberate you but to get you into his keeping. He is a very great man here and let me tell you that your safety depends on his dexterity in the use of his prestige rather than on his power which he cannot use.
>
> (273)

Lingard's involvement in politics at this mundane level rather than at a more removed or exalted level, as a suer of small favours rather than as an organizer of great enterprises, marks the beginning of his demise as supreme commander on the Shore of Refuge.

There is a certain degree of irony, of course, in Conrad's use of the word 'diplomacy', as there is in his use of the word 'gentleman' in *The Rescue*. In the real world of human affairs, as opposed to the romantic world of his dreams, Lingard cannot maintain his integrity and plain-dealing; his behaviour must sooner or later qualify, or shatter, his conception of himself as the restorer of kingdoms, as did Lord Jim's. Even Heyst discovers that, in order to confront the forces of evil that invade his island, he must stoop to trickery, intrigue, and diplomacy. 'I am not much of a diplomatist' (318), he admits to Lena in *Victory*; later he confesses to having 'dissembled my dismay at the unforeseen result of my idiotic diplomacy' (325). 'A diplomatic statement', he tells her, 'is a statement of which everything is true but the sentiment which seems to prompt it. I have never been diplomatic in my relation with mankind—not from regard for its feelings, but from a certain regard for my own. Diplomacy doesn't go well with consistent contempt. I cared little for life and still less for death' (325). Lingard's diplomacy does not go well with his romantic dreams of friendship and the restitution of thrones; his true métier, like Jorgenson's, is action, not diplomacy and backroom intrigues. To quote an anonymous reviewer writing more than a hundred years ago in *Saturday Review* (September 13, 1862), 'The hero must, to give meaning to a meaningless phrase, fight for an idea. . . . There is very little room for heroes in wars carried on to settle successions, to rectify frontiers, or to maintain balance of power.' Like other heroes from the simpler worlds of the epic and the romance, Lingard cannot survive the secularization or commercialization of his vision; that is why a conflict between his sense of honour and his passionate impulses destroys him morally.

Conrad goes to great lengths in *The Rescue* to establish the image of Lingard as a figure from a simpler, more heroic age; or, rather, as a hero with values that are larger than the petty, artificial world of the *Hermit*. That is the reason for his alterations in the original manuscript, where Lingard's character had been more complex and his motives somewhat darker; the simplifications are all in the service of artistic integrity, not signs that Conrad no longer wanted to face the darker side of human nature. We know, for example, of Lingard's humble origins; we know, too, that in the Malay archipelago he is called Rajah Laut, or King Tom. His brig, which is the fastest thing afloat and appears to the Wajo watchmen as a mysterious bird from the sky, is called the *Lightning*. D'Alcacer describes Lingard in terms which leave the reader in no doubt about Conrad's intentions: 'A knight as I live! A descendant of the immortal hidalgo errant upon the sea' (142). Mrs. Travers dreams of Lingard 'in chain-mail armour and vaguely recalling a Crusader' (458); when he first appears to her at their final meeting on the sandbar, he has in the distance 'a human form that isolated and alone appeared to her immense: the shape of a giant outlined amongst the constellations' (463). When she hears at first-hand the story of his rescue of Hassim and Immada and his commitment to restore them to their kingdom, Edith marvels at the nature of the events; but she is even more impressed with the manner in which they have been expressed: 'They outlined themselves before her memory with the clear simplicity of some immortal legend. They were mysterious, but she felt certain they were absolutely true. They embodied artless and masterful feelings; such, no doubt, as had swayed mankind in the simplicity of its youth' (153).

Edith Travers herself is described in *The Rescue* as the true female counterpart to Lingard:

She was tall, supple, moving freely. Her complexion was so dazzling in the shade that it seemed to throw out a halo around her head. Upon a smooth and wide brow an abundance of pale fair hair, fine as silk, undulating like the sea, heavy like a helmet, descended low without a trace of gloss, without a gleam in its coils, as though it had never been touched by a ray of light; and a throat white, smooth, palpitating with life, a round neck modelled with strength and delicacy, supported gloriously that radiant face and that pale mass of hair unkissed by sunshine.

(139)

D'Alcacer observes to himself that 'of all the women he knew, she alone seemed to be made for action. . . . Her supple figure was not dishonoured by any faltering of outlines under the plain dress of dark blue stuff moulding her form with bold simplicity' (139). Mrs. Travers is, like Lingard, of a romantic nature, but she has been disenchanted by the discovery that her ideal of a 'great passion' (151) cannot be attained in the prudent world of society; in Lingard she sees the possibility of fulfilling that once discarded romantic dream. In Immada she sees, perhaps, a vision of herself as a young woman, before the compromises of civilized life had touched her; and her confrontation with Immada on the deck of the *Hermit* is one of the key passages in the novel:

Mrs. Travers fixed her eyes on Immada. Fair-haired and white she asserted herself before the girl of olive face and raven locks with the maturity of perfection, with the superiority of the flower over the leaf, of the phrase that contains a thought over the cry that can only express emotion. Immense spaces and countless centuries stretched between them: and she looked at her as when one looks into one's own heart with absorbed curiosity, with still wonder, with an immense compassion.

(140)

The battle which she must fight in *The Rescue* is with the centuries, with time itself; this queen of the 'palatial drawing rooms' (140) must try to throw off the manacles of sophistication and indifference in order to embrace her naked feelings, her primitive impulses and instincts, at whatever cost.

Another way of expressing Edith Travers' dilemma is to say she must discard her education, or *feel* her way back into life. The narrator informs us that, when Lingard immersed himself in the destinies of Hassim and Immada, the centre of his life 'shifted about four hundred miles—from the Straits of Malacca to the Shore of Refuge—and where he felt himself within the circle of another existence, *governed by his impulse, nearer his desire*' (99, italics mine). So, too, does Edith feel herself drawn away from the artificial world of the yacht *Hermit*, grounded literally and figuratively, as she immerses herself in Lingard's affairs and emotions. For Lingard himself the problem is to maintain his distance from this world, which he had only glimpsed briefly from the decks of a trawler as a youth. The appearance of the *Hermit* in the Shallows throws him off balance, acts as a magnet that pulls him away from his impulsive enterprise. Before the arrival of his countrymen he had drifted into an entirely different world, where his identity, his reputation, and his social status bore no relation to the facts of his previous existence; but this unexpected encounter with shapes from his past throws Lingard out of gear mentally:

> To the unconscious demand of these people's presence, of their ignorance, of their faces, of their voices, of their eyes, he had nothing to give but a resentment that had in it a germ of reckless violence. He could tell them nothing because he had not the means. Their coming at this moment, when he had wandered beyond that circle which race, memories, early associations, all the essential conditions of one's origin, trace round every man's life, deprived him in a manner of the power of speech. He was confounded. It was like meeting exacting spectres in a desert.
>
> (121–22)

Faced with Travers' refusal to shake hands, with his growing suspicion and unconcealed disgust, Lingard is, to put the matter in the simplest terms, socially at a loss. Travers demands to be treated as a great man, but he is unprepared to grant the same respect to King Tom; he regards the affair as an unnecessary intrusion on his privacy and spares no effort to insult Lingard. The breakdown or, rather, the failure of communication between the two worlds is most savagely mirrored in the insulting words addressed by the ignorant sailing-master to Lingard's royal friends, Hassim and Imada: 'Hey! Johnny! Hab got fish? Fish! One peecee fish! Eh? *Savee?* Fish—' (136).

Lingard's loss of the power of speech at the exact moment of his encounter with the Europeans is extremely important, both as an image of the ultimate conflict between two worlds— that of plain-dealing and straight-talking and that of double-dealing and diplomacy—and as a clue to another of Conrad's central concerns in *The Rescue*. If *The Arrow of Gold*, with its images of painting, is about various ways of seeing experience, *The Rescue* is about various ways of hearing or listening; it is a novel with vast silences, silences which correspond to the spaces between people. What is important in *The Rescue* is the way in which a thing *sounds*; the interpretation of events hangs upon the way a greeting is made. Ears are attuned to catch the slightest hint of friendliness or animosity or sarcasm; significantly, simple heroic Lingard seldom indulges in irony, though the natives and Europeans frequently do. This is a world that can be lost if, for a moment, a character ceases to listen, especially to the sound of his own inner voice. Lingard's tone of voice, as much as his rugged appearance, puts Travers off; it is not sufficiently deferential. And what makes Lingard attractive to d'Alcacer and to Edith Travers is the fact of his earnestness, his complete lack of pretence.

In *The Rescue* Conrad is concerned to explore, as he was somewhat in *Victory*, the relation between speech and sentiment, between statement and meaning. The problem is summed up in Lena's statement to Heyst—'I hear what you say; but what does it mean' (325)—which triggers off his discussion of the meaning of diplomacy. To ascertain what a statement means, a listener must know something about the nature of language and the way in which it is being used, or abused; he must catch the speaker's intonation. *The Rescue*, more than any other Conrad novel, takes as its operative metaphor speech itself—or, more generally, language; it is replete with illusions to tone of voice. Daman, we are told, speaks in 'an ironic and subdued tone' (223). Belarab, the pious statesman, 'talked, low-voiced and dignified, with now and then a subtle intonation, a pervasive inflexion or a half-melancholy smile in the course of an argument' (435). In contrast, Tengga the bully 'discoursed loudly and his words were the words of a doomed man' (446). Jorgenson admits to Lingard, 'I can speak English, I can speak Dutch, I can speak every lingo of these islands—I remember things that would make your hair stand on end—but I have forgotten the language of my own country' (103). Yet Edith Travers says of him: 'That man has no tone, and so much depends on that' (307). Inevitably, Jorgenson's tonelessness, his voice from the grave, makes Edith distrust him and not give the crucial ring-message to Lingard. After the ensuing explosion that shatters lives and illusions on the Shore of Refuge, Carter tries to rouse the defeated Lingard by 'raising his voice without altering its self-contained tone' (424); later, he resorts to his 'gentlest tone' (427). Finally aroused, Lingard orders Carter 'in a stern voice' (429) to send for the faithful Wasib, but he addresses the old man 'in a low cautious tone as though he were afraid of the sound of his own voice' (448). The list seems endless once one becomes conscious of this particular dimension of the novel. What needs to be recognized is the extent to which this is a novel about voices—some passionate and some disembodied, some tender and some coldly cruel—about people listening, pondering, meditating, probing the silence that is at the centre of their lives. As Conrad says in *Last Essays*, concerning his relationship with Stephen Crane: 'with us it was the intonation that mattered. The tone of a grunt could convey an infinity of meaning between us' (110).

The opening pages of *The Rescue* set the scene—perhaps one should say, tune the ear—for this drama of voices. The *Lightning* is becalmed, a silent ship in a silent universe; everything is reflecting and reflective in the mirror of the sea: 'To the south and east the double islands watched silently the double ship that seemed fixed amongst them forever, a hopeless captive of the calm, a helpless prisoner of the shallow sea' (3). The silence is broken by the first mate Shaw, who curses the calm and chatters to a canary below decks. Shaw is an abusive boor and insists on asserting himself by giving a senseless order to shift the helm. When Lingard inquires what is happening, Shaw puts on an amiable expression and affects a 'tone of surprise' (8). We are told that Shaw is 'abrupt in manner and grumpy in speech' (12), that he has a 'gossiping tone' (20), and that his 'discourse' (23) consists of inaccurate bits of history and gossip which he does not understand. His speech is highly mannered, larded with malapropisms and clichés, one of which is, ironically, that when trouble comes he will be found to be 'all there' (12). An intolerant windbag, he refers to the non-white races as 'Chinamen' (23), 'niggers' (23), 'savages' (24), and 'flat-nosed chaps' (24); his speech is plodding and deliberate, because of stupidity but also by design, 'accentuating the meaning of his words by the distinctness of his utterance' (4). Apart and watchful sit the crew, 'dark-faced, soft-eyed silent men' (13), who eat with decorum and some reserve. They are alert, respectful, sensible enough to natural phenomena to feel a wind coming while Shaw is still cursing the calm and to spot a boat between the islands after he has seen nothing with the glass. When the helmsman and *serang* discuss the boat, their exchange is conducted in 'a gentle tone', with a 'tender obstinacy' (16), and with some irony.

Out of the darkness that settles upon the *Lightning*, eliminating entirely the visible universe, Lingard hears the fatal 'English words—deliberate, reaching him one by one; as if each had made its own difficult way through the profound stillness of the night' (28). The voice of Carter registers a 'deliberate drawl' and 'a tinge of disappointment in its deliberate tone' (28). Throughout *The Rescue* words themselves have a palpable existence; they assume forms that can wound or heal, excite or depress, challenge or discourage. After his long conversation with Belarab, we are told that 'The faint murmur of the words spoken on that night lingered for a long time in Lingard's ears, more persistent than the memory of an uproar' (111). One can almost feel the intense silence that follows the disastrous encounter between Lingard and Travers:

> Mrs. Travers and d'Alcacer seemed unable to shake off a strong aversion to talk, and the conversation, like an expiring breeze, kept on dying out repeatedly after each languid gust. The large silence of the horizon, the profound repose of all things visible, enveloping the bodies and penetrating the souls with their quieting influence, stilled thought as well as a voice. For a long time no one spoke. Behind the taciturnity of the masters the servants hovered without noise.
>
> (146–47)

Travers' dinner-talk contrasts in every way with the restrained talk of the insulted natives, Hassim and Immada.
D'Alcacer and Edith Travers feel themselves 'assailed by
official verbiage' (147); while Travers rants, his stewards
wait, 'stoical in the downpour of words like sentries under a
shower' (148). Shortly after the exasperating dinner, Edith
finds herself deep in conversation with Lingard and discovers
that the words, the names of native chieftains, 'seemed to
possess an exceptional energy, a fatal aspect, the savour of
madness' (163); she perceives that Lingard's confession has
'stripped her at once of her position, of her wealth, of her
rank, of her past' (167). Even Shaw, who has so effectively
murdered the language, loses his head and begins to spout
about his fears and frustrations to Lingard: 'the native gross-
ness of his nature came clattering out like a devil out of a trap.
He would blow the gaff, split, give away the whole show, he
would back up honest people, kiss the book, say what he
thought, let all the world know . . . and when he paused to
draw breath, all around him was silent and still. Before the
impetus of that respectable passion his words were scattered
like chaff driven by a gale and rushed headlong into the night
of the Shallows' (191). As this Biblical echo suggests, Shaw's
pearls turn into swine and are driven into the night, into the
sea.

In the world of *The Rescue* speech is the miracle that
bridges the separateness of men, but it is an unstable medium
of communication. Shaw speaks of 'evil communications
corrupting good manners' (229), but bad manners, including
speech, can corrupt communications beyond help. In Part
VI, chapter V, d'Alcacer talks frankly and pointedly to Lingard about life and about the fate of men lost in mazes. Lingard does not take offence at, or heed, this barely disguised
warning; in fact, he hardly bothers to listen to his companion
in captivity. 'I can think of nothing,' he replies. 'I only know
that your voice was friendly; and for the rest—' (412). Lingard attends not to the meaning of what is said but to the sentiment—that is, to the impulse that drives one man to address
another. The norm in human conversation that one finds rendered in *The Rescue*, as in the plays of Chekhov and Pinter,
includes broken monologues, dead-ends, and non-sequiturs
that communicate more or less than the words themselves on

a rational level. There are two notable passages in the novel in
which Conrad employs what might be called a verbal or conversational realism. The first is a conversation between Shaw
and his captain, Lingard, in which neither character commu-
nicates with the other but in which a great deal is communicated to the reader. While Lingard reminisces about a French
skipper he had chummed with in Ampanam, in a story the
significance of which only becomes clear to the reader in retrospect, Shaw tries to interject comments to reinforce his image of himself as a knowledgeable man; one of his comments
is a delightfully prosaic modernization of the fall of Troy:

> 'Women are the cause of a lot of trouble', he said, dispas-
> sionately. 'In the *Morayshire*, I remember, we had once a
> passenger—an old gentleman—who was telling us a yarn
> about them old-time Greeks fighting for ten years about
> some woman. The Turks kidnapped her or something.
> Anyway, they fought in Turkey; which I may well be-
> lieve. Them Greeks and Turks were always fighting. My
> father was master's mate on board one of the three-deck-
> ers at the battle of Navarino—and that was when we went
> on to help those Greeks. But this affair about a woman
> was long before that time.'
>
> (22)

Shaw's comment, which sounds rather like Huck Finn giving
Jim a lesson in history, serves an important function in *The
Rescue*: not only is it an off-handed reminder of the relation
between Lingard's affairs and those of epic literature, but also
it is an historical parallel of kidnapping and bloodshed and diplomacy that throws yet another light on events on the Shore
of Refuge, in which there is a woman of considerable beauty
and a hero whose fine conscience proves to be his Achilles
heel.

A better example of Conrad's close attention to the psychology of speech and communication in *The Rescue* may be
found in Part V, chapter III, where Lingard and Edith Travers
engage in a conversation which is ostensibly about opera, but
which is really about their respective views of reality. Edith
says that her departure from Belarab's stockade had seemed
like 'walking upon a splendid stage in a scene from an opera,
in a gorgeous show fit to make an audience hold its breath.
You can't possibly guess how unreal all this seemed, and how

artificial I felt myself. An opera you know . . .' (300). Lingard, to whose simple mind metaphor is an unknown quantity, adds that he and some mates once saw an opera in Melbourne. When Edith questions him concerning his response to this travesty, this 'defiance of all truth' (301), Lingard declares that 'of the few shows I have seen that one was the most real to me. More real than anything in life' (301). While the dialogue here is realistic in terms of its underlying psychology, it clearly functions on a symbolic level; and the opera image connects with the other theatrical images that Edith Travers employs in her efforts to explain her immersion in a strange new experience. When Lingard asks her to bring the *Hermit*'s company on board the *Lightning*, even if it means playing a part, he tells Edith: 'It's no play either' (159). For her part, she sees Lingard in terms of a 'great actor' (282) moving 'on a darkened stage in some simple play' (282). When she goes with Lingard in the hope of gaining the freedom of her husband and d'Alcacer, Edith Travers has the 'sensation of acting in a gorgeously got up play on the brilliantly lighted stage of an exotic opera whose accompaniment was not music but the varied strains of the all-pervading silence' (295). She tries to explain to Lingard that she has never before had his capacity to lose herself in life, to become, as it were, unconscious of the spectacle: 'Do you know the greatest difference there is between us? It is this: That I have been living since my childhood in front of a show and that I never have been taken in for a moment by its tinsel and its noise or by anything that went on on the stage' (305). Eventually, she loses her sense of apartness, her self-consciousness, and has a sense of the reality of what is happening to her: 'She saw, she imagined, she even admitted now the reality of those things no longer a mere pageant marshalled for her vision with barbarous splendour and savage emphasis. She questioned it no longer—' (367). When she goes to meet Lingard in the stockade, carrying a torch literally and figuratively, she finally abandons herself to her illusion, to the destructive element of her passionate involvement. But even then, dressed in native costume and protected by the dark, she has only 'a moment of self-forgetfulness' (395); she abandons herself to Lingard's embrace 'Not instinctively but with resignation and as it were from a sense of justice' (395).

What Conrad seems to be working at in *The Rescue* is a language of notation, in which speech itself is many-faceted and functions at both the real and the symbolic levels; as was evident in many of the conversations between Heyst and Lena in *Victory*, meaning or sentiment are the sub-text that must be searched for behind the words. Although he does not elaborate on the subject, this seems to be what Jocelyn Baines has in mind in his observations on *The Rescue*: 'More, perhaps, than in any of his other novels Conrad relies, at least in two parts, on what is implied rather than what is explicitly stated.'[1] Conrad is clearly more interested in the linguistic and psychological possibilities of his material than he is in plot. Readers who find *The Rescue* static might consider Stanislavsky's famous justification of the plays of Chekhov, whose work has also been described as static: 'His plays are full of action, not in their external but in their inner development. In the very inactivity of his characters a complex inner activity is concealed.'[2] There is in *The Rescue*, as in most of the later novels, a good deal of inner activity. Gesture, understatement, irony, circumlocutions, non-sequiturs—these are the tips of the iceberg; they are the notations by which we perceive the complex inner space that has always been Conrad's primary concern. As he reminds us in the Author's Note to *Within the Tides*:

> To render a crucial point of feeling in terms of human speech is really an impossible task. Written words can only form a sort of translation. And if that translation happens, from want of skill or from over-anxiety, to be too literal, the people caught in the toils of passion, instead of disclosing themselves, which would be art, are made to give themselves away, which is neither art nor life. Nor yet truth! At any rate, not the whole truth; for it is truth robbed of all its necessary qualifications which give it its fair form, its just proportions, its semblance of human fellowship.
>
> (viii–ix)

The very difficulty of the 'translation' seems to have inspired Conrad to finish this troublesome novel and to incorporate into its structure, its form, the actual matter of style that had so long delayed its appearance in print. Throughout *The Rescue* he is concerned not only with speech and its limitations, but also with other related aspects of human behaviour, which I described initially as manners. Closely related to the matter of diplomacy in *The Rescue* is a considerable emphasis on etiquette or decorum. Each character has a clear, though possibly absurd, sense of what is required of him, or her, in a given situation. Lingard believes, quite rightly, that his failure to come to any understanding with Travers stems from the fact that, as he says to Edith Travers, 'No! I suppose I didn't look enough like a gentleman' (164). His forthright manner and rugged appearance offend the diminutive scholar-politician, for whom appearance is everything. Travers' indignation, like his Kurtzian hatred of 'inferior' (148) races, has nothing whatever to do with morality. 'I own with regret that I did in a measure lose my temper,' he confesses, 'but then you will admit that the existence of such a man is a disgrace to civilization' (147). Travers rejects the possibility that Lingard is right about the danger of the situation and declares, pompously: 'It is the social aspect of such an incident I am desirous of criticizing' (147). All of his social pretensions, including monocle, silver tea-service, and brass-buttoned stewards, stand juxtaposed with his insensitivity and indirection; in fact, the contradiction which he represents is perfectly embodied in the position of his yacht *Hermit*, grounded on the Shallows.

Lingard has a very different notion of what constitutes a gentleman. He redefines the word in terms of morals rather than manners, attitudes and actions rather than appearances. 'And I would know what a gentleman would do,' he says to Edith Travers. 'Come! Wouldn't he treat a stranger fairly? Wouldn't he keep his word wherever given?' (164). Though Travers fails the test, Lingard does find a gentleman in the Travers' guest and travelling-companion, d'Alcacer. As he observes to Edith: 'He was trying to make it up between me and your husband, wasn't he? I was too angry to pay much attention, but I like him well enough. What pleased me most was the way in which he gave it up. That was done like a gentleman. Do you understand what I mean, Mrs. Travers?' (258–59). What he means is that d'Alcacer has a sense of style, a sensitivity to occasion, which Lingard himself understands and appreciates. We know, for example, that Lingard's burial proceedings for the Lascar, slain at the time of his first meeting with Hassim, impress both his crew and his guests from

Hassim's prau: 'In such acts performed simply, from conviction, what may be called the romantic side of his nature came out; that responsive sensitiveness to the shadowy appeals made by life and death, which is the groundwork of a chivalrous character' (74). Like Lingard, d'Alcacer has a 'chivalrous respect' (124) for the feelings and privacy of others. Travers, on the other hand, has not a generous or chivalrous bone in his body; he is described as a man 'whose life and thought, ignorant of human passion, were devoted to extracting the greatest possible amount of personal advantage out of human institutions' (123).

Decorum and style are not inappropriate terms to bring to a discussion of *The Rescue*; indeed, the matter of decorum, or style, is seldom absent from the description of Lingard's chivalric proceedings. When Hassim has been insulted by Travers' sailing-master, Lingard explains to his friend that 'They take a rajah for a fisherman' (136); Hassim's cool, ironic reply—'A great mistake, for, truly, the chief of ten fugitives without a country is much less than the headman of a fishing village' (136)—serves to heighten the contrast between the tasteless, crude world of Travers and the dignity and restraint of Lingard and his friends. Conrad would have felt quite at home, I suspect, with the simple ideas, such as courage, fidelity, and etiquette, that are central to heroic and romance literatures; and, considering the epic scope of *The Rescue*, the heroic mould in which Lingard and Edith Travers are cast, and the frequent allusions to the world of chivalry, it seems natural to consider the elements that his novel has in common with these literatures.

One thinks of the formal speeches that occur when Beowulf meets one by one the coast-warden, Wulfgar, Hrothgar, and Unferth. These speeches are in the heroic style and contain considerable formulaic material. Beowulf addresses the coast-warden with a formal account of his own genealogy, the manner of his father's life and death, the purpose of his mission, and not without a few mild boasts. His tact, however, is always beyond question: 'We are people of the Geatish nation and hearth-companions of Hygelac. My father was renowned among peoples, a noble leader in battle named Ecgtheow. He tarried many winters before he, an old man, passed away from the dwellings of men; each of the wise men far and wide throughout the earth recalls him readily. We have come to seek thy lord, the son of Healfdene, the protector of the people, with honourable intent; give us good counsel! We have a great errand to the famous ruler of the Danes, nor shall aught of it be kept secret, as I think.' This quotation has all the ingredients, the inflated rhetoric, the concern for propriety, and so on, found in the formal greetings between Lingard and the native chieftains. The meeting with Daman is described largely in terms of Daman's regal bearing and appearance; and Lingard, having already required his companion, Edith Travers, to dress appropriately for the occasion, hastens to remind her of the proper gesture to make to an Arab chieftain. 'Great is your power,' Daman begins, typically; then he proceeds to define the nature of his political alliance with Lingard:

> But you and I are men that have real power. Yet there is
> a truth that you and I can confess to each other. Men's
> hearts grow quickly discontented. Listen. The leaders of
> men are carried forward in the hands of their followers;
> and common men's minds are unsteady, their desires
> changeable, and their thoughts not to be trusted. You are
> a great chief they say. Do not forget that I am a chief, too,
> and a leader of armed men.
>
> (294)

There is at work on the Shore of Refuge in *The Rescue*, as in *Beowulf*, something akin to classical restraint, a self-imposed control which is in itself one small stay against the anarchy, self-interest, and cruelty of the historical process. Lingard's heroic cast, like Beowulf's, is matched by numerous graces, including a sensitivity to decorum and ritual as well as an emotional and verbal control remarkable in a white European. What C. S. Lewis has said of ritual applies equally well to the idea of style in *The Rescue*: 'It is a pattern imposed on the mere flux of our feelings by reason and will, which renders pleasures less fugitive and griefs more endurable, which hands over to the power of wise custom the task (to which the individual and his moods are so inadequate) of being festive or sober, gay or reverent, when we choose to be, and not at the bidding of chance.'[3] When Lingard is jolted out of his familiar context and its rituals, he loses his sense of his own identity, his style, so that he no longer knows how to react, how to deal with the issues that confront him; as long as he deals with concrete problems he can function, but the unknown, the unexpected, troubles him beyond his capacities.

Conrad had no doubt about the importance of style in men's lives. He was himself a great stickler for decorum, known to be fastidious about dress and unusually polite in his dealings, even with fools. The details of his life were as important to him as the details of his art; in the Author's Note to *The Shadow Line*, he speaks of 'the shame, and almost the anguish with which one remembers some unfortunate occurrence, down to mere mistakes in speech, that have been perpetrated by one in the past' (vii). In fact, this great stylist in prose and seamanship stated the matter quite clearly in the Familiar Preface to *A Personal Record*: 'And in this matter of life and art it is not the Why that matters so much to our happiness as the How. As the Frenchman said, "*Il y a toujours la manière*" ' (xix).

In *The Rescue* it is a Spaniard, not a Frenchman, who best embodies this principle of style. When Lingard is rendered impotent by his susceptibility to pressures of conscience (in the form of conflicting loyalties) and to his passions (in the delightful form of Edith Travers), d'Alcacer emerges as another possibility, indeed the only one, open to us in a world that is sadly out of joint. Conrad seems to be saying, as I suggested earlier, that the world is too complex to support such active manifestations of the heroic. Conrad has great sympathy for the ideal of fidelity to which Lingard has pledged himself, but it is with d'Alcacer that he feels most at home in *The Rescue*. This civilized Spaniard is the consciousness through which his most important observations are made in the novel.

D'Alcacer represents a centre of calm (not indifference) between the passive, sterile society of the *Hermit* and the tragically active and doomed world of the *Lightning*. He must not be seen as a carbon copy of Decoud in *Nostromo*, whose scepticism ends in suicide; nor is he a Hamlet or a Prufrock, detached and disenchanted like Heyst in *Victory*. That role belongs more to Edith Travers than to d'Alcacer. If he is a sceptic, he is one who has come through the Centre of Indifference, not with the affirmation and gusto of Carlyle but at least with sufficient irony and perspective to be somewhat amused and indulgent with life. I make this point because of its significance to *The Rescue* and to a reading of the later fiction generally. Many critics complain about Conrad's so-called later affirmations. I would be disposed to reject any critical preoccupation with, or demand for, either *angst* or affirmation in art, since what really matters is the way in which an author makes use of his chosen materials. At the same time, I believe that Conrad's later fiction is far less affirmative, in the superficial sense in which Hewitt and Moser and Guerard employ the term, than is generally admitted. There are affirmations in *Victory* and *Chance*, to be sure, but they are only limited affirmations (all illusions, Conrad can be heard whispering), such as fidelity, courage, and sympathy, with which men cling to one another and to this earth. One reason for the failure to understand the later novels is the tendency to read a novel solely in terms of action, or plot, to the exclusion of other possibilities of meaning. The *whole* world of a novel, not just a single character or chain of events, is a metaphor for the author's vision and must be seen in its entirety before anything significant can be said about affirmation or *angst* or apathy. The road to salvation that may be glimpsed through the fabric of a work of art must be tested in relation to *each* of the characters that struggle to find it—whether a Heyst or a Marlow or a Lord Jim. *The Rescue* is not a happy, or even superficially affirmative, novel. As Jocelyn Baines has observed: 'It is a melancholy but moving book. Its mood of defeatism and world-weariness is even more pronounced than that of *Victory*, which does at least contain a positive admonition.'[4] Read solely in terms of Lingard, the novel ends in despair and in moral death; and in terms of Edith Travers, in romantic disillusionment. That is why the epigraph from Chaucer's *The Frankeleyn's Tale*—'Allas!' quod she, 'that ever this shold happe! For wende I never, by possibilitee, that swich a monstre or merveille might be!'—seems so much less appropriate for this Romance of the Shallows, as Conrad subtitles *The Rescue*, than does the obvious and relevant quotation from *Julius Caesar* (Act IV, Scene III):

There is a tide in the affairs of men
Which taken at the flood leads on to fortune;
Omitted, all the voyage of their life
Is bound in shallows and in miseries.

D'Alcacer, however, escapes the shallows; he is the one character who, although virtually a pawn in the game of life and death that is played on the Shore of Refuge, nevertheless remains somewhat removed and aloof from it. And it is precisely his position between the Scylla of passion and the Charybdis of paralysis that makes him an important centre of interest in the novel.

Our first glimpse of d'Alcacer is as a tall white-clad figure, in attendance upon Edith Travers, standing with his arm entwined around an awning stanchion on the deck of the *Hermit*. He seems to have stepped off the set of a Wilde play, insisting that it doesn't matter what you do so long as you do it with style. Everything about the man gives the impression of good taste, not artificial like that of Blunt and his mother in *The Arrow of Gold*, but perfectly natural. When he and Travers are released from their imprisonment by Daman's henchmen, we are told that d'Alcacer 'advanced smiling, as if the beach were a drawing-room' (298). In terms of manners and dress, d'Alcacer is not showy or affected; he is a master of understatement. He asks Edith Travers to warn him of any bad turn of events by simply raising her left hand to her forehead, a gesture as subdued as the stylized manifestation of grief in a Japanese Noh play. His dignity (and here Conrad is smiling not laughing) is such that he even tips his hat to Edith as he goes over the side of the *Emma* to a probable death. And yet d'Alcacer is not a chivalrous fop with an impeccable set of manners; he has a sense of his own presence that supports him in the most trying circumstances. While Lingard slumps helplessly and mournfully beside him during their internment in Belarab's stockade, d'Alcacer exhibits a studied calm; he restrains his impulses and emotions and decides, after some deliberation, to smoke one of his three remaining cigarettes, leaving one at least for his departure the following day through the gates of the stockade to his death. And this for the reason that 'A cigarette soothed, it gave an attitude' (411). His style, including this little ritual, supports him in the face of an irrational universe; the poetry in his nature, to use Robert Frost's words about poetry, provides 'a momentary stay against confusion'.

Although Travers considers d'Alcacer unprincipled, Lingard sees him as a man of honour, a gentleman. D'Alcacer responds with great sympathy and tact to the simple idealism of Lingard and to Edith's fatal attraction to it. 'Not everyone deserves to be touched by fire from heaven' (130), he tells her. On at least two occasions he refrains from questioning decisions that he believes were made on the basis of Lingard's sense of honour, even though these decisions affect his life immensely. 'A point of honour is not to be discussed' (349), he confides, unless it is at the expense of ordinary humanity. We are informed that d'Alcacer 'had that truly aristocratic nature which is inclined to credit every honest man with something of its own nobility and in its judgment is altogether independent of class feeling' (309). The narrator's insistence on d'Alcacer's nobility is without irony in *The Rescue*, perhaps because there are sufficient alternatives or polarities in the other characters to provide a spectrum of views on the subject. In *Victory* both Heyst and his infernal counterpart, plain Mr. Jones, are described as gentlemen, Heyst sympathetic and fastidious to a sin and Jones unbearably aloof and affected. Conrad places most of the remarks about the qualities of a gentleman, ironically, on the cunning and bewhiskered lips of Mr. Jones' henchman, Martin Ricardo, which serves as an effective undercutting. In *The Arrow of Gold* the upper classes fare rather badly, too, although some distinction is made between the natural sympathies of M. George and Mills and the vulgar sentiments and values of Don Juan Blunt and his mother. Mrs. Blunt is described in satiric terms that render her so-called aristocratic connection disgusting and absurd. Where she lives by vanity and excess, d'Alcacer conducts himself with humility and restraint.

There is nothing blunt about d'Alcacer. His motto would be that which Conrad quotes so frequently in his work: *tout comprendre est tout pardonner*. His immense sympathies are a product, the narrator informs us, of his 'natural gift of insight' (309–10) into situations and people around him. He is 'acutely observant and alert to the slightest hint' (346); he looks with 'profound attention' (412) at every aspect of his immediate world. From his discriminating consciousness come the most interesting observations about events in *The Rescue*. He coins the phrase 'Man of Fate' (312) for Lingard and describes him as 'a rough man naively engaged in a contest with heaven's injustice' (346); he perceives that Lingard is 'lost in a maze' (412) and will eventually die of a broken heart or be killed morally. About women in general and Edith

Travers in particular, he is insatiably curious; of those women who are truly great, like Edith and her counterpart Rita de Lastaola in *The Arrow of Gold*, d'Alcacer makes a comment to Lingard that brings together both the heroic and the theatrical allusions which we have discussed:

> No, there are not many of them. And yet they are all. They decorate our lives for us. They are the gracious figures on the drab wall which lies on this side of our common grave. They lead a sort of ritual dance, that most of us have agreed to take seriously. It is a very binding agreement with which sincerity and good faith and honor have nothing to do. Very binding. Woe to him or to her who breaks it. Directly they leave the pageant they are lost.
>
> (412)

Disgusted at the thought of not being able to face his death at the hands of thugs with 'calm dignity' (408), d'Alcacer comes to the ironic conclusion that civilization has at least *one* advantage: it does not allow one to be crudely speared in the back. 'It was a shudder of disgust because Mr. d'Alcacer was a civilized man and though he had no illusions about civilization he could not but admit to the superiority of its methods. It offered one a certain refinement of form, a comeliness of proceedings and definite safeguards against deadly surprises' (408). D'Alcacer is more interesting because more highly characterized than his close relative Marlow in *Chance*, but he shares with Marlow an unusual degree of sensitivity to natural and moral phenomena. He is struck with awe and wonder not only by the immensity of the passions of Edith and Lingard, but also by the responses of the diminutive, cringing Travers; 'All this was not very impressive. There was something pitiful in it: whisper, grip, shudder, as of a child frightened in the dark. But that emotion was deep. Once more that evening, but this time aroused by the husband's distress, d'Alcacer's wonder approached the borders of awe' (357).

D'Alcacer is, in short, one of Conrad's fine consciences. And he shares with his creator an alertness to the spectacle of the universe, a curiosity about its things, events, and people. Like Conrad, d'Alcacer would subscribe to those sentiments expressed in *A Personal Record* about the universe being, not ethical in its purpose, but rather 'purely spectacular: a spectacle for awe, love, adoration, or hate, if you like, but in this view—and in this view alone—never for despair' (92); he, too, possesses 'the high tranquillity of a steeled heart' and 'the detached curiosity of a subtle mind' (92). D'Alcacer's function in *The Rescue* is to provide a counterbalance to the beautifully impossible romanticism of Lingard and Edith Travers; without him the novel would be incomplete. As Conrad says in his essay on Henry James: 'The range of a fine conscience covers more good and evil than the range of a conscience which may be called, roughly, not fine; a conscience, less troubled by the nice discrimination of shades of conduct. A fine conscience is more concerned with essentials; its triumphs are more perfect, if less profitable, in a worldly sense' (*NLL*, 17). D'Alcacer's function is not unlike that of Marlow in *Chance*, the first-person narrator in *Victory*, the mature captain who narrates his youthful experiences in *The Shadow Line*, and the outside editor-narrator in *The Arrow of Gold*. His irony and worldly wisdom serve as a moderating influence in the narrative, counterbalancing the romance elements and rendering *The Rescue* more acceptable to the modern temperament, which tends to be sceptical of romance.

Considering Conrad's concern for style, or expression, in *The Rescue*, and his efforts to render credible his ironic romance, this novel has fared rather badly at the hands of his critics. Frederick Karl, for example, criticizes *The Rescue* for 'over-blown phrases', 'overwriting', and for 'the pretentious solemnity' of the chapter headings; the novel, he says, is a 'hodge-podge of Conrad's major techniques and themes' which loses its claim to the reader's attention by 'purple passages that denigrate the quality of the novel. That Conrad allowed these passages to stand after the numerous revisions the book underwent, is testimony to his loss of critical power.' Karl quotes five passages which, though 'not the worst of Conrad's writing', are nevertheless unimpressive and 'establish a cheap style for *The Rescue*'; he even dismisses Lingard for not being a Faust or, at least, a Lord Jim. Nowhere does Karl explain precisely what it is about these passages that makes them cheap and unsatisfactory; he merely assumes that readers will understand what he means by 'effective language' and 'an effective chief character'. That there are elements well worth a reader's attention in *The Rescue* seems unquestionable. Even Karl admits at the outset of his discussion that the book 'contains everything good' in Conrad, though he does not say what these good things are; and he observes, with no sense of contradiction or paradox in his argument, that 'the language, the setting, the pace of the novel' all have much in common with Conrad's most ambitious work, *Nostromo*.[5]

I mention Karl's remarks, not because his analysis of *The Rescue* is without merit, but because they are typical of the kind of two-handed Johnsonian criticism that has plagued Conrad since his earliest days as a novelist, by critics who are more sensitive to the larger components of fiction, such as character and action, than they are to specifically linguistic matters. In 1896, H. G. Wells made a similar kind of remark in his review of *An Outcast of the Islands* for *Saturday Review*. He described the novel as 'perhaps the finest piece of fiction that has been published this year', but went on to qualify his praise in a most absurd fashion: 'One fault it has, and a glaring fault . . . Mr Conrad is wordy; his story is not so much told as seen intermittently through a haze of sentences. He has still to learn the great half of his art, the art of leaving things unwritten. . . . he writes despicably. He writes so as to mask the greatness that is in him.'[6] Wells' distaste for impressionistic prose is understandable and it anticipates the reaction to metaphor and anthropomorphic analogy that characterizes much of the fiction and criticism of fiction of this century, especially in Europe; but his habit of praising with faint damns is quite unacceptable because it ignores one of the major technical preoccupations of Conrad, the interrelation or blending of form and content. For Conrad, as well as for modern critics like Wayne Booth and David Lodge, there is no sense in saying that a book is both fine and despicably written. Conrad's own reply to Wells' criticism makes this point clearly: 'Something brings the impression off—makes its effect. What? It can be nothing but the expression—the arrangement of words, the style—Ergo: the style is not dishonourable.'[7]

Conrad was more faithful than Lingard to his rescue work, 'this snatching of vanished phases of turbulence, disguised as fair words, out of the native obscurity into a light where the struggling forms may be seen, seized upon, endowed with the only possible form of permanence in this world of relative values—the permanence of memory' (*NLL*, 13). Although it took him twenty-two years to bring this 'rescued fragment' (*NN*, x) to light, when he did finish *The Rescue* he had found a style; he had found, as he confesses in the Author's Note to the novel, 'the proper formula of expression, the only formula that would suit' (viii). With proper Conradian irony, it seems to have taken critics more than twice as long to take Conrad at his word and to gain some inkling of the message he struggled to deliver in *The Rescue*.

6 The Rover
'Brevity Ab Initio'

Writing to John Galsworthy about his last finished novel, *The Rover*, Conrad described it as an 'interlude' which he had paused to write during his long pursuit of his 'runaway' Napoleonic novel, *Suspense*. 'I have wanted for a long time to do a seaman's "return" (before my own departure),' he wrote, 'and this seemed a possible peg to hang it on' (*LL*, II, 339). This interlude proved to be a most successful one, because it appealed to Conrad as a kind of swan-song and because it enabled him to give immediate shape to the visions of spilt blood with which his head was reeling from his research for the never-to-be-finished Mediterranean novel. Like *Heart of Darkness*, another piece composed very quickly, *The Rover* was written with absolute conviction about the nature of its political components; Conrad was as certain about the horror and degradation of the revolutionary impulse in France as he had been about the baseness of the colonial presence in Africa years before. As he said in a fascinating essay, 'Autocracy and War', written in 1905:

> The end of the eighteenth century was, too, a time of optimism and of dismal mediocrity in which the French Revolution exploded like a bomb-shell. In its lurid blaze the insufficiency of Europe, the inferiority of minds, of military and administrative systems, stood exposed with pitiless vividness. And there is but little courage in saying at this time of day that the glorified French Revolution itself, except for its destructive force, was in essentials a mediocre phenomenon. The parentage of that great social and political upheaval was intellectual, the idea was ele-

vated; but it is the bitter fate of any idea to lose its royal form and power, to lose its 'virtue' the moment it descends from its solitary throne to work its will among the people. It is a king whose destiny is never to know the obedience of his subjects except at the cost of degradation. The degradation of the ideas of freedom and justice at the root of the French Revolution is made manifest in the person of its heir; a personality without law or faith, whom it has been the fashion to represent as an eagle, but who was, in truth, more like a sort of vulture preying upon the body of Europe which did, indeed, for some dozens of years, resemble a corpse. The subtle and manifold influence for evil of the Napoleonic episode as a school of violence, as a sower of national hatreds, as the direct provocateur of obscurantism and reaction, of political tyranny and injustice, cannot well be exaggerated.

(*NLL*, 85–86)

The events of *The Rover* take place in the troubled wake of the French Revolution and illustrate dramatically what Conrad considered to be the effects of that 'bomb-shell' on the social fabric of the country and on the personal lives of a number of Frenchmen in an obscure coastal community near Toulon. *Suspense*, which was intended as a larger canvas, was to chart the moral and psychological climate of Europe during Napoleon's exile on Elba; had it not been left unfinished at his death, *Suspense* might well have been Conrad's most interesting and ambitious novel, a passionate statement about the sad legacy of the intellect and a reaffirmation of Conrad's Polish-British conservatism. On the other hand, the very abstractions that he was pursuing with such a vengeance in *Suspense* might have turned upon Conrad, finally, and consumed his art; in fact, as the letters suggest, he does seem to have lost for a time all sense of purpose and direction in that novel. His task in *The Rover*, however, was more specific, more humble, and altogether more personal; it was more in the spirit of that suggested pause to observe the motions of the solitary labourer in his field struggling with a stump, which Conrad claims in the Preface to *The Nigger of the 'Narcissus'* to be the task of the artist.

Although the temperamental rightness of his subject and the readiness to hand of the background materials account for much of the tautness of Conrad's narrative and the intensity and concreteness of his images in *The Rover*, Conrad goes to considerable lengths in his letter to Edward Garnett on December 24, 1923, to point out that he had consciously tried to give *The Rover* a special quality of precision and economy: 'I gather like a real treasure all the words of commendation you give to Catherine, Arlette, and the doctrinaire Réal. I gather them the more eagerly because what I feared most in the secret of my heart was an impression of sketchiness. This is perhaps my only work in which brevity was a conscious aim. I don't mean compression. I mean brevity *ab initio*, in the very conception, in the very manner of thinking about the people and the events' (*LL*, II, 326). Conrad discusses Garnett's notion that Scevola was not sufficiently formidable as an adversary for Peyrol, stating that the pitiful creature was not really a revolutionary at all but a 'pathological case', 'a creature of mob psychology'; then his argument shifts back to the matter of artistic intention:

> Yes, my dear, I know you will believe me when I tell you that I had a momentary vision of quite a great figure worthy of Peyrol; the notion of a struggle between the two men. But I did deliberately shut my eyes to it. It would have required another canvas. No use talking about it. How long would I have had to wait for that moment? —and the mood of the other was there, more in accord with my temperament, more also with my secret desire to achieve a feat of artistic brevity, once at least, before I died. And on those grounds I believe you will forgive me for having rejected a greater thing—or perhaps only a different one.
>
> (*LL*, II, 327)

In another letter, this time to his Polish translator Bruno Winaver, Conrad replied in similar terms to a suggestion that *The Rover* be adapted to the stage: 'As to its adaptability for the stage, I was at first surprised. But on thinking it over I see the possibility, though of course I do not see the way in which it could be visibly presented or spiritually rendered in spoken words. But it is a fact that the book has got very little description, very few disquisitions, and is for the most part in dialogue *en forme parlée*' (*LL*, II, 335). If one remembers the speeches, the invocations to the shades, the large cast of characters, and the exotic setting of Conrad's Malayan epic, *The Rescue*, his claim to have achieved something different in *The Rover* can be more easily appreciated. Conrad described *The Rover* initially as 'a sort of long short story' over which he felt 'a certain sense of mastery'; but, in contrast with his experience with *Lord Jim*, another extended short story, Conrad never lost his sense of direction and mastery as *The Rover* grew to its present length.[1]

No discussion of *The Rover*'s technique, its form, can afford to ignore Conrad's claims to have aimed for a 'feat of artistic brevity'; as is so often the case with the clues that he gives to his novels in the letters, essays, and prefaces, this claim of brevity provides a key to the relation between content and form in *The Rover*. And it provides the key to *The Rover* in much the same manner that the references to 'brush strokes', 'portraiture', and the 'detailed manner of a study' in the letters provide the key to understanding Conrad's artistic intentions in *The Arrow of Gold*. In the following pages I will try to suggest the nature of this feat as it is manifested in the various aspects of the novel.

The strong situation which Conrad explores in *The Rover* is not so much the matter of Peyrol's return from his wanderings and adventures, in answer to his homing instincts and desire for rest, as the conditions which he finds when he sets foot again in France—a state of wretchedness and suspicion and bureaucracy in the city of Toulon and a state of stunned silence and moral and emotional paralysis in the surrounding countryside, all of which is the legacy of the Revolution. After the collapse of institutions and values, and the subsequent witch-hunts and blood-letting, France seems to be in a state of shock; every character, except for Michael, the fisherman of the Madraque lagoon who remained untouched by events, bears wounds from the holocaust. 'We are all savages here'(20), Michael tells Peyrol. Arlette, whose parents were murdered in Toulon and who had been forced by Scevola to run with the *sans-culottes* in their savage raids, has suffered a moral shock that makes her withdraw into herself; in her own home she is a prisoner not only of Scevola, but also of her horrific memories. She is a lost soul, 'a wild sea-bird . . . not to be grasped' (22); she has 'clear eyes that had been smitten on the very verge of womanhood by such sights of bloodshed and terror as to leave in her a fear of looking steadily in any direction for long, lest she should see coming through the air some mutilated vision of the dead' (49). Interfered with, like Flora de Barral in *Chance*, Heyst in *Victory*, and Rita de Lastaola in *The Arrow of Gold*, Arlette becomes speechless, struck dumb by experience. 'I did not feel myself exist,' she confesses to the priest. 'Something was gone out of me' (155). Lieutenant Réal, son of a *ci-devant* couple murdered by patriots, is another orphan of the Revolution who has seen too much. When Peyrol suggests that Réal has been 'bewitched in [his] cradle', the lieutenant replies: 'No, I don't think it was so early as that' (206). Réal is described as 'a man who on emerging from boyhood had laid for himself a rigidly straight line of conduct amongst the unbridled passions and the clamouring falsehoods of revolution which seemed to have destroyed in him all capacity for the softer emotions' (209).

Peyrol returns, in other words, to a moral and emotional wasteland, full of 'wretched quill-drivers' (5), 'boastful and declamatory beggars' (2), and 'ragamuffin patriots' (5) and lacking all traditional social graces. Scevola, the blooddrinker, is in possession of Escampobar, 'where at one time they would give you a glass of wine' (10); little or no real work is being done on the land; and even the priest's garden is 'choked with weeds' (147). The landscape itself, like the inhabitants, seems to have been bled of all colour, except for a 'clump of dark pines with blood-red trunks in the sunset' (6); the rest consists of a 'barren flat expanse of stones and sombre bushes' (6). From his room at the Escampobar farm, where he is described as being a 'satisfactory inmate' (34), Peyrol senses the 'immobility of all things' (30). Of the local craft he observes, 'theirs was not the stillness of death but of light slumber, the immobility of a smiling enchantment' (31). These words—'stillness', 'immobility', and 'enchantment'— recur with great frequency in the pages of *The Rover*; they are part of the romance pattern of the novel, and serve to heighten the sense of inertia and paralysis that has been left on the land and its people by revolution. Conrad employs two myths primarily: the myth of the Gorgon's head, the sight of which turns the beholders to stone; and the myth of Pygmalion, who falls in love with the statue he has sculpted. Naturally, the Gorgon's head is the French Revolution; a glimpse of its atrocities has quite petrified Réal and Arlette. But Conrad is too honest to attribute all of the ills of the community to the Revolution: Scevola, we learn, was born hollow and was therefore easy prey for the prevailing ideas and sentiments, 'a creature of the universal blood-lust of the time' (48); Catherine, *la fiancée du prêtre*, has given herself up to a hopeless love and to a life-denying campaign of chastity at Escampobar; even Peyrol, himself an orphan of poverty and disease, has had to school his emotions in the difficult classrooms of sailing-ships.

In order to convey the dreadful paralysis which has settled upon this French community and in perfect accord with the myths that he sees underlying this situation, Conrad employs throughout *The Rover* numerous images associated with sculpture or statuary. Peyrol's face is described as 'clean, like a carving of stone' (101); he seems to be 'a carven image of grim dreaminess' (116) and is said to have an 'uncanny living-statue manner' (116). At one point during the conversation with Réal, the narrator says that Peyrol's 'stone-effigy bearing had become humanized against his will' (118); then, quite as suddenly, he seems to be 'turning into stone as if by enchantment' (119). Réal himself is described off-handedly in terms of Pygmalion, the 'poor devil who fell in love with a picture or a statue' (212); Peyrol observes that Réal acts as if he 'were made of a different clay' (106). Réal and Arlette stand still 'as if both had been changed into stone', 'a pair of enchanted lovers bewitched into immobility' (223). Aunt Catherine's face is 'finely carved' (166), 'a sharp carving of an old prophetess of some desert tribe' (174); it 'might have been a carving in the marvellous immobility of its fine wrinkles' (80). More often than not the characters seem locked in a pose like stone-figures, like statuary; they appear, even when engaged in such limited communion as Réal has with Peyrol, to be lifeless, to be inanimate like the landscape of stones and shrubs. At one point in *The Rover* time itself seems to have stopped: 'Among the unchangeable rocks at the extreme end of the Peninsula, time seemed to stand still and idle while the group of people poised at the southernmost point of France had gone about their ceaseless toil' (40). The 22-gun sloop *Amelia*, a reminder of the presence of the English fleet in the area of Cape Esterel, appears 'bereft of all motion . . . more like a white monument of stone dwarfed by the darkling masses of land on either hand than a fabric famed for its swiftness in attack or in flight' (52). When Captain Vincent leans over the rail to scan the coastline sometime after midnight, he observes that 'in the pervading stillness the moon, riding on a speckless sky, seemed to pour her enchantment on an uninhabited planet' (52).

This sense of immobility belongs to the very shape and detail of *The Rover*; it functions both structurally and stylistically in the novel. Considering the emphasis on rhetoric in *The Rescue* and painting in *The Arrow of Gold*, it is fitting that *The Rover* also should recall those fictional aims which Conrad had set down so many years before in his Preface to *The Nigger of the 'Narcissus'*. Just as *The Rover* embodies a vision of human community in which the paralysing (one might even say petrifying) effects of psychic shock may be relieved, or at least minimized, by the exercise of sympathy and courage, so also the novel aspires, in terms of form, to what Conrad so described as 'the plasticity of sculpture' (*NN*, ix). In his remarks on this aspect of *The Rover*, Thomas Moser seems to have ignored entirely the patterns of myth and romance which underlie the treatment of character and event:

> Finally we find in *The Rover*, as in *The Arrow of Gold*, a pervading sense of weariness which infects all of the characters. It has perhaps a certain appropriateness in *The Rover* since the central figure and one of the important minor figures, Catherine, are both old. Nevertheless, their weariness results not only from age but also from despair. As in *The Arrow of Gold*, the most characteristic pose of the characters is seated, head in hand. At various points in the book we find Peyrol, Catherine, and Arlette in that position.[2]

Albert Guerard seems also to have missed the point; he describes *The Rover* as 'a coarse-grained study of feeble-minded and inarticulate people' which somehow makes a 'recovery . . . after two hundred and fifty pages of extreme dullness and ineptitude'.[3] The final pages of *The Rover* are not a recovery from ineptitude, but the culmination of a movement that builds from the earliest descriptions of character and place in the novel. The stone figures gradually come to life again as a sense of solidarity is slowly re-established at Escampobar. Catherine explains to Peyrol that his arrival has worked a miracle in Arlette, making her speak for the first time and arousing some sentiment in her. Arlette, in her turn, brings Réal 'the sense of triumphant life' (260). Réal, who is 'cold-blooded as a fish' (232), finds himself disconcertingly committed to 'an unworthy passion for a mere mortal envelope stained with crime and without a mind' (210); he describes his loss of control as a 'moral disaster' (213), but understands fully that it has given him back his life. The old rover himself, who from the first page of the novel has been called 'undemonstrative' (1) and unemotional, discovers that he has an 'uneasiness . . . a sense of the endangered stability of things' (122); he discovers that he cannot, after all, bury himself in obscurity. Following his talk with Catherine about the 'sign from death', he finds himself unsettled:

> Melancholy was a sentiment to which he was a stranger; for what has melancholy to do with the life of a sea-rover, a Brother of the Coast, a simple, venturesome life, full of risks and leaving no time for introspection or for that momentary self-forgetfulness which is called gaiety. Sombre fury, fierce merriment, he had known in passing gusts, coming from outside; but never this intimate inward sense of the vanity of all things, that doubt of the power within himself.
>
> (173)

Réal fails to shake Peyrol's mildness, 'as though he had tried to shake a rock' (67); but later, in the face of Arlette's embrace and vitality, Peyrol loses his control: 'The rover, whom only that morning the powerful grasp of Lieutenant Réal found as unshakable as a rock, felt all his strength vanish under the hands of that woman' (175). After he has kissed the unconscious Arlette and sent her back to the house in the arms of Réal, Peyrol feels a breeze on his neck and is 'grateful for the cool touch which recalled him to himself, to his old wandering self which had known no softness and no hesitation in the face of any risk offered by life' (250).

The movement towards liberation, towards life and action, begins most obviously with the arrival of the *Amelia* and with the capture of one of its boat-crew by Peyrol. Lieutenant Réal, who arrives from Toulon to watch the *Amelia*'s movements and to plan some strategy to trick the English fleet out of position, adds to the complications at Escampobar. While Peyrol's patriotism is aroused by seeing this pride of French craftsmanship in the hands of the English and in command of the coastal waters, Arlette's passions are aroused by the French lieutenant. Chapter ten, the literal centre of the book, marks the actual turning point in the action of the story. Events leading up to this moment cover a period of several years, but, with the exception of the postscript which tells of the changes at the Escampobar farm, the events that follow from this chapter take only a matter of hours. Here Peyrol's rage at the impudence of the English reaches a point where he is prepared to assist in Réal's plan to put false dispatches into their hands:

> The disinherited soul of that rover ranging for so many years a lawless ocean with the coasts of two continents for a raiding ground, had come back to its crag, circling like a sea-bird in the dusk and longing for a great sea victory for its people: that inland multitude of which Peyrol knew nothing except the few individuals on that peninsula cut off from the rest of the land by the dead water of a salt lagoon; and where only a strain of manliness in a miserable cripple and an unaccountable charm of a half-crazed woman had found response in his heart.
>
> (142–43)

In this chapter also Arlette recovers fully from her psychic shock: 'I am awake now' (146), she cries out. She whispers Eugene Réal's name 'for the pleasure of hearing the sound' (146) and sets out for the church in the hope of receiving some moral support in her changed condition.

Conrad attends closely to detail in this chapter. The weather, which had heretofore been oppressively bright and uniform, changes in a fashion which quite alters the scenery of the peninsula: 'This grey vapour, drifting high up, close against the disc of the sun, seemed to enlarge the space behind its veil, add to the vastness of a shadowless world no longer hard and brilliant but all softened in the contours of its masses and in the faint line of the horizon, as if ready to dissolve . . .' (139). This new softness corresponds to the softness that en-

compasses Arlette and to the emotion which Peyrol feels.
Arlette finds herself unconsciously drawn towards the village
by the 'church-tower, where, in a round arch, she could see
the black speck of the bell which escaping the requisitions of
the Republican wars, and dwelling mute about the locked-up
empty church, had only lately recovered its voice' (147); the
church-tower serves as an objective counterpart of her own
recovery of speech. At the church itself the mortar had begun
to crumble and 'the beds of the plot were choked with weeds,
because the abbé had no taste for gardening' (147). With this
image Conrad captures deftly the abbé's rigidity, the coldness
and austerity of his religion, in contrast to the sensuality, that
'something provokingly pagan' (149), which he senses in
Arlette. Appropriately, the bulk of Arlette's experience
among the *sans-culottes* in Toulon is related here, as part of her
confession, heightening the effect of her deliverance from the
spell or possession from which she has suffered for years.
After her confession, the narrator tells us, Arlette 'never
looked back'; significantly, after the changes which come
about in chapter ten, the narrative looks backward no more,
but moves with great speed and force towards its remarkable
climax.

This concern for texture, for descriptive detail, is one of
the special features of *The Rover*. In this novel Conrad seems
to have developed a kind of descriptive short-hand, which
enables him to invest every detail with just the right colouring and significance. *The Rover* is the most graphic and cin-
ematic of the later novels, more so even than *The Arrow of
Gold* where the tableaux and the compositional elements in
various scenes are always seen in a dim light or shadow; in
The Rover every image stands out as if invested with its own
energies. Perhaps the very starkness of the landscape, in contrast to the dense forests of the Shore of Refuge in *The Rescue*
and the plush gallery-like drawing-rooms of the *Rue des Consuls* in *The Arrow of Gold*, makes each detail more sharply
outlined and present to the situation; so few sounds are heard,
so few signs of human habitation are seen, that whatever details Conrad chooses to provide assume an elemental quality,
almost an unreality. One thinks of the care with which Conrad selects and renders the descriptive detail of Peyrol's jour-
ney from Toulon to Escampobar:

The slopes were covered with scanty grass; crooked
boundary walls of dry stones ran across the fields, and
above them, here and there, peeped a low roof of red tiles
shaded by the heads of delicate acacias. At a turn of the
ravine appeared a village with its few houses, mostly with
their blind walls to the path, and, at first, no living soul in
sight. Three tall platanes, very ragged as to their bark and
very poor as to foliage, stood in a group in an open space;
and Citizen Peyrol was cheered by the sight of a dog
sleeping in the shade. The mule swerved with great determination towards a massive stone trough under the village fountain. Peyrol, looking round from the saddle
while the mule drank, could see no signs of an inn. Then,
examining the ground nearer to him, he perceived a ragged man sitting on a stone. He had a broad leathern belt
and his legs were bare to the knee. He was contemplating
the stranger on the mule with stony surprise. His dark
nut-brown face contrasted strongly with his grey shock of
hair.

(15–16)

This description is intensely visual and concrete; it has none
of the abstraction and adjectival excess which critics have
found so distracting in the early fiction of Conrad. Everything is spare, economical, right down to the ironic description of Michael's expression as one of 'stony surprise', which
links him to but differentiates him slightly from the rocky,
inanimate terrain.

The Rover is replete with specific images (I am tempted in
discussing this novel to say *shots*) that remain fresh in the
mind long after the specific context has faded, such as the image of a 'hen manoeuvring her neck pretentiously on the
doorstep' (38) at the beginning of chapter four and the image
of the miserable cripple, 'that twisted scrap of humanity' who
keeps Peyrol company while he repairs the tartane and who
can be seen 'making his way on his crutches with a pendulum
motion towards the hull' (93) each morning. Conrad here
uses description in a minimal sense; he does not pile on detail
after detail, in the manner of the realist-naturalist writer, to
convince us of the material reality of his imagined world; nor
does he blur the edges and outlines by one or another kind of

verbal excess, in the manner of the impressionists, to convince us of the reality of the perceiving consciousness. By establishing setting and mood firmly in the early pages of the novel, Conrad is then free to recall this mood or setting with the slightest allusion, the smallest detail; such, for example, is the significance and value, artistically speaking, of the image of the manure fork and the tartane. Once their association with the violence and blood-letting of the Revolution has been established, it is sufficient for the most passing reference to the objects to remind us of this association. In other words, these images act as verbal anchors that keep the reader from drifting beyond the political realities that are responsible for conditions at Escampobar.

Perhaps the most interesting piece of furnishing in *The Rover* is Peyrol's tartane. Frequent references are made to the boat throughout the novel and it functions at both a local and a structural level as a focus for certain associations with the blood-baths of the Revolution and as an actual prop for the events of the story. Arlette's parents go to their deaths in Toulon on board the tartane, which, according to Scevola and probably with thanks to him as well, is later filled with mangled bodies of *ci-devants* who have tried unsuccessfully to flee the scourge; and this same tartane brings their daughter Arlette and Citizen Scevola back to Escampobar. Later, Peyrol obtains and renovates the tartane, washing out the dried blood in that 'empty charnel house' (87). Conrad's description of Peyrol's first glimpse of the cabin is superb for its restraint and for its subtle concentration on one item that tells the story more poignantly than many words:

> He wrenched off the enormous padlock himself with a bar of iron and let the light of day into the little cabin which did indeed bear the traces of the massacre in the stains of blood on its woodwork, but contained nothing else except a wisp of long hair and a woman's earring, a cheap thing which Peyrol picked up and looked at for a long time. The associations of such finds were not foreign to his past. He could without very strong emotion figure to himself the little place choked with corpses. He sat down and looked about at the stains and splashes which had been untouched by sunlight for years. The cheap little ear-

ring lay before him on the rough-hewn table between the lockers, and he shook his head at it weightily. He, at any rate, had never been a butcher.

(87)

Later, the tartane serves as a prison for the captured English seaman, Symons, as it is tied up in the cove at Escampobar; and, finally, Peyrol uses the tartane to outsmart Vincent, the *Amelia*'s captain, and to deliver the false dispatches into English hands. Significantly, the tartane becomes again a 'floating hearse' (279), this time for the bodies of Peyrol and Michael and Scevola. Symons himself has the dubious honour of being its coxswain until the tartane, French ensign flying, is sunk by the *Amelia*'s guns. As 'an immense suddenly created solitude' (281) settles upon the sea above the vanished tartane, all the images associated with the vessel re-surface in one's imagination, including the initial reference to Peyrol's sea-life, which began when 'he hid himself on board a tartane' (7) after his mother's death.

A similar use is made of the manure fork, which serves throughout *The Rover* as a continual reminder of the presence of Scevola, 'the purveyor of the guillotine' (26), who believes that 'there hasn't been enough killing' and that 'Pity may be a crime' (27). The fork is usually seen in Scevola's hands or leaning against a wall; it seems, by association, more a weapon than a tool of labour, as if to say that the ploughshares have been beaten back into swords. Symons, who had been threatened with the fork by Scevola in a confusion of identities, describes it as 'a devil of a weapon' (195). When Peyrol finds the fork at the foot of the ravine, he asks himself, 'How on earth did this thing come here?' (201), and then carries it back to the house, shouldered like a rifle. During the final sea-chase, Scevola, without his murderous weapon as a crutch, becomes even more animal-like, adopting 'the mode of progression on all fours' (264); after he has been shot by the Marines on the *Amelia*, his legs can be seen 'sliding nervelessly to and fro to the rolling of the vessel' (268). The fork is an ambiguous image in *The Rover*, as I have suggested, because of its dual function; ironically, the first reference to this object is made, not in connection with Scevola at all but in connection with Peyrol's mother, whom he remembers 'shaking down olives, picking stones out of a field, or handling a manure fork like man, tireless and fierce, with wisps of greying hair flying about her bony face' (7).

Conrad's attention to such details and his capacity to invest each image with its own energies, seems to me to justify his claim to Edward Garnett, not only that he had tried to achieve 'a feat of artistic brevity' in *The Rover*, but also that he had been concerned with 'the *slightest shades*, the *faintest flavours*, the *simplest indications of sentiment underlying the action*' (*LL*, II, 326). *The Rover* is the work of a writer very much at one with his art. In this novel Conrad handles his materials with the deftness and assurance of the professional story-teller, sensing just the right moment for advancing the plot, for divulging relevant information about the characters, and for using the setting to create and to sustain mood. Consider, for example, the manner in which information is conveyed to the reader. The mysterious fabric of the life of Peyrol, one-time pirate and gunner of the Republic, is unfolded slowly and deftly, not in self-conscious lumps here and there in the narrative, but unobtrusively as it is called to mind by image and event—that is, our understanding of his character develops naturally and organically with the unravelling of the events of the story. One particularly fine example that comes to mind is the digression of the sea-chest, which is not really a digression at all. In the course of describing Peyrol's efforts to pack away his retirement loot in an old sea-chest, Conrad takes one and a half pages to give us the history of the chest, its acquisition, loss, and recovery by the rover; Peyrol has so few possessions that the 'digression' is clearly important only insofar as it tells us something about the events that shape the life and character of this retired Brother of the Coast. We learn, in short space, a little of the extent of his travels, his association with all and sundry types of person, and of the wound 'which laid him open and gushing like a slashed wine-skin' (36) and which had such a sobering effect on his character. The chest, unlike the tartane and the manure fork, has only a local significance in *The Rover* but is a most appropriate vehicle for the conveying of necessary information to the reader.

Conrad believed that a work of art 'should carry its justification in every line' and that the artist must be capable of an 'unremitting never discouraged care for the shape and ring of sentences' (*NN*, vii, ix). The history of his novels is the history of his efforts to master, not only the grouping and perspective of his materials, but also words themselves. His letters to Clifford, Galsworthy, and Cunninghame Graham reveal, in their general observations about writing as well as in their specific criticism of texts, Conrad's acuteness and meticulousness in the matter of style. In a letter to Hugh Clifford, for example, he declares:

> You do not leave enough to the imagination. I do not mean as to facts. . . . I am alluding simply to the phrasing. True, a man who knows so much . . . may well spare himself the trouble of meditating over words, only words, groups of words, words standing alone, are the symbols of life, have the power in their sound or their aspect to present the very thing you wish to hold up before the mental vision of your reader. The things 'as they are' exist in words; therefore words should be handled with care lest the picture, the image of the truth abiding in facts, should become distorted—or blurred.
>
> These are the considerations of a mere craftsman—you may say; and you may also conceivably say that I have nothing else to trouble my head about. However, the *whole* of the truth lies in the presentation; therefore the expression should be studied in the interest of veracity. This is the only morality of *art* apart from the *subject*.
>
> (*LL*, I, 279–80)

This passage is followed by the most detailed examination of words and phrases in Clifford's *In a Corner of Asia*, which Conrad says that he had received only three hours previously. The letter reveals, as if Conrad's prose were not sufficient evidence of the fact, that he was concerned, like Mallarmé and Eliot, to purify the dialect of the tribe.

The Rover, Conrad's last completed novel, is a testament to his continuing interest in words, in style; it is a model of precision and clarity. Its outlines and delineations have an almost classical strength and exactness; the prose is pared to the bone, with very little adjectival heaviness, inversion, pile-up of descriptive phrases, and almost no long convoluted sentences such as can be found in early novels like *Almayer's Folly* and *An Outcast of the Islands*. The prose does, in fact, bear the marks of Conrad's interest in brevity: it seems to possess a special kind of restraint, a filter that eliminates all but the most economical and suggestive words and groups of words. Here is a passage from the first chapter:

> Citizen Peyrol refused to take up a defensive attitude. He merely mentioned in a neutral voice that he had delivered his trust to the Port Office all right, and as to his character he had a certificate of civism from his section. He was a patriot and entitled to his discharge. After being dismissed by a nod he took up his cudgel outside the door and walked out of the building with the calmness of rectitude. His large face of the Roman type betrayed nothing to the wretched quill-drivers, who whispered on his passage. As he went along the streets he looked as usual everybody in the eye; but that very same evening he vanished from Toulon. It wasn't that he was afraid of anything. His mind was as calm as the natural set of his florid face. Nobody could know what his forty years or more of sea-life had been, unless he told them himself. And of that he didn't mean to tell them more than what he told the inquisitive captain with the patch over one eye. But he didn't want any bother for certain other reasons; and more than anything else he didn't want to be sent perhaps to serve in the fleet now fitting out in Toulon. So at dusk he passed through the gate on the road to Fréjus in a high-wheeled cart belonging to a well-known farmer whose habitation lay that way. His personal belongings were brought down and piled up on the tailboard of the cart by some ragamuffin patriots whom he engaged in the street for that purpose. The only indiscretion he committed was to pay them for their trouble with a large handful of assignats.
>
> (5–6)

Conrad avoids here the doubt and ambiguity of the subjunctive mood, with its conditional clauses, which characterizes his early work; he prefers the straightforwardness of the indicative mood. The passage reads easily not only because of the normality of the syntax (subject-predicate-object) and the absence of any sort of verbal gymnastics, but also because it has a discernible rhythm and movement which is achieved, in large part, through the use of short sentences and simple con-

junctives. It has the certainty of perspective, of mature editing, that omits the inessential, leaving, as Conrad said to
Clifford, the rest to imagination. With the exception of the
phrase 'calmness of rectitude', the diction is simple and concrete. The colloquial expression 'all right' and the construction 'looked as usual everybody in the eye' have a distinctly
French flavour which seems appropriate for this returned
rover of the seas.

There is another passage early in the novel which is interesting for the way in which it carries the eye in and out of
descriptions of scenery, changing focus from present to past,
and then shifting without a false note into details of personal
history:

> At that spot Citizen Peyrol had made up his mind to
> leave the high road. Every feature of the country with the
> darkly wooded rises, the barren flat expanse of stones and
> sombre bushes to his left, appealed to him with a sort of
> strange familiarity, because they had remained unchanged
> since the days of his boyhood. The very cartwheel tracks
> scored deep into the stony ground had kept their physiog-
> nomy; and far away, like a blue thread, there was the sea
> of the Hyères roadstead with a lumpy indigo swelling still
> beyond—which was the island of Porquerolles. He had an
> idea that he had been born on Porquerolles, but he really
> didn't know. The notion of a father was absent from his
> mentality. What he remembered of his parents was a tall,
> lean, brown woman in rags, who was his mother. But
> then they were working at a farm which was on the main-
> land. He had fragmentary memories of her shaking down
> olives, picking stones out of a field, or handling a manure
> fork like a man, tireless and fierce, with wisps of greyish
> hair flying about her bony face; and of himself running
> barefooted in connection with a flock of turkeys, with
> hardly any clothes on his back. At night, by the farmer's
> favour, they were permitted to sleep in a sort of ruinous
> byre built of stones and with only half a roof on it, lying
> side by side on some old straw on the ground. And it was
> on a bundle of straw that his mother had tossed ill for two
> days and had died in the night. In the darkness, her si-
> lence, her cold face had given him an awful scare.
>
> (6–7)

Past and present co-exist here; there is a beautiful sense of historical overlay. The personal history, while remaining appropriately vague and fragmented for the character of the mysterious rover, takes on a genuine reality through the use of specific concrete details, such as rags, straw, and manure fork. Conrad's artistry, his fine control of words, can be seen clearly enough in his knowing when to use an indefinite phrase like 'in connection with a flock of turkeys' rather than all of the other possible phrases that come to mind to describe a boy's activities and chores; also, it is evident in his use of understatement when describing the young Peyrol's reaction to the devastating fact of his mother's death and the spectre of his grim future: 'her cold face had given him an awful scare'.

The passages which Thomas Moser quotes to prove that the prose in *The Rover* is rhetorical and subject to 'mechanical faultiness' hardly justify the harshness of his criticism.[4] The first is a rather typical, if not inspired, description of the romantic heroine who figures prominently in the later fiction; what redeems this particular passage, it seems to me, is the rather humorous contrast suggested by the comparison between Arlette's vitality and gunner Peyrol's complete lack of control in the face of her seductiveness. The other bits that Moser quotes, throwing them together when in fact they are from different parts of the novel, apparently offend because they begin with the construction 'as to' and because Conrad chooses, in the first instance, to break his sentence with a dash in order to interject a piece of information about Peyrol's character into the description of his return to France in charge of a prize taken by the French navy. If there is an occasional flaw in the prose of *The Rover*, it will be found mainly in an awkward construction, or punctuation, such as the following: 'As, directly the ropes had been let go, the tartane had swung clear of the shore, the movement given her by Michael carried her towards the entrance by which the basin communicated with the cove' (251). The construction is less faulty than awkward to read; it impedes somewhat the movement of the prose. One might also argue that the word 'communicated' (meaning 'to be connected with') is somewhat fanciful at this point in the narrative, although such a criticism may merely reflect its infrequent usage at present. No, it seems to me that there is sufficient merit in the prose of *The Rover* and in the later fiction generally to call into question such summary dismissals as Moser's. John Palmer's remarks on this question bear consideration, although he too reiterates the traditional attitudes to the later fiction in his admission that 'There is little doubt that Conrad's artistic judgment had deteriorated by the time of *The Rover*.'[5] Palmer suggests that some of the 'technical features which have seemed weaknesses may actually be organic to Conrad's later attitude: the angular syntax, the absence of a militant motive toward originality (a willingness to use clichés, for example, with only the slightest irony), and the gently undercut romanticism of the later fiction may amount to a subtle affirmation of human community—the same commitment which, seen earlier in a more defensive and energetically moralistic way, had helped to define the assumptions of works like *Lord Jim* and *The Secret Agent*.'[6] Palmer's attitude to the later fiction is, by comparison with the summary denunciations of so many critics, encouraging; and his remarks about the matter of prose style sound, at least, a note of integrity: 'In its humility of diction, *The Rover* even approaches the stoical immediacy of a Hemingway or Camus. . . . The whole question of Conrad's later style is a difficult one, and must be approached first of all in the context of his later artistic aims.'[7]

The Rover, it must be admitted, does not carry its justification in every line—no novel does—but it does maintain a sufficiently high standard to establish its author's credibility and integrity as a writer of fiction. At times, the prose of *The Rover* recalls not only the poetic quality of *The Shadow Line*, but also the clarity and profundity of those final pages of *The Nigger of the 'Narcissus'*, where there is a perfect marriage of understatement and symbolic suggestiveness. The prose of *The Rover* also brings to mind Conrad's words in 'A Familiar Preface' to *A Personal Record*: 'You perceive the force of a word. He who wants to persuade should put his trust not in the right argument but in the right word. The power of sound has always been greater than the power of sense. . . . Give me the right word and the right accent and I will move the world' (xii).

In what sense does Conrad wish to 'move the world' in his final completed work? *The Rover*, on one level, is an attempt to say something about the politics of force and violence. In the essay 'Autocracy and War', with which this discussion began, Conrad calls revolution 'a short cut in the rational devel-

opment of national needs in response to the growth of world-
wide ideals' (*NLL*, 101); he also argues that 'The true greatness of a state' does not arise from fear and oppression, but 'is
a matter of logical growth, of faith and courage' (91). In *The
Rover* Conrad makes no pretence at fairness in his treatment
of the French Revolution; he ignores most of its currents and
concentrates almost solely on the atrocities of the *sans-culottes*,
the list of which disturbs even at this distance in time. Conrad's patriots are all wretched ragamuffins or dangerous ani-
mals, who scorn pity and cannot get enough killing. They at-
tract to their cause hollow men like Scevola, who has 'a lack
of resolution in his bearing' (26), the 'air of being a manifestation' (39), and sleeps well because of his 'first-class fireproof
Republican conscience' (44). Citizen Scevola, who has a 'gaping mouth' (181) and resembles a sort of 'dwarf hugging a
bucket' (48), seems to Peyrol to be no more than 'a creature
of the universal blood-lust of the time' (48). Peyrol himself
considers politics a farce; all of the issues are 'not distinct
enough' (25) and revolutionary jargon is worthy only of his
'secret contempt' (25). Contemporary history (and its political happenings) is characterized not by progress but by a
complete breakdown in the social order, by 'mutiny and
throwing officers overboard' (25). Throughout the novel
there are ironic or satiric references to the 'Immortal Principles' (25); there is even a juxtaposition that is worthy of the
venom of Alexander Pope: 'Republic, Nation, Tyranny, Liberty, Equality and Fraternity, and the Cult of the Supreme
Being' (8). The presence of the word 'tyranny' in this rag-bag
of abstractions, not to mention the ironic associations of the
word 'cult', throws into confusion the values which the list
ought to suggest.

It should be understood, however, that in *The Rover* Conrad's main concern is not with the French Revolution but
with the damage that has been wrought by such a manifestation of cruelty and violence. As he says in 'Autocracy and
War' of Russian autocracy: 'The worst crime against humanity of that system we behold now crouching behind vast
heaps of mangled corpses is the ruthless destruction of innumerable minds' (*NLL*, 99). The French Revolution must be
seen primarily as a metaphor for man's internal state which,
Conrad believed, could easily assume an aggressive aspect

and run amuck. The blood-letting which has wreaked havoc
in the lives and minds of Réal and Arlette could have taken
place in the Congo or in the Malay archipelago, as well as in
Europe; in fact, it is just another, perhaps more grotesque,
manifestation of the forces of dehumanization at work in the
sick cultural circles of *The Arrow of Gold*. Against the ideas
and principles of bloody revolution, the 'unbridled passions
and clamouring falsehoods' (209), Conrad sets the Brothers
of the Coast, a mysterious fraternity of freebooters, not at all
respectable but with a code that appears almost noble, or
chivalric when compared to that of the patriots. When the
captain in the Port Office abuses Peyrol and calls the Brother-
hood 'an abominable lot of lawless ruffians' (5), the rover reminds him that they 'had practised republican principles before a republic was thought of; for the Brothers of the Coast
were all equal and elected their own chiefs' (5). What differentiates the Brothers from the landsmen is their commitment to
the sea, to the service of an exacting mistress. Peyrol's resistance to the ideas of the French Revolution, the 'invention
of landsmen' (8), stems from his experience of hard work and
exacting conditions of survival; he has been too busy to formulate fixed ideas, so that he has the advantage of a 'slowly
developed intelligence' (8) which is not easily swayed or distracted by fashion, whether political or intellectual. Consequently, he is the only one equipped to accomplish the mission of tricking the English and to restore peace and order to
the small community of Escampobar.

The restraint which Conrad embodies in Peyrol permeates
The Rover at every level. In terms of action, Conrad avoids
the potential for sensationalism and melodrama that the material offers; the romance pattern provides a convenient psychological framework within which to analyse the social and
psychological components of his story. The characters themselves are drawn simply and economically; only Peyrol's
character is kept, by necessity, fluid and mysterious by a subtle combination of realistic detail and mythic allusion. Conrad's descriptions in *The Rover* bear the stamp of his special
short-hand: objects and places are invested with unusual energies and powers of evocation; certain recurring images give
the novel shape and cohesion, taking on a greater, almost
symbolic, dimension by virtue of their structural signifi-

cance. The prose itself, as I have suggested, is, at times, homely and idiomatic; at other times it is a model of precision and clarity, sculpturesque in its outlines and delineations. There is no more evocative passage in all of Conrad's fiction than the few lines describing Peyrol's death:

> Peyrol, sinking back on the deck in another heavy lurch of his craft, saw for an instant the whole of the English corvette swing up into the clouds as if she meant to fling herself upon his very breast. A blown seatop flicked his face noisily, followed by a smooth interval, a silence of the waters. He beheld in a flash the days of his manhood, of strength and adventure. Suddenly an enormous voice like the roar of an angry sea-lion seemed to fill the whole of the empty sky in a mighty and commanding shout: 'Steady!' . . . And with the sound of that familiar English word ringing in his ears Peyrol smiled to his visions and died.
>
> (269)

Coming as it does at the end of an exciting chase, this passage is remarkably well modulated; the understatement which characterizes so much of the entire novel is echoed in the word 'Steady', which also serves as Conrad's advice to a world just torn apart by a war that was 'like the explosive ferment of a moral grave' (*NLL*, 86).

It is not surprising that *The Rover* is such a powerful work, a moving testament to Conrad's artistic integrity; for him, as for the rover Peyrol, there could be no real sleep this side the grave. As he says in his essay on Henry James:

> When the last aqueduct shall have crumbled to pieces, the last airship fallen to the ground, the last blade of grass have died upon a dying earth, man, indomitable by his training in resistance to misery and pain, shall set this undiminished light of his eyes against the feeble glow of the sun. The artistic faculty, of which each of us has a minute grain, may find its voice in some individual of that last group, gifted with a power of expression and courageous enough to interpret the ultimate experience of mankind in terms of his own temperament, in terms of art.
>
> (*NLL*, 13–14)

Locked in his own silences, confronted with his own terrifying visions, Conrad struggled to find a voice, to give imaginative expression to his vision of reality. 'The artist creates', he insisted, 'because he must. He is so much of a voice that, for him, silence is like death' (*NLL*, 14). Conrad found a voice: it was in a foreign language and subject to unimaginable difficulties of mastery. Each new novel he embarked on was a new struggle with that language. And *The Rover*, with its descriptive short-hand, its blending of romance pattern and imagistic detail, is a fitting tribute to his success.

Postscript

Faced with the task of summarizing Conrad's achievement in the later novels, the critic feels rather like Lieutenant Réal, Arlette, and the cripple of Madrague trying to arrive at a satisfactory assessment of the life and character of Peyrol, after the heroic events at the conclusion of *The Rover*: 'He had a great heart', 'he was not a bad Frenchman' (286). Perhaps some such understatement is in order at this stage in Conrad studies, considering the relatively unexplored reaches of the later fiction. One must begin, simply, by insisting upon Conrad's artistic integrity, since so much of the criticism of the later novels treats that work not only as if it were written by a different individual altogether, but also as if its author were some sort of bull crashing from room to room through the House of Fiction. The fact is, however, that the same author who dropped his pen and rose from his writing table after the arduous task of composing *Under Western Eyes* sat down again at that table and took up his pen—probably the same pen—to complete work on *Chance*, first of the so-called later novels; then, later, as if to provide further proof that he had not been transformed overnight into an artistic failure, he wrote the almost universally praised novel *The Shadow Line*, mid-way between the larger, more difficult works of the later period. Although the record of conflicting opinions concerning the nature and degree of his success in the later period indicates that the critical problems will not be quickly or easily resolved, a number of important conclusions may be drawn from the foregoing discussions.

First, the later novels are considerably more interesting and complex than has been admitted by achievement-and-decline critics. As I have argued throughout this study, Conrad neither suppressed his awareness of the heart of darkness, nor lost his interest in the craft of fiction. In fact, not only have the psychological and individualist concerns of works such as *Lord Jim* and *Under Western Eyes* been transmuted, in the later novels, into complex and multifaceted analyses of man-in-community, with all the problems of moral failure and success contingent thereon, but also, in terms of technique, Conrad's vigorous pursuit of the elusive ideals of psychological realism has shifted somewhat towards the creation of a richly textured and subtly symbolic fictional mode. These novels of Conrad's last years can neither be dropped, as Guerard has recommended in the case of *Victory*, nor omitted from serious consideration as part of Conrad's contribution to the art of fiction, as so many critics have chosen to do.

Between 1890 and 1915, according to Malcolm Bradbury, there was a body of novels and aesthetic statements that substantially defined the nature of modernism, at least in its first stage:

> The emphasis on technique, or the perpetual resources of the artist himself as a high subjective consciousness; the emphasis on rendering, or the heightened resonance that might be attached to certain observed objects; the emphasis on tactics of presentation through the consciousness of characters rather than through an objective or materialistic presentation of the material; and the emphasis on the medium of art as the writer's essential subject matter—these were all laid down before the First World War.[1]

The later works contribute to this definition as surely as any of Conrad's novels. As a matter of fact, the conception of style which informs *The Rescue* at every level serves as a useful indicator of Conrad's continued preoccupation with matters of technique. The descriptive short-hand of *The Rover*, the portraiture and tableaux of *The Arrow of Gold*, the mixed modes of *Victory*, the character relations and point of view in *Chance* and *The Shadow Line*—these aspects of technique in the later novels remind us that Conrad was as unremitting a stylist in prose as he was in seamanship, always scheming for effects, always trying for that extra longitude. Similarly, his concreting, his blending of structural and linguistic elements, and, most importantly, his invention of, and experimentation with, the form of the ironic romance recall his insistence upon technique and the temperamental basis of his art in the letters, essays, prefaces, and in *A Personal Record*.

Conrad believed, with Pound and the modernists, that technique is the test of an artist's sincerity. Skill, he said in a letter to Arnold Bennett, is the 'word in my mind embracing everything' (*LL*, I, 306); and to his French translator, in reference to the difference between his own work and Kipling's, he wrote: '*Son intérêt est dans le sujet, l'intérêt de mon oeuvre est dans l'effet qu'elle produit.*'[2] This sentiment also finds expression in a letter to Conrad's friend and fellow-writer Hugh Clifford: 'the whole truth lies in the presentation. . . . This is the only morality of *art* apart from the *subject*' (*LL*, I, 279–80). Conrad also believed that art must make its appeal through the senses; in the later novels, as in such imagistic early works as *Heart of Darkness*, he is concerned to speak via the image, as well as through his 'unconventional grouping and perspective' (*LL*, II, 317). Much of the 'art' of *The Shadow Line* and *The Rover* derives from Conrad's unique capacity to translate thought and feeling into appropriate image. However, as a result of his reading and his own fictional experiments, Conrad came to believe that great art often had a 'symbolic character' (*LL*, II, 205) and that certain patterns of myth and romance, such as the descent and the rescue, could also move hearts and minds; in fact, he became increasingly drawn, in his later works, to such structurally useful and psychologically charged archetypal patterns.

The patterns of myth and romance in the later fiction represent an important direction in modern literature. As Barbara Seward explains, 'The current probing of myth, lore, and pagan letters is a part of the whole contemporary attempt to integrate the artist's deepest impulses with those of humanity at large; for such integration offers relief from a tendency to be overly subjective and from a prevailing sense of aloneness in the modern mechanistic world.'[3] Although he was instrumental, with James and Ford, in making the novel a 'direct impression of life', which involved the shift towards a more fluid, or temperamental, shaping and ordering of materials, Conrad, like Yeats, Eliot, and Joyce, recognized the dangers inherent in undue subjectivity, and the role which myth and history might play in transforming the personal into the universal, in art.[4] *Victory* rises above the potential limitations of the romance pattern, not only by virtue of the

irony generated by the first-person narration, which belongs
to the realistic mode, but also by the mythic patterns introduced in the early pages and brought sharply into focus in the
second half of the novel. Similarly, the story of a seaman's
'return' and the romance pattern of the rescue of the damsel
in distress, both of which Conrad employs in _The Rover_, are
transformed by the use of the Pygmalion myth. In terms of
their extensive use of the patterns of myth and romance, always undercut by some form of irony, the later novels represent an important stage in the evolution of Conrad's art, but a
stage that is not likely to be appreciated by those critics who
regard psychological realism as the zenith in the development
of the novel.

Although he tends to favour a more objective mode in the
later novels, and seems to have felt increasingly at home with
a perspective of mythic omniscience, Conrad by no means
eschews the methods and advantages of psychological realism. _Chance_, _Victory_, _The Shadow Line_, and, to a lesser degree, _The Arrow of Gold_ enjoy, in their perspective as well as
in their grouping, the benefits (mainly a sense of intimacy
and a greater illusion of reality) of Conrad's impressionistic
techniques. Of greater importance, however, is his related attempt to establish in each novel a 'consciousness', whether
the narrator or a character, with whom the reader can identify
and who, by implication, represents the figure of the artist. In
this respect, _Chance_ provides the pattern for all of the later
novels. Considerable effort has been made to underline the
parallel between Marlow's pursuit of the 'truth' of Flora's situation and the artist's pursuit and ordering of his fictional
materials, a parallel which serves not only to heighten the
emotional intensity of the novel, but also to render it more
significant as a source for understanding Conrad's artistic
aims. Detachment, curiosity, imaginative sympathy, fidelity
to the task—these are the qualities associated with the 'consciousnesses' created in the later novels, all characteristics that
Conrad demands for the artist in his non-fiction writings.

At times, as in _Victory_ and _The Arrow of Gold_, this 'consciousness' is a composite figure: a combination of the detached curiosity of the first-person narrator and the sympathetic imagination of Davidson in _Victory_; or the combined
wisdom of the mature M. George who has written his life

and the editor-narrator who puts it into order and further perspective in *The Arrow of Gold*. In *The Shadow Line* the mature captain who narrates, with a uniquely indulgent self-irony, the adventures of his neurotic and rebellious youth is the sympathetic 'consciousness'. In *The Rescue* the qualities I have mentioned are part of the characterization of d'Alcacer, the Spaniard who embodies the principle of style and who provides a much needed perspective on the romance of Edith and Lingard, as well as on the political intrigues on the Shore of Refuge. In *The Rover*, a certain amount of curiosity, detachment, and sympathy attaches itself to ex-gunner Peyrol, who has been schooled by a hard life at sea; but it is also embodied in the very fabric of the novel, in the descriptions, in the grouping, and in the perspective of the omniscient narrator who, as Flaubert said of the artist, is 'everywhere felt but nowhere seen'.[5]

Critics who accuse Conrad of turning, in the later novels, to less interesting figures—dullards, as Guerard says of Davidson in *Victory*—would do well to re-read these works with a view to distinguishing between the figures of romance and the ironic narrators, or 'consciousnesses', through whom the romance pattern is either filtered or otherwise modified. These 'consciousnesses' are by no means dull or uninteresting.

In the later novels, therefore, Conrad's own 'fine conscience' (*NLL*, 17) is consistently revealed, perhaps more so than in the works of any other period. That is why these novels are indispensable to an understanding of Conrad's vision of human community, and the artist's role therein. As Alan Friedman suggests, it was not technique so much as vision which changed the course of fiction:

> The shift to which I refer was gradual, but it took place, I will suggest, with greatest velocity at about the turn of this century. . . . It was not merely plot, or characterization, or technique, or thought, or symbolic organization that changes; it was not a matter of irreconcilable meanings, conflicting themes, or difficult problems. The change in the novel took place at a more fundamental level than any of these; it left the novel 'open' in another sense and in another aspect, though in a respect that inevitably touched, now here, now there, all other matters.

The process which underlay the novel was itself disrupted and reorganized. The new flux of experience insisted on a new vision of existence; it stressed an ethical vision of continual expansion and virtually unrelieved openness in the experience of life.[6]

Conrad shared this vision to a limited extent. He had seen enough in his travels to the Orient, Latin America, and the Congo, in his readings of European history, and in his meditations upon the social and philosophical climate of the late nineteenth and early twentieth centuries to know that the foundations of conduct and belief were crumbling, that a new age of insecurity and flux was being ushered in. The more convinced he became of the inevitability of this shift the greater his determination to broaden his fictional canvas and to avail himself of whatever fictional techniques were necessary to give imaginative expression to his vision of reality.

Conrad entertained certain convictions, in his novels as well as in his letters, essays, and prefaces, about the value of work, fidelity, and solidarity in the face of a universe that is without meaning, but his vision is best expressed in that passage from *A Personal Record* to which I have often referred in this study:

The ethical view of the universe involves us at last in so many cruel and absurd contradictions, where the last vestiges of faith, hope, charity, and even of reason itself, seem ready to perish, that I have come to suspect that the aim of creation cannot be ethical at all. I would fondly believe that its object is purely spectacular: a spectacle for awe, love, adoration, or hate, if you like, but in this view—and in this view alone—never for despair! Those visions, delicious or poignant, are a moral end in themselves. The rest is our affair—the laughter, the tears, the tenderness, the indignation, the high tranquillity of a steeled heart, the detached curiosity of a subtle mind—that's our affair! And the unwearied self-forgetful attention to every phase of the living universe reflected in our consciousness may be our appointed task on this earth. A task in which fate has perhaps engaged nothing of us except our conscience, gifted with a voice in order to bear true testimony to the

visible wonder, the haunting terror, the infinite passion
and the illimitable serenity; to the supreme law and the
abiding mystery of the sublime spectacle.

(92)

This is not a sentimental vision, a vision which, according to
Hewitt and Moser, is characterized by appeals to romantic
love and simple affirmations. The works of the later period
are endowed, at least, with a tough-minded humanism that
anticipates the writings of Albert Camus; at their most extreme, they are devastatingly bleak portraits of the failure of
religious sentiment, intellect, culture, diplomacy, and the instinct for social change. The affirmations of the later fiction
are carefully qualified: the healing doctrine of work, which is
embodied in *The Shadow Line*, has as its sobering footnote
the reminder that there is, after all, little rest for anyone in
life; similarly, the heroic conclusion to *The Rover* includes the
English captain's advice to hold steady. And in *Victory*, one of
the least understood novels of the later period, Heyst's education in the dangers of reason or intellect remains, at best, ambiguous: he ironically transfers his allegiance from one abstraction about the meaninglessness of life to another
abstraction about love and putting one's trust in life, as a pre-
lude to committing suicide.

Conrad's moral centre in the later novels has not gone soft,
to use Mr. Jones' term for the age in which he and Heyst are
living. Rather, he has come to a greater understanding of the
relation between individual destiny and the destiny of that
larger community of ideas, actions, values, and institutions
which is the primary concern of the later period. The later
novels represent, as I suggested in my reference to Palmer
and Zabel in the Introduction, not failure or betrayal, but
continuity, a fulfilment of those aims expressed as early as
1897 in the Preface to *The Nigger of the 'Narcissus'*. This preface, which is surely one of the key aesthetic statements which
Bradbury says defined modernism, is replete with analogies
to those elements which are most important in the later novels.

The Preface to *The Nigger of the 'Narcissus'* anticipates the
later novels at every turn, but nowhere more significantly
than in proving the fundamental metaphor of the rescue. The
rescue of the damsel in distress, or some variation on that

theme, parallels the role of the artist, rescuing the materials of history, or memory, from obscurity. The language, the tone, the sentiments, including the appeal to solidarity and the view of the artist's function, all reflect the passage I have just quoted from *A Personal Record* as a comment on the vision of the later novels. Furthermore, Conrad's statement that fiction 'must strenuously aspire to the plasticity of sculpture, to the colour of painting, and the magic suggestiveness of music' (*NN*, ix), as well as give 'unremitting never-discouraged care for the shape and ring of sentences' (ix), not only anticipates the modernist preoccupation with technique, including Huxley's interest in the musicalization of fiction, but also provides basic metaphors with which Conrad shapes his last three novels: images of painting and theatre, for the absurdly unreal events which take place in the drawing-rooms and amphitheatres of culture and politics in *The Arrow of Gold*; constant allusions to the nature and problems of verbal communication, for the jungles of diplomatic intrigue and unspeakable passion in *The Rescue*; and images of sculpture and statuary, for the psychologically frozen and brutalized world of post-revolutionary France in *The Rover*. Even the basic rhythm of romance, embodied in the Spenserian epigraph to *The Rover*—'Sleep after toyle, port after stormie seas,/ Ease after warre, death after life, does greatly please'— and often mistaken as a sign of an exhausted vision, is anticipated in the pages of this remarkable Preface, in the anecdote about the solitary labourer working in his field and in the final comment about the shape and evanescence of the artistic effort: 'And when it is accomplished—behold!—all the truth of life is there: a moment of vision, a sigh, a smile—and the return to an eternal rest' (*NN*, xii).

Conrad once wrote to his publisher William Blackwood to explain that the endings of his stories were of great importance: '. . . and in the light of the final incident, the whole story in all its descriptive detail shall fall into place, acquire its value and significance. This is my method based on deliberate conviction. I've never departed from it.'[7] In this letter Conrad instances 'Karain: A Memory' and *Heart of Darkness*, the endings of which cast a profoundly sombre and ironic light over the preceding events. As I have suggested, particularly in my discussions of *Chance*, *Victory*, *The Shadow Line*, and *The Rover*, no interpretation of the novels can afford to ignore the light cast on events by the final incident, couched as it inevitably must be in circumstances and perspective that qualify, or ironically alter, the implications of the patterns of myth and romance. So it is with the body of the later novels, with which Conrad's life and literary career ended; these controversial novels cast an important light on his entire *oeuvre*, in all its range and variety. They add considerably to our understanding of Conrad's mind, just as they testify to the energy and constant evolution of his art. The later novels, furthermore, are evidence that Conrad, like his fictional creation Peyrol, had not only a great heart, but also a great talent, that his endings were as mysterious as his beginnings. And, to quote from the last lines of *The Rover*: ' "Everything's in that," murmured the cripple, with fervent conviction in the silence that fell' (286).

Notes

Preface—(pages ix–x)
1. The three papers—George II. Thomson, 'Conrad's Later Fiction', Avrom Fleishman, 'Conrad's Last Novel', and Gary Geddes, 'The Structure of Sympathy: Conrad and the Chance that Wasn't'—were published in advance of the seminar in *English Literature in Transition*, 12, no. 4 (1969).

Introduction—(pages 1–10)
1. Henry James, *The Art of Fiction and Other Essays*, and John Galsworthy, *Castles in Spain and Other Screeds*.
2. Thomas Moser, *Joseph Conrad: Achievement and Decline*, p. 102.
3. Ibid., p. 180.
4. Albert Guerard, *Conrad the Novelist*, p. 275.
5. Ibid., p. 55.
6. Bernard Meyer, *Joseph Conrad: A Psychoanalytic Biography*, p. 243.
7. Morton Zabel, 'Chance and Recognition', in Mark Schorer, ed., *Modern British Fiction*, p. 82.
8. G. Jean Aubry, *Joseph Conrad: Life and Letters*, II, p. 205.
9. David Thorburn, *Conrad's Romanticism*, pp. 47, 50.
10. Frederick Karl, *Joseph Conrad: The Three Lives*, p. 805.
11. This discussion of spatial and sequential forms, including the reference to Hogarth, I owe to Robert Scholes and Robert Kellogg, *The Nature of Narrative*.
12. Moser, *Joseph Conrad: Achievement and Decline*, p. 180.

Chapter 1 *Chance*—(pages 11–40)
1. Edward Garnett, *Letters from Joseph Conrad*, p. 245.
2. Edward Crankshaw, *Joseph Conrad: Some Aspects of the Art of the Novel*, p. 125.
3. Frederick Karl, *A Reader's Guide to Joseph Conrad*, pp. 237, 241.
4. Royal Roussel comes to a similar conclusion in *The Metaphysics of Darkness*, p. 175: 'This method is the subject of the novel.' I

presume that Roussel was not aware of my essay on *Chance*, published in *English Literature in Translation* in 1969, where this idea was first advanced.

5. Karl, *A Reader's Guide to Joseph Conrad*, p. 238.
6. Edward Curle, *Conrad to a Friend*, p. 142.
7. William York Tindall, 'Apology For Marlow', in Robert Rathburn and Martin Steinmann, eds., *From Jane Austen to Joseph Conrad*, pp. 274–85.
8. Douglas Hewitt, *Conrad: A Reassessment*, p. 90.
9. David Lodge, *The Novelist at the Crossroads*, p. 46.
10. Jocelyn Baines, *Joseph Conrad: A Critical Biography*, p. 382.
11. John Palmer, *Joseph Conrad's Fiction*, pp. 198ff.

Chapter 2 *Victory*—(pages 41–80)
1. Roussel, *The Metaphysics of Darkness*, p. 178.
2. Ibid., p. 164.
3. Guerard, *Conrad the Novelist*, pp. 255, 275.
4. Muriel Bradbrook, *Joseph Conrad: England's Polish Genius*, p. 62.
5. Palmer, *Joseph Conrad's Fiction*, p. 169.
6. Ibid., 180–81.
7. Hewitt, *Conrad: A Reassessment* (1969 edition), p. 109.
8. Ibid.
9. Palmer, *Joseph Conrad's Fiction*, 169; R. W. B. Lewis, 'The Current in Conrad's *Victory*', in Charles Shapiro, ed., *Twelve Original Essays on the Great English Novels*, p. 209.
19. Ibid., p. 228.
11. Guerard, *Conrad the Novelist*, p. 275.
12. Bradbrook, *Joseph Conrad: England's Polish Genius*, p. 66.
13. Northrop Frye, *Anatomy of Criticism*, p. 140.
14. Albert Camus, *The Rebel*, p. 264.
15. Ibid.
16. Ibid., p. 261.
17. Ibid., p. 267.
18. Garnett, *Letters from Joseph Conrad*, p. 125.
19. T. S. Eliot, *Selected Poems*, p. 12.
20. Mary McCarthy, *The Humanist in the Bathtub*, p. 175.
21. Ibid., pp. 188–89.
22. Guerard, *Conrad the Novelist*, p. 259.
23. Numerous analogies might be drawn profitably between the psychology of *Victory* and the view of human nature expressed in eighteenth-century literature. The character relations, in particular, with their corresponding triangles of Heyst-Lena-Wang and Jones-Ricardo-Pedro, could be discussed in terms of either the mind-body conflict or images of the Great Chain of Being

so prominent in European literature since the Renaissance. A passage from Pope's 'Essay on Man' will serve to illustrate this point:

Placed on this isthmus of a middle state,
A Being darkly wise, and rudely great:
With too much knowledge for the Sceptic side,
With too much weakness for the Stoic's pride,
He hangs between; in doubt to act, or rest;
In doubt to deem himself a God, or Beast;
In doubt his Mind or Body to prefer;
Born but to die, and reasoning but to err;
Alike in ignorance, his reason such
Whether he thinks too little, or too much:
Chaos of Thought and Passion, all confused;
Still by himself abused, or disabused;
Created half to rise, and half to fall;
Great lord of all things, yet a prey to all;
Sole judge of Truth, in endless Error hurled:
The glory, jest, and riddle of the world!

This passage seems to have been written exclusively for Heyst: his squeamishness, his inability to act, the conflict he feels between his passion and his intellect, his ironic position as ineffectual Number One on Samburan. Heyst remarks, in connection with the rather unfortunate acquisition of Pedro as cook, that 'A creature with an antediluvian lower jaw, hairy as a mastodon, and formed like a prehistoric ape, has laid this table' (358). Human nature, too, according to the metaphor of the Chain of Being, has been laid by the brute, primitive forces that must be accommodated but kept in check for the survival of the organism, or species. Heyst has gone too far in the opposite direction; like Swift's Yahoos, he has lost his sense of proportion in the pursuit of reason. When he becomes distracted by the infernal trio and by his incapacity to retrieve the stolen revolver from Wang, Heyst snatches off his cork helmet, symbol of his rational control (like the white umbrella of Professor Moorsom in 'The Planter of Malata'), and dashes it to the ground (346–47).

24. Baines, *Joseph Conrad: A Critical Biography*, p. 398.
25. Scholes and Kellogg, *The Nature of Narrative*, p. 82ff.
26. Sharon Kaehele and Howard German, 'Conrad's *Victory*: A Reassessment', *Modern Fiction Studies*, 10 (Spring 1964), 68.
27. Ibid., p. 67.
28. Scholes and Kellogg, *The Nature of Narrative*, p. 99.
29. Alain Robbe-Grillet, 'Old "Values" and the New Novel', *Evergreen Review*, 3, no. 9 (Summer 1959), reprinted in James L.

Calderwood and Harold E. Toliver, eds., *Perspectives On Fiction*, p. 186.

30. Ibid.
31. Ibid., p. 182.
32. Ibid., p. 188.
33. Camus, *The Rebel*, p. 269.
34. Scholes and Kellogg, *The Nature of Narrative*, p. 108; Malcolm Bradbury, *Possibilities: Essays on the State of the Novel*, p. 263.

Chapter 3 *The Shadow Line*—(pages 81–113)
1. Quoted in Zabel, 'Chance and Recognition', *Modern British Fiction*, p. 26.
2. John A. Gee and Paul J. Sturm, *Letters from Joseph Conrad to Marguerite Poradowska, 1880–1920*, p. 45.
3. Zabel, as above, pp. 27–28.
4. Guerard, *Conrad the Novelist*, p. 30.
5. Missing this point, Guerard argues that 'the first two chapters are seriously defective, perhaps because they are dependent upon literal recall: of the material difficulties of getting the *Otago* underway, of a period of undefined anxiety. The irritability of the narrator becomes finally irritating to the reader' (ibid., p. 32).
6. Said makes a similar comparison in *Joseph Conrad and the Fiction of Autobiography*, p. 170.
7. Scholes and Kellogg, *The Nature of Narrative*, p. 157.
8. Said, *Joseph Conrad and the Fiction of Autobiography*, p. 165ff.
9. Ibid., pp. 194, 196.
10. Ibid., p. 197.
11. Lawrence Graver, *Conrad's Short Fiction*, p. 179.
12. The best source for this information is Norman Sherry, *Conrad's Eastern World*.
13. Dale B. J. Randall, ed., *Joseph Conrad and Warrington Dawson: The Record of A Friendship*, p. 169.

Chapter 4 *The Arrow of Gold*—(pages 115–143)
1. Quoted in Borys Conrad, *My Father: Joseph Conrad*, p. 114.
2. Ibid., pp. 118, 122.
3. Quoted in Baines, *Joseph Conrad: A Critical Biography*, p. 408.
4. Neville Newhouse, *Joseph Conrad*, p. 138.
5. Eloise Knapp Hay, *The Political Novels of Joseph Conrad*, p. 322.
6. Leo Gurko, *The Two Lives of Joseph Conrad*, pp. 189–90.
7. Quoted in Baines, *Joseph Conrad: A Critical Biography*, p. 409.
8. Walter Wright has written sympathetically about the symbolism in *The Arrow*, which he says is 'not abstruse but intended to accentuate the unity of focus', *Romance and Tragedy in Joseph Conrad*, p. 85. He argues that the novel 'lacks contrast of tone as

it keeps striving to be more and more subtle on the kind of theme normally given short space in a novel', ibid., p. 75. Wright's observation is acute, but his conclusions seem to me mistaken. Conrad's aim is not merely to 'identify love in terms of its effects on man's imagination, the faculty through which he apprehends the nature of human destiny and of the universe', ibid.; his aim is, among other things, to push the novel in new directions, which in this case includes shifting attention away from plot.

9. Karl, *A Reader's Guide to Joseph Conrad*, p. 277.
10. Gurko, *The Two Lives of Joseph Conrad*, p. 190.
11. Paul Wiley, *Conrad's Measure of Man*, p. 163.
12. Ibid., p. 170.

Chapter 5 *The Rescue*—(pages 145–171)
1. Baines, *Joseph Conrad: A Critical Biography*, p. 417.
2. Stanislavsky, *My Life and Art*, quoted in Elisaveta Fen's introduction to *Plays, Anton Chekhov*, p. 7.
3. C. S. Lewis, *A Preface to Paradise Lost*, p. 22.
4. Baines, *Joseph Conrad: A Critical Biography*, p. 417.
5. Karl, *A Reader's Guide to Joseph Conrad*, p. 281ff.
6. Quoted in Baines, *Joseph Conrad: A Critical Biography*, p. 166 and David Lodge, *Language of Fiction*, pp. 27–28. Lodge calls this the 'Argument from Bad Writing.'
7. Garnett, *Letters from Joseph Conrad*, p. 53.

Chapter 6 *The Rover*—(pages 173–195)
1. Garnett, *Letters from Joseph Conrad*, p. 284.
2. Moser, *Joseph Conrad: Achievement and Decline*, p. 201.
3. Guerard, *Conrad the Novelist*, p. 284.
4. Moser, *Joseph Conrad: Achievement and Decline*, pp. 200–201.
5. Palmer, *Joseph Conrad's Fiction*, p. 253.
6. Ibid.
7. Ibid.

Postscript—(pages 197–205)
1. Bradbury, *Possibilities*, p. 85.
2. Aubry, *Joseph Conrad: Lettres Françaises*, p. 87.
3. Barbara Seward, *The Symbolic Rose*, p. 9.
4. James, *The Art of Fiction and Other Essays*, p. 8.
5. Gustave Flaubert, *Lettres*, p. 98.
6. Alan Friedman, *The Turn of the Novel: The Transition to Modern Fiction*, pp. 14–15.
7. Paul Blackburn, *Joseph Conrad: Letters to William Blackwood and David S. Meldrum*, pp. 152–56.

Bibliography

Primary Sources

Conrad, Joseph. *Collected Edition of the Works of Joseph Conrad.* 21 vols. London: Dent, 1946–1955. This edition follows the pagination of the 'Uniform' and 'Medallion' editions.

Aubry, G. Jean, ed. *Joseph Conrad: Lettres Françaises.* Paris, 1930.

———. *Joseph Conrad: Life and Letters.* 2 vols. New York: Doubleday, 1927.

Blackburn, William, ed. *Joseph Conrad: Letters to William Blackwood and David S. Meldrum.* Durham, N.C.: Duke University Press, 1958.

Curle, Richard, ed. *Conrad to a Friend.* London: Sampson, Low and Marston, 1928.

Garnett, Edward, ed. *Letters from Joseph Conrad.* Indianapolis: Bobbs-Merrill (Charter Books), 1956.

Gee, John A., and Sturm, Paul J., trans. and eds. *Letters from Joseph Conrad to Marguerite Poradowska, 1880–1920.* New Haven: Yale University Press, 1940.

Randall, Dale B. J., ed. *Joseph Conrad and Warrington Dawson: The Record of a Friendship.* Durham, N.C.: Duke University Press, 1968.

Secondary Sources
Books

Allen, Walter. *The English Novel: A Short Critical History.* Middlesex: Pelican Books, 1958.

———. ed. *Writers on Writing.* London: Phoenix, 1949.

Allott, Miriam. *Novelists on the Novel.* New York: Columbia University Press, 1966.

Andreach, Robert F. *The Slain and Resurrected God: Conrad, Ford, and the Christian Myth.* New York: New York University Press, 1970.

Baines, Jocelyn. *Joseph Conrad: A Critical Biography.* London: Weidenfeld, 1960.

Bate, Walter J., ed. *Criticism: The Major Texts*. New York: Harcourt, 1952.

Booth, Wayne. *The Rhetoric of Fiction*. Chicago: University of Chicago Press, 1961.

Boyle, T. E. *Symbol and Meaning in the Fiction of Joseph Conrad*. Hague: Mouton, 1965.

Bradbrook, Muriel. *Joseph Conrad: England's Polish Genius*. Cambridge: University Press, 1942.

Bradbury, Malcolm. *The Novel Today*. Glasgow: Fontana/Collins, 1977.

———. *Possibilities: Essays on the State of the Novel*. London: Oxford University Press, 1973.

Camus, Albert. *The Myth of Sisyphus*. New York: Random House (Vintage Books), 1955.

———. *The Rebel*. New York: Random House (Vintage Books), 1956.

Cassell, Richard. *Ford Madox Ford, A Study of his Novels*. Baltimore: Johns Hopkins Press, 1961.

Conrad, Borys. *My Father: Joseph Conrad*. London: Calder and Boyars, 1970.

Conrad, Joseph. *Heart of Darkness*. Edited by G. Geddes. Toronto: Thomas Nelson and Sons, 1970.

Copland, Aaron. *Music and Imagination*. New York: The New American Library (Mentor Books), 1959.

Crankshaw, Edward. *Joseph Conrad: Some Aspects of the Art of the Novel*. London: Lane, 1963.

Eliot, T. S. *Selected Poems*. London: Faber and Faber, 1961.

Flaubert, Gustave. *Lettres*. Edited by Richard Humboldt and translated by J. M. Cohen. London: Weidenfeld, 1950.

Ford, F. M. *Joseph Conrad: A Personal Remembrance*. London: Duckworth, 1924.

———. *Thus to Revisit: Some Reminiscences*. London: Chapman and Hall, 1921.

Forster, E. M. *Abinger Harvest*. New York: Harcourt, 1947.

Friedman, Alan. *The Turn of the Novel: The Transition to Modern Fiction*. New York: Oxford University Press, 1966.

Frye, Northrop. *Anatomy of Criticism*. New York: Atheneum, 1966.

Galsworthy, John. *Castles in Spain and Other Screeds*. New York: Scribners, 1927.

Geddes, Gary, ed. *20th-Century Poetry & Poetics*. Toronto: Oxford University Press, 1969.

Gekoski, R. A. *Conrad: The Moral World of the Novelist*. London: Paul Elak, 1978.

Ghiselin, Brewster, ed. *The Creative Process*. New York: The New American Library (Mentor Books), 1955.

Graver, Lawrence. *Conrad's Short Fiction*. Berkeley: University of California Press, 1969.

Guerard, Albert. *Conrad the Novelist*. Cambridge: Harvard University Press, 1958.

Gurko, Leo. *Joseph Conrad: Giant in Exile*. New York: Macmillan, 1962.

———. *The Two Lives of Joseph Conrad*. New York: Crowell, 1965.

Hart Davis, Rupert. *Hugh Walpole: A Biography*. London: Macmillan, 1952.

Hay, Eloise Knapp. *The Political Novels of Joseph Conrad*. Chicago: University of Chicago Press, 1963.

Hewitt, Douglas. *Conrad: A Reassessment*. Cambridge: Bowes and Bowes, 1952 (2nd ed., 1969).

James, Henry. *The Art of Fiction and Other Essays*. Edited by M. Roberts. New York: Oxford University Press, 1948.

Johnson, Bruce. *Conrad's Models of Mind*. Minneapolis: University of Minnesota Press, 1971.

Karl, Frederick. *Joseph Conrad: The Three Lives, A Biography*. New York: Farrar, Straus, and Giroux, 1979.

———. *A Reader's Guide to Joseph Conrad*. New York: Farrar, Straus and Giroux (The Noonday Press), 1960.

Langer, Susanne. *Problems of Art*. New York: Scribner's, 1957.

Leavis, F. R. *The Great Tradition*. Middlesex: Penguin Books (Peregrine), 1962.

Lewis, C. S. *A Preface to Paradise Lost*. London: Oxford University Press (Galaxy Books), 1960.

Lewisohn, Ludwig, ed. *A Modern Book of Criticism*. New York: Modern Library, 1919.

Lodge, David. *Language in Fiction: Essays in Criticism and Verbal Analysis in the English Novel*. London: Routledge and Kegan Paul, 1966.

———. *The Novelist at the Crossroads and Other Essays on Fiction and Criticism*. London: Routledge and Kegan Paul, 1966.

McCarthy, Mary. *The Humanist in the Bathtub*. Toronto: Signet Books, The New American Library of Canada, 1964.

Macauley, Robie, and Lanning, George. *Technique in Fiction*. New York: Harper and Row, 1964.

Meyer, Bernard. *Joseph Conrad: A Psychoanalytic Biography*. Princeton, N.J.: Princeton University Press, 1967.

Moser, Thomas. *Joseph Conrad: Achievement and Decline*. Cambridge: Harvard University Press, 1957.

Newhouse, Neville. *Joseph Conrad*. London: Evans Brothers Ltd., 1966.

Palmer, John. *Joseph Conrad's Fiction, A Study in Literary Growth*. New York: Cornell University Press, 1968.

Roussel, Royal. *The Metaphysics of Darkness*. Baltimore and London: The Johns Hopkins Press, 1971.

Said, Edward. *Joseph Conrad and the Fiction of Autobiography*. Cambridge: Harvard University Press, 1966.

Saveson, John E. *Conrad, The Later Moralist*. Amsterdam: Rodopi N.V., 1974.

Scholes, Robert and Kellogg, Robert. *The Nature of Narrative*. New York: Oxford University Press, 1966.

Schorer, Mark, ed. *Modern British Fiction: Essays in Criticism*. New York: Oxford University Press, 1961.

Seward, Barbara. *The Symbolic Rose*. New York: Columbia University Press, 1960.

Shahn, Ben. *The Shape of Content*. New York: Vintage, 1957.

Sherry, Norman. *Conrad's Eastern World*. Cambridge: The University Press, 1966.

Stallman, R. W., and West, R. B., eds. *The Art of Modern Fiction*. New York: Rinehart and Co., 1949.

————, ed. *The Art of Joseph Conrad: A Critical Symposium*. East Lansing: Michigan State University Press, 1960.

Thorburn, David. *Conrad's Romanticism*. New Haven and London: Yale University Press, 1974.

Tindall, William York. *The Literary Symbol*. New York: Columbia University Press, 1955.

Wiley, Paul. *Conrad's Measure of Man*. Madison: University of Wisconsin Press, 1954.

Wright, Walter F., ed. *Joseph Conrad on Fiction*. Lincoln: Nebraska University Press (Regent's Critics Series), 1964.

————. *Romance and Tragedy in Joseph Conrad*. New York: Russell and Russell, 1966.

Yelton, Donald. *Mimesis and Metaphor, an inquiry into the genesis and scope of Conrad's symbolic imagery*. Hague: Mouton, 1967.

Articles

Curle, Richard. 'The History of Mr. Conrad's Books', *Times Literary Supplement*, August 30, 1923, p. 570.

Fen, Elisaveta. Introduction to *Plays, Anton Chekhov*. Harmondsworth: Penguin Books, 1959.

Fleishman, Avrom. 'Conrad's Last Novel', *English Literature in Transition*, 12, no. 4 (1969), 189–94.

Gatch, Katherine Haynes. 'Conrad's Axel', *Studies in Philology*, 48 (1951), 98–106.

Geddes, Gary. 'Clearing the Jungle: The Importance of Work in Conrad', *Queen's Quarterly*, 73, no. 4 (Winter 1966), 559–72.

————. 'Conrad and the Darkness Before Creation', *The Antigonish Review*, no. 7 (Autumn 1971), 93–104.

————. 'Conrad and the Fine Art of Understanding', *The Dalhousie Review*, 47, no. 4 (1967), 492–503.

————. 'That Extra Longitude: Conrad and the Art of Fiction', *University of Windsor Review*, 3, no. 2 (Spring 1968), 65–81.

————. 'The Rescue: Conrad and the Rhetoric of Diplomacy', *Mosaic*, 7, no. 3 (Spring 1974), 107–25.

————. 'The Structure of Sympathy: Conrad and the Chance That Wasn't', *English Literature in Transition*, 12, no. 4 (1969), 175–88.

Haugh, Robert F. 'Conrad's Chance: Progression D'Effet', *Modern Fiction Studies*, 1, no. 1 (February 1955), 9–15.

Howarth, Herbert. 'The Meaning of Conrad's *The Rover*', *The Southern Review*, 6, no. 3 (Summer 1970), 682–97.

Johnson, Bruce. 'Conrad's "Falk": Manuscript and Meaning', *Modern Language Quarterly*, 26 (June 1965), 267–84.

Karl, Frederick. 'Joseph Conrad's Literary Theory', *Criticism*, 2 (1960), 317–35.

Kreiger, Murray. 'Conrad's "Youth": A Naive Opening to Art and Life', *College English*, 20 (March 1959), 175–80.

Leavis, F. R. 'Joseph Conrad', *Sewanee Review*, 76 (Spring 1958), 179–200.

Lewis, R. W. B. 'The Current of Conrad's Victory', in Charles Shapiro, ed., *Twelve Original Essays on the Great English Novels*, pp. 103–231. Detroit: Wayne State University Press, 1970.

Perry, John Oliver. 'Action, Vision, or Voice: The Moral Dilemmas in Conrad's Tale-Telling', *Modern Fiction Studies*, 10, no. 1 (1964), 3–14.

Robbe-Grillet, Alain. 'Old "Values" and the New Novel'. *Evergreen Review*, 3, no. 9 (Summer 1959). Reprinted in James L. Calderwood and Harold E. Toliver, eds., *Perspectives On Fiction*, pp. 183–89. New York: Oxford University Press, 1968.

Stallman, R. W. 'Conrad and "The Secret Sharer"', in *The Art of Joseph Conrad*, listed above, pp. 275–88.

————. 'Victory', in *The Art of Modern Fiction*, listed above, pp. 607–21.

Stankiewicz, Edward. 'Poetic and Non-Poetic Language', in Donald Davey and Others, eds., *Poetics*, pp. 11–23. Warsaw: Panstwowe Wydawnictwo Nankowe, 1961.

Symons, Arthur. *Saturday Review*, 85 (1898).

Tate, Allen. 'Techniques of Fiction', in William Van O'Connor, ed., *Forms of Modern Fiction*, 30–45. Bloomington: Indiana University Press, 1964.

Thomson, George H. 'Conrad's Later Fiction', *English Literature in Transition*, 12, no. 4 (1969), 165–74.

Tindall, William York. 'Apology for Marlow', in Robt. C. Rathburn, and Martin Steinmann, eds., *From Jane Austen to Joseph Conrad: Essays Collected in Memory of James T. Hillhouse*, pp. 274–85. Minneapolis: University of Minnesota Press, 1958.

Watt, Ian. 'Story and Idea in Conrad's *The Shadow Line*', in Mark Schorer, ed., *Modern British Fiction: Essays in Criticism*, pp. 119–36. New York: Oxford University Press, 1961.

Worth, George J. 'Conrad's Debt to Maupassant in the Preface to *The Nigger of the "Narcissus"*', *Journal of English and Germanic Philology*, 54 (1955), 700–704.

Wright, Elizabeth Cox. 'The Defining Function of Vocabulary in Conrad's *The Rover*', *South Atlantic Quarterly*, 59 (Spring 1960), 265–77.

Zabel, Morton. 'Chance and Recognition', in R. W. Stallman, ed., *The Art of Joseph Conrad*, listed above, pp. 19–35.

Zuckerman, Jerome. 'Contrapuntal Structure in Conrad's *Chance*', *Modern Fictional Studies*, 10 (Spring 1964), 49–54.

Index